Dusty

Also by Lucy O'Brien

*She Bop: The Definitive History of
Women in Popular Music*

Annie Lennox

Madonna: Like an Icon

Dusty

A Biography of
Dusty Springfield

Fully revised and updated

LUCY O'BRIEN

Michael O'Mara Books Limited

This paperback edition published in Great Britain in 2024 by
Michael O'Mara Books Limited
9 Lion Yard
Tremadoc Road
London SW4 7NQ

First published by Sidgwick & Jackson, an imprint of Macmillan Publishers
Ltd in 1989; Revised by Pan Books in 2000, an imprint of Macmillan
Publishers Ltd, 25 Eccleston Place, London SW1W 9NF.

A CIP catalogue record for this book is available from the British Library.

This product is made of material from well-managed, FSC®-certified forests
and other controlled sources. The manufacturing processes conform to the
environmental regulations of the country of origin.

ISBN: 978-1-78929-586-3 in paperback print format
ISBN: 978-1-78929-157-5 in ebook format

1 2 3 4 5 6 7 8 9 10

Typeset by Ed Pickford
Printed and bound at CPI UK

www.mombooks.com

Acknowledgements

Many thanks to John McElroy and Paul Howes of the Dusty Springfield Bulletin, Fred Dellar, Stuart Cosgrove, Alan Jackson, Vicki Wickham, Mike Gill, Charles Shaar Murray, Tony Byworth, Pam Lewis, John Lomax, Daryl Sanders, Wendy Fonarow, Vicky Germaine, Gill Paul, Penny Valentine, Kris Kirk, Graham Lock, Jimmy Henney, Steve Rowley, Murray Chalmers, Len Brown, Nick Fiveash, Ray Owen, Caroline Rust, Mandy Merck, Catherine Bell, Chris May, Jane Garcia, Naomi Kooker, Jim Melly, Mum, Dad and the luscious Malcolm Boyle.

Thanks also to interviewees: Brooks Arthur, Steve Barri, Vic Billings, Simon Bell, Roisin Brozozowski, Dave Clark, Riss Chantelle, Gene Chrisman, Gary Coleman, Frankie Culling, Billie Davis, Angela Dean, Norman Divall, Sister Agnes Dempsey, Jo Donnelly, Tom Dowd, Nathan East, Bobby Emmons, Julie Felix, Paddy Fleming, Jackie Forster, Denise Garvey, Ed Greene, Dan Hartman, Jonathan Harvey, Mike Hurst, Tom Jones, Kip Krones, Dennis Lambert, Alan LeCoyte, Lulu, Arif Mardin, Brian Poole, Howard Portugais, Ivor Raymonde, Pat Rhodes, Gillian Rodgerson, Tom Saviano, Tom Shapiro, Sid Sharpe, Dave Shrimpton, Shelby Singleton, Bob Stanley, Liz Thwaites, Clive Westlake, Jerry Wexler, Allee Willis, David Wolfert and Bobby Wood.

The following articles were helpful during research: Mick Brown, 'You Don't Have to Say You Love Me', *Daily Telegraph*, 27 May 1995; Andrew Duncan, '"This is my last shot. How many times can I come back?"', *Radio Times*, 30 April 1994; Louette Harding, '"Suddenly my life is valuable to me ..."', *You* magazine, 28 May 1995; Tom Hibbert, 'Blondes Have Less Fun', *Q*, Issue 31, 1989; Chrissy Iley, 'Why Dusty Came Home', *Daily Mail*, 12 June 1990; Alan Jackson, 'Dusty's road back on track', *The Times*, 7 June 1995; Jon Savage, 'Brand New Dusty', *Observer*, 12 February 1989.

Also helpful were David Evans, *Scissors and Paste: A Collage Biography of Dusty Springfield* (Britannia Press Publishing, 1995), and Pat Griffin, *Strong Women, Deep Closets: Lesbians and Homophobia in Sport* (Human Kinetics, 1998).

Thanks also to: *New Musical Express*, *Melody Maker* (Disc), *Q*, *Scotland on Sunday*, *The Times*, the BBC (City Nights), Canadian TV, LBC, *Gay Times*, *Gay News*, *Rolling Stone*, *Record Collector*, *Sunday Express*, *Daily Express*, *Daily Mirror*, *Evening Standard*, the *Sun*, *News of the World*, *TV Times*, *That Will Never Happen Again* fanzine, *BB Review*, *City Limits*, *Variety*.

Contents

'Sometimes the ladies involved give too much of them-selves, sometimes not enough. This song is for all those women, no matter where they are.'

Dusty, Royal Albert Hall, 1978

Introduction

One of the Ones

I FIRST BECAME AWARE of Dusty's enigmatic power as a teenager, listening to poignant ballads like 'I Close My Eyes and Count to Ten' and 'You Don't Have to Say You Love Me', and it was as if there was this beautiful, sad lady singing from far across a room. That sense of yearning was compounded by a striking image – bouffant silver-blonde hair, fine features and heavily mascaraed eyes.

Dusty was an intriguing mystery. She had a decade of delicious fame in the sixties with a string of UK hit singles. Then she went to America and disappeared. What happened?

Then in 1987 she reappeared on *Top of the Pops* and had a huge hit with the Pet Shop Boys, the wittily titled 'What Have I Done to Deserve This?'. I got the opportunity to interview her, and spent two hours talking with her by phone at her home in LA. She was funny, unguarded and friendly. What stood out to me was the way she answered questions. Many pop artists 'perform' themselves in interviews, giving practised answers – but she didn't. She thought hard about each question and gave me an honest, smart, observant response. Dusty spoke with the same application she gave to her singing. She was resistant to cliché, in every respect. While recording, if she felt there was an ounce of insincerity, she would do the take again. That attention to detail was part of the sixties mod scene that spawned her, and even though she went on to become a celebrated international star, Dusty's aesthetic was always about expressing true authentic emotion.

I was so fascinated by her story that in 1988 I began researching the first edition of this book. It was a challenging task. Although Dusty now has the attention and recognition she deserves, back then little was really known about her. There was no internet, so it was impossible to do a Google search. I had to do months of detective work, combing through back issues of the music press in the British Library, compiling a list of names, phoning people and writing letters. Gradually, gradually I began to meet friends, musicians, songwriters, producers – people who had worked with her, known her and, despite her difficult reputation, loved her. It was a journey that started with her childhood home in West Hampstead, and led me to the US, travelling to New York, Nashville, Memphis and LA, retracing her steps in the Springfields and in her solo career.

There were some high points. Talking to Atlantic producer Jerry Wexler about the recording of Dusty in Memphis was inspirational. 'There were no traces of black in her singing, she's not mimetic. Whatever she gets from black is transmogrified with her own sensibility. She has a pure silvery stream,' he said to me. I also remember Arif Mardin driving me in his car through downtown Manhattan, polite and elegant, reminiscing about the arrangements on those Memphis sessions, and Tom Dowd laughing uproariously at the memory of a frustrated Dusty throwing an ashtray across the studio. He also told me that she had the jazz singer Blossom Dearie as one of her reference points. 'I realized that she had obscure avant-garde genius as her goal,' he recalled.

It was these conversations that helped me construct the picture of Dusty as a highly unconventional and gifted singer. I also spent an afternoon with Vic Billings, her manager through the sixties, a man with large, puppy-brown eyes and a camp, dry wit. He gave me such insight into her Goon-ish, mischievous humour, as did her friends Pat Rhodes and Simon Bell.

I also discovered a darker side to her story, and as I travelled through the US it was distressing to hear from friends like Howard Portugais and Brooks Arthur how much Dusty disintegrated during those lost LA years. The music industry has never been a kind place for people with mental health issues, but back in the seventies there was even less support and understanding for an artist who fell through the cracks. It's a testament to her will and inner strength that Dusty found a way through again. Even though her sense of well-being was precarious, in the years before her death Dusty did find some hard-won peace of mind.

Many of the people I interviewed for the first editions of *Dusty* have since passed away. Dusty herself is gone, but what is remarkable is the enduring nature of her legacy, that her pop icon status has grown. Part of this is the recognition of her anti-racist work – introducing Motown artists to Britain, speaking up about civil rights, refusing to play to segregated audiences in South Africa. She also spoke out in support of gay rights at a time when there was deep and impervious opposition to gay culture. 'Being a lesbian was not seen as a nice thing. We'd been fed dreadful misinformation about what lesbians were, and how we always lurked around lavatories or railway stations to pick up poor little defenceless women,' said the late Jackie Forster. I am grateful to her and Frankie Culling for giving me such an evocative picture of the subterranean 'very dark, very welcome and very sexy' lesbian world that Dusty was a part of in the fifties and sixties. Although for years she hid her sexuality, in 1970 Dusty risked losing commercial popularity by acknowledging she loved women as well as men. Dusty's fierce loyalty to her gay fans meant that she was one of the first LGBT icons.

Maybe the pain of hiding her gay sexuality was expressed in her singing, and that fine sense of melancholy. There was a precision with which she sang, an economy of vocal style that showed she understood the essence of soul music. She didn't try to copy Aretha Franklin, or Martha Reeves, or Bessie Smith, the black singers she was inspired by. She expressed the rigidity of a post-war suburban upbringing, insecurity, mental health torture, emotional fragility and inspirational joy at the sheer power of music all together, through a musical idiom that wasn't 'hers' originally, but which she somehow transposed to a very English experience. If soul was about testifying, she testified.

What she has left us is remarkable, and it resonates through generations. At a dubstep party in Hackney in the 2000s, a young man came up to me through the crowd to talk about Dusty. 'It's her voice. It's just her *voice*. Everyone knows it. You can't explain what it is, but you just know it. She's one of the ones,' he said. She was one of the ones indeed.

Lucy O'Brien
February 2024

Prologue

IMAGINE THE PICTURE. In 1955 a sixteen-year-old girl from north London looked at herself in the mirror. Staring back at her was the face of a chubby tomboy with unflattering round National Health glasses, short mousy-red hair and an awkward smile. She wore a battered convent gymslip and tie. She exuded all the finesse of an unhappy, gawky schoolgirl. A misfit. Someone who would never belong. 'You'll never make it, Mary O'Brien,' she said to herself. 'You'll never make it, Mary. You're dull, boring and destined for librarianhood.'

She reached up to a picture that had been wedged firmly into the corner of the mirror. It was a movie still of Hollywood star June Haver, whose wide open face and vivacious eyes were framed with the blondest hair Mary had ever seen. June Haver symbolized a world seemingly out of reach – rich, glittering and forbidden. 'It's no good, Mary,' she vowed. 'Be miserable or become someone else.'

In a gesture of teenage daring that changed the direction of her life, Mary tore off the gymslip, the regulation school shirt and the flat, uninspiring shoes. She scrubbed her face clean and began applying thick peaches and cream foundation. Pursing her lips, she slowly and deliberately smeared on pink lipstick. She put up her hair in a French chignon, slipped into a black sheath dress and glamorous high heels. Then she stood up, pretended to hold a microphone and sang, low and soft, a half-remembered vaudeville blues song, adapting it in her head to the fifties crooning she heard daily on the radio. Warming to her performance, she tilted her head and raised her hands with each powerful intonation.

Within the next ten years she would metamorphose into a glorious parody of femininity, with a tall blonde beehive wig and layers of heavy black mascara around her eyes. Like Dorothy, she would go in search of Oz. With that first radically thought-out change of style in 1955, the imaginary had become real. She put Mary O'Brien tidily away.

Pop has rarely seen such a reinvention of self. Long before Ziggy Stardust, long before Annie Lennox's man in a suit, long before Prince and his panoply of personalities, Mary O'Brien transformed herself into somebody who impressed the world. She injected a feisty soul sensibility into moribund British pop, she entertained audiences with her dry wit, she challenged preconceptions, was rumoured to be a lesbian and left a trail of smashed crockery behind her.

In a bedroom in 1950s London she created a girl called Dusty.

1

Catholic Girl

'HELL, HAVE I been a hellraiser,' said Dusty in 1968, 'but now I'm settling.' For a woman who had negotiated the highs and pitfalls of stardom with a wayward, gifted and restless spirit, those words sounded like wishful thinking. A self-confessed 'malcontent', her desire for peace of mind had continually been undermined by the drive for perfection, which had taken her to the heart of political controversy and personal pain. Part playful schoolgirl, part sophisticated star, she was born slap bang in the middle of Britain's preparations for war. Later this served as a metaphor for her troubled life.

When Dusty was born on 16 April 1939, countries were rearming throughout Europe, in the face of Hitler's expansionism. Russia was holding talks in Moscow with Western powers, and in the US President Roosevelt called for peace while at the same time urging military defence against aggression. In London girls of eighteen were required for a new 100,000-strong army of nurses, the Territorial Army was mobilized in the parks, blackout curtains were hung at windows and basements were transformed into air-raid shelters. Despite talk of 'peace in our time', the Civil Defence Bill was rushed through Parliament.

Against this backdrop of excitement and feverish conjecture, Mary Isobel Catherine O'Brien was born in a large, draughty Victorian house in north London. Her birth certificate registers the family home as 87 Fordwych Road, a tree-lined street in West Hampstead that, in the 1930s, represented middle-class mobility. Near to working-class Kilburn, with its large Irish immigrant population, the detached houses of West Hampstead and Cricklewood marked a 'step up'.

Dusty's mother, Catherine Anne Ryle, or Kay to her friends, was a spirited, independent Irishwoman. A flapper girl in the 1920s, she had a pointed pixie face and vivacious eyes. She also came from good stock. Her father was a parliamentary reporter for the *Irish Times*, while her grandparents had reputedly been members of a travelling Gilbert and Sullivan company. Although Kay herself nursed fierce ambitions to become a world-class entertainer, she never got further than dancing in amateur dramatic shows. For a decent Catholic girl in the 1920s, the stage was deemed an unsuitable career: an actress, after all, was seen as only one step above a prostitute. Marriage and motherhood were the ultimate goals for the Catholic girl, but Kay put them off for as long as possible.

Kay met and married Dusty's father when she was thirty-one. A shy, lumbering Scotsman with a moon face, Gerard Anthony O'Brien was five years younger than Kay, and better known by his initials OB. When Dusty was born he worked as an income-tax accountant at Lauderdale Mansions, Paddington, and earned a good salary. Later he became a tax consultant to successful clients. This steady office work, however, cramped his spirits, and his real aspiration to be a classical concert pianist remained thwarted. Solidly middle class, OB had been in India and, according to Dusty, 'shoved off to public school at the age of seven'. Then he was shuttled back and forth between India and Britain until he left school. Such an erratic, unsettled childhood left him reserved and withdrawn.

The O'Briens waited four years before they started a family. Kay gave birth first to Dion, later known as Tom, who was followed four years later by Mary, now Dusty.

Although Kay and OB had been initially attracted to each other by a shared love of music, their temperaments were unsuited. Kay was restless, full of quick wit and dreams. She would keep late hours and hold tea parties at five in the morning, catching up on sleep during the day. Dusty did that too, claims Pat Rhodes, Dusty's personal secretary and one of her closest friends. 'She'd be mooching around, sitting watching telly after we had gone to bed at twelve. She honestly could not sleep normal hours, regardless of what time she was meant to get up. That was bred into her.'

OB's slow-burning sensitivity irritated Kay and, says Pat, 'led to terrible arguments. They were very unhappy, but they were Catholic, so they'd never dream of splitting up, even though they didn't hit it off and were rowing all the time. Dusty used to listen to this and I felt that, deep down, that was what put her off marriage.' As a girl, Dusty had tantrums and was jealous of her brother. She had no recollection of warmth or affection. 'Somehow I took whatever criticism there was very much to heart. I have an ambivalent relationship with my brother. Our house was full of ambivalence. Raging ambivalence! None of us wanted to be there,' she said later.

She criticized her father as a 'lazy sod' with a 'great deal of anger'. His verbal abuse would crush her. 'I remember going into the front room and holding on to the hot-water pipes until they scalded me, until my palms turned bright red. And no one ever noticed,' Dusty said. 'I don't know why I was doing that. I'd picked up on the tension, and maybe I thought I was the reason.' Dusty's first cousin, Angela Hunter, countered this just before the singer's death, telling me that OB was a 'gentle, sweet, very humorous man. I can remember him going to collect Dusty, night after night, from a nightclub in Chelsea where she had been singing, to take her back on the last Tube to Ealing.' While growing up, however, Dusty must also have experienced a sense of self-destructiveness that became a blueprint for the family.

'Mother blundered through life. Nothing bad ever happened to her until she married. She wasn't cut out for it and would've liked to have been a flapper for ever, but at thirty-one thought it was time to do the right thing, married, and resented it for the rest of her life,' Dusty later told journalist Andrew Duncan in the *Radio Times*. 'She would ponce off to the south of France and send my father postcards saying, "Having a great time … Regards". It was never "Love".'

Dusty lived with a permanent restlessness: when the family moved out into the home counties, her parents never unpacked, because they missed London so much. 'My father never cut the grass – the neighbours' chickens used to go in there. They kept saying, "We're going back to London." They were trapped into being suburban without having suburban minds.'

Dusty inherited her mother's voluble, impulsive nature, with her father's tense shyness and angry self-discipline. The two sides of her personality declared war at a young age. Her mother was ready with Irish truisms and stern moral asides such as 'Ingratitude will show on your face' and 'The best things you can do are for other people'. She was also given to hurling objects around the room and once slapped a trifle very hard with a spoon, saying, 'You'll get it quicker this way.' Caught between highly talented parents and her Catholic upbringing, Dusty battled continuously between a desire to please and to be utterly selfish.

Her brother Tom was a shy, musically gifted boy. He inherited his father's sensitivity and developed a polite reserve as a form of protection, channelling his feelings into music. At an early age he and Dusty began to experiment with different sounds. 'They had thought of nothing but show business since the age of four,' ex-Springfield Tim Feild later remarked. Tom and Dusty would put together a beat with 'found' instruments, notably saucepans and spoons, and bash out songs on the kitchen table. From the beginning they had different musical ideas, and it was this friction that later provided the creative spur for the Springfields.

They had a robust childhood. Taking after her active mother, Dusty was a bouncy baby, forever falling out of things. Once she hit the pavement after dive-bombing from her pram, another time she plummeted from the table on to the kitchen floor. She brimmed with an energetic awareness of the world around her. 'I remember the low drones of planes after a bombing raid,' she once said. 'I remember the end of the war, dressed up in a white baby siren suit for the victory celebrations. There was a long table in the road, piled high with cakes for the party ... happy faces again. I also remember the end of rationing and the sight of my first banana when the fruit supplies started again.'

Up to the age of seven Dusty was a 'pretty girl in pretty frocks', playing on the swings in the park and enjoying raucous family holidays in Bognor. Then she caught measles and,

'Everything seemed to change. I got fat and horrible.' Putting on weight made her self-conscious and awkward, and to add to the ignominy, her short-sightedness meant that she had to wear the hated round pebble glasses.

Although painfully aware of her appearance, Dusty disguised her sense of inadequacy with practical jokery and a cheery disposition. She had a low boredom threshold, convincing herself that her family was reticent, dull and lacked the courage they needed to startle the world. In fact, she thought they weren't capable of startling the world. 'We didn't have much confidence in ourselves,' she said. 'I was a nothing kid. Not particularly good. Not particularly bad. Maybe it was the middle class coming out in me, but I never had the courage to be really bad.'

At ten she became 'pure St Trinian's', the archetypal cheeky schoolgirl with uniform askew and an impudent gleam in the eye. She inherited this from her parents too: although they were outwardly staid and suburban, they often let off steam in Marx Brothers fashion, hurling chocolate swiss rolls and crockery against the walls of their living room.

Dusty started school when her family moved to High Wycombe, a small manufacturing town in Buckinghamshire. Many black migrants from Jamaica and Trinidad had settled there after the war, and it was then that Dusty first came into contact with the West Indian culture and black American music that fascinated her. In 1949 St Augustine's Catholic Primary was a small school situated in the town centre. Forty years later, the teaching principal at the time, Sister Agnes Dempsey DJ, then Mother Marie Louise, fondly remembered her former pupil Dusty: 'I can still see her as a vibrant little nine-year-old, in her blue blazer. Her hair was a rust-gold colour, with a quiff, not curly but soft and silky. She had gold-rimmed spectacles and twinkling eyes. Her speech and laughter were musical.' Well into her seventies, Sister Agnes still retained a clear picture of Dusty: 'Study for her was no real problem, her application and interest were consistent. Sometimes she would linger on after school to clean the blackboard and have a chat. I used to think what a lovely missionary she would make, with her happy, outgoing and generous personality. Naturally I did not mention this to her.'

Although at one point she considered becoming a nun (what good Catholic girl doesn't?), Dusty believed she could never be 'good' enough, so abandoned the idea of a religious vocation. At eleven she passed her entrance test for St Bernard's Convent in London Road. Sister Agnes was sad to see her go and thought of her with motherly concern: 'At eleven she had already become a beautiful lady, with a different hairstyle. Later on, when I heard about her success in the entertainment world, I was glad for her. This old world is in constant need of little boosts of joy.'

Dusty didn't recall her schooldays with much affection: 'I didn't think they were the happiest days of my life and I still don't. There were a lot of hard times, too.'

She attended St Bernard's Convent for only a short time before the family moved back to London. Run by a congregation called the Daughters of Jesus, St Bernard's was a close-knit private school with slightly eccentric teaching methods. Roisin Brozozowski, a pupil in the sixties, remembers a ramshackle building opposite a large park near the Rye river with around two hundred fee-paying girls. 'It had to close down in the end because it failed a building inspection,' she says. 'I remember there was a history book from when Florence Nightingale was still alive. The standards of education were not impressive. There was a lot of religious instruction and philosophizing about hell.'

Emphasizing the importance of practical and merciful works, the Daughters of Jesus encouraged their charges to care for the sick and underprivileged. Roisin recalls 'war houses' – tithe cottages on the edge of the school grounds – where 'decrepit' old people were cared for by the order. 'The nuns were full of good works. They tried to instil in you a sense of helping. I bet they turned out a lot of social workers.' One sister had a wooden leg, and it was rumoured that the stern headmistress, Sister Fidelias, smoked a pipe. Despite the eccentric atmosphere, though, there were strict rules: 'There was a system of points, and you'd lose a point, say, for not having your hat on in public or talking when you weren't meant to. If you lost so many points you had to stand up in assembly while they read out your misdemeanours. It was quite intimidating.' Roisin concedes that the experience was also 'character-building' for the pupils, most of whom were of Polish, Irish or Italian extraction.

From St Bernard's, Dusty was pitched into St Anne's: a busy fee-paying West London convent with over five hundred pupils. Like many convent schools in Britain in the eighties and nineties, St Anne's closed its doors in 1987. There had been a gradual 'vocation crisis', with fewer and fewer nuns taking vows and entering teaching orders. When Dusty went to the school in 1951, however, the convent was thriving, run by a small but prosperous order, the Sisters of Charity of St Jeanne-Antide Thouret.

The school was at the centre of the local community, and its magazine, with photographs of resourceful girls in gymslips, became a rallying point. In 1953 a 'Spiritual Bouquet' was sent to Queen Elizabeth on her coronation day, 'as a mark of our affection ... God's blessing on her reign'. During the school's Golden Jubilee celebrations that year, editor Angela Talbot White mused: 'We wonder whether the school will develop as much as it has in the last fifty years the great and indefatigable spirit of the Sisters, who continually set us the excellent example of practising the school motto, *virtus sola nobilitas est* [Goodness Is Excellence].'

Within two years a new note had crept into the school magazine. 'We must live up to our reputation' was the exhortation. 'A keener sense of loyalty to individual Houses must be developed, members tend to be too casual and not sufficiently self-sacrificing.' By now, though, the first currents of the beat movement and rock 'n' roll were drifting over the Atlantic, sparking a new sense of self-definition for the post-war teenage generation. Duty-bound to honour the school motto, Dusty was torn between being a model pupil and letting rip; convent schooling taught good works and sexual sublimation in equal measure. Throughout her life Dusty was caught up in the dilemmas of many an ex-convent girl in veering between nun-like eccentricity and wild rebellion. 'The expectation was that even if you had a career you would get married within a few years and definitely have children,' recalls Margaret Regan, who went to a London convent school at the same time as Dusty. 'The official line was that the prime aim of marriage was the begetting of children, pleasure was secondary. According to the Church, there was no birth control apart from the rhythm method. And there was a minimum of sexual contact before marriage, along with modesty of dress. You didn't do anything to encourage or inflame your young man.' However, 'Having a vocation was made quite attractive. The Virgin Mary was held up as an example, and although very few girls actually had a vocation, you got the feeling that marriage was considered second best,' continues Regan. During Dusty's schooldays in the early fifties, the pressure to be a good Catholic girl was strong. This was pre-Vatican II, the great shake-up of the Catholic Church that happened in the mid-sixties. In the fifties the Church was strictly hierarchical, with the Pope at the top, the ranks of the clergy in the middle and the laity at the bottom. Although the whole world was changing around it, the Church kept to its traditions, remaining timeless, static and frozen. The faithful learned well-defined rituals – whether that was eating fish on Friday, saying prayers in Latin or, if you were a woman, being modest and covering your head during Mass.

This was anathema to someone as questioning as Dusty. She had no intention of settling into marriage, let alone becoming a nun: she had plans for a singing career. Outwardly she conformed, but within was a dissatisfied girl, resentful of the Church's moral strictures. Yet although she resisted the Church's call, many close to her say that she could never shake off the sense of responsibility and guilt her education imposed.

After she became famous, Dusty went back to her old school as guest of honour at a fête organized by her former teachers. In the early sixties the *Sunday Mirror* published a picture of her surrounded by nuns wearing full habits, under the caption: 'Dusty and Her Swinging Nuns'. The occasion raised a thousand pounds, a considerable sum in those days, for a new school chapel. From her mother Dusty had acquired an enduring sense of moral obligation.

St Anne's showed a liberal awareness in the face of a changing world. Girls were encouraged to attend the Debating Society and outings to the House of Commons, as well as making a pilgrimage to the shrine of St Bernadette at Lourdes. They learned to value an open mind alongside a sense of propriety. On 6 November 1954 the magazine reported guardedly that, 'Douglas Hyde gave us a talk on Communism, which was both interesting and informative.'

'There was a homely, friendly atmosphere,' recalls Liz Thwaites, a former scholarship pupil in Dusty's year. 'The nuns were old-fashioned and strict, but they weren't vicious. They didn't cane you – just gave you black marks and detention.' Thwaites remembers Mary O'Brien as an approachable girl who was friendly and laughed a great deal. 'She seemed confident and fun-loving. She didn't shine at anything academically, but she didn't get into trouble. She was never one to get a lot of praise and glory. I don't think the school truly appreciated what talent was passing through their hands.'

At the time Dusty was having trouble sloughing off the puppy fat. 'She was stodgy with very straight, chubby little legs, and her favourite shoes were those awful sandals with a bar and punching on the front,' says Thwaites. 'You'd never in a hundred years have picked her out as someone who was going to be famous. She wasn't at all worried about her appearance.' The memory of the bloated schoolgirl plagued Dusty as she continued to struggle with a weight problem later in life: prone to anxiety, she quelled it with large amounts of chocolate.

Liz Thwaites and Dusty were in the same school house, St Jeanne-Antide's, which was proud of its co-operative spirit, although there was often dismay at the number of black marks the girls notched up. 'At studies we are steadily improving ... Let's hope this will continue and that the number of black marks gained by the House will fall at the same time,' house captain Cecilia Trasler remarked briskly in 1954.

Though St Jeanne-Antide's competed regularly on scholastic and sporting terms with the other houses, St Anne's and St Michael's, Dusty was not sporty. Her only notable period of exertion was in her fourth year, when she played in the school hockey team. In the team photograph she sits up straight, with short hair and glasses, grinning and holding her hockey stick between her knees. But it was not a good year: 'We played very few hockey matches last Easter term owing to lack of practice, and unfortunately those we did play were not very successful,' snarled the games captain in the school magazine. 'At the beginning of the new school year, we lost all but three members of the 1st XI and consequently most of the new team had had only a year's experience of hockey. This, perhaps, was the reason for the failure in our only match.'

Despite her brave efforts on the hockey pitch, Dusty was not a sports lover and left athletics to the more agile girls. Even as a consummate tennis fan in the seventies, she took lessons but avoided playing whenever she could. 'She'd get onstage and sweat for an hour and work really hard, but she wouldn't run round a field,' declares her friend Pat Rhodes. Neither was Dusty interested in becoming an academic high-flyer. She never liked lessons but didn't have the courage to cheat. 'Not that it's a courageous thing anyway,' she said. 'I liked history, geography,

French and English. I struggled through to O Level, but I got a hate on about English because the book they gave me to read was *Mansfield Park*, which I didn't like. I was too wrapped up in American Hollywood writer Budd Schulberg.'

Her maths teacher, Mrs Denise Garvey, had a different impression of Dusty's intellectual worth. 'She was very clever, good at maths, and a real all-rounder,' Mrs Garvey recalls. 'She was keen on sport and very outgoing – into practical jokes. Wherever there was fun there was Mary.' Dusty might not have enjoyed school, but she was adept at pleasing the teachers while remaining popular with her peers. However, her real interest lay in music: 'Any chance she got she'd be strumming the guitar and practising country-and-western tunes,' adds Mrs Garvey.

An enterprising Dusty formed a band with the leading soloists in the school choir, classmates Angela Patten (now Dean) and Jean MacDonald. They rehearsed in the school cloakroom and gave special performances on feast days, complete with a guitar. Angela Dean remembers a school talent show one November: 'It was a celebration for Sister Stanislaus's feast day. For our performance Mary did all the arrangements, the guitar and the harmonies. She chose "St Louis Blues" [a song immortalized in 1929 by vaudevillian mama Bessie Smith] which we in all our innocence sang. The headmistress and five others walked out in disgust. They thought it too raunchy.'

According to their former classmates, Dusty, Angela and Jean harmonized well. 'They sang really corny songs including "Scarlet Ribbons (for Her Hair)", a song about a child who's died and the parents find ribbons on her bed,' says Liz Thwaites. 'It was very sickly, but the nuns lapped it up. It was actually

Mary's pièce de résistance. She was very good, we were quite impressed.'

To Angela, Dusty's performance was not that of an amateur: 'For us it was just a case of enjoying ourselves at school. For Mary it was going on to the Big Time.'

By the age of ten Dusty's determination to pursue a musical career was clear. When asked by a teacher what she wanted to do when she grew up, Dusty replied, 'I want to be a blues singer.' In a world where the options open to most girls were nursing, secretarial or shop work, this caused a stir. Dusty's bluesy singing and strangely adult delivery were considered outrageous. It was the one area in which she shone. 'Well, it sounded good, it sounded exotic,' she admitted, years later. 'It certainly wasn't what any of the other kids wanted to be. They wanted to be really sensible things like radiographers. And "blues singer" had a certain exoticism to it, and it also meant "black". I was fascinated with black faces and black voices … I had no idea what it meant!'

Throughout her teenage years Dusty was also fascinated by the lives of Hollywood movie stars. 'She was very interested in films. She'd always point out if a girl at school resembled a certain film star,' says Thwaites. Dusty's mother, Kay, often took her daughter to the local cinema to escape the frustration of household chores. They shared a love of trashy Tinseltown glamour, idolizing female stars like June Haver and Marilyn Monroe. Dazzled by such shimmering blondes, Dusty figured that peroxide meant fun, glamour and entertainment. Later she dyed her hair blonde in an attempt to eradicate the vestiges of the drab schoolgirl Mary O'Brien.

'My mother was so tired, poor thing,' Dusty once said. 'She

was never meant to be a housewife so she would sit through the afternoon showing twice, which made it even better because we could sit there from two o'clock when the pictures opened to well after five o'clock and we got to see B movies in the middle, and that was the best. Then we'd go home and have tea.' Dusty collected hundreds of film magazines, stowing them in tin trunks and vowing never to throw them away. 'It was the sheer glamour and gaudy Technicolor, the Betty Grable red-lips look – a slash of scarlet – that was absolutely marvellous.'

In a bleak post-war Britain, still affected by rationing, Hollywood presented a lush, rich fantasy world, and her trips to the movies bred in Dusty a highly developed sense of camp and glittering artifice. It was one reason why she moved to Hollywood in the seventies. 'It was just the whole glitz of it,' she said. 'It was everything I wanted to be and would never be, but I wanted to be in there with them doing it.' Dusty enjoyed leaping off school desks to dance Gene Kelly routines when no one was looking. Dusty described her outer teenage self as an overweight blob with National Health glasses, while inside she was 'a seething mass of ambition, ready to claw my way to the top'.

Relief came in her mid-teens when she formed a musical duo with her brother Tom, who had left the local Catholic boys' school, St Benedict's, and was working as a Lloyds Bank clerk. 'We always knew her brother was in the music business,' recalls Thwaites. 'He must have helped her. He was tall, clean-shaven and pleasant-looking, and he used to meet her after school sometimes.'

Dusty began to accompany Tom on nightclub dates, playing the folk and Latin material that would become the base of the Springfields' sound. They rehearsed in their father's garage with the aid of an old tape recorder, a pair of maracas and a frying pan, in an approximation of Latin rhythms. Tom allowed Dusty onstage with him at drinking clubs in Chelsea or Belgravia so that she could practise her singing. They worked hard, often performing a hundred songs a night, and played to film stars like Rita Hayworth and Jack Lemmon. They also did debutante balls and restaurants, where audiences either mocked them, ignored them or, at best, clapped faintly. 'It's a rotten job, it really is a rotten job. But it's a way to make a buck,' said Dusty. 'Also, I had this feeling, and I don't know whether it was conceit or naivety, but I knew it was going to be all right.'

Dusty and Tom's musical partnership was fruitful, but as brother and sister they were never particularly close. She was the more outgoing and outrageous of the two – the 'natural' performer – while he preferred to concentrate on songwriting. Yet Dusty was sensitive about his school achievements: he had done well at GCEs, while she had left school as soon as she could, convinced that she wasn't very bright. 'It was too much for me, I used to get very upset that I wasn't good enough,' she told the *Daily Mail's* Chrissy Iley in 1990. 'The feelings of inadequacy followed me through my life. Now I'm grateful to my brother because it was he who unwittingly started me off singing. I started because he started, and I wanted to be better than him at something.'

Tom had a succession of jobs: he moved from banking to stockbroking, and eventually to the Army, where he joined the Royal Artillery. He was later transferred to the Intelligence Corps, where he became a Russian interpreter/translator. When he left in 1958 he could speak nine languages, which influenced the Springfields' internationalist style. By 1955,

Dusty was finding school tedious and restrictive, and was eager to launch her pop career. In July that year, a group of fifth-formers made a pact to meet on the same date five years later in Trafalgar Square, London. 'I'll see if I can make it from rehearsal,' Dusty quipped optimistically. 'Bighead,' retorted fellow pupil Doreen Rulton.

Dusty's prediction came true. It had to happen: she had spent years single-mindedly planning it. At sixteen she decided that the person looking back at her from the mirror was not going to make it as she was. 'She would have ended up a librarian,' Dusty sniffed. It was then that she metamorphosized from dowdy schoolgirl to glamorous womanhood.

Liz Thwaites remembers this transformation as shocking. 'Obviously she didn't like her image because when she left school she changed it completely. You wouldn't have recognized her. We went back to a reunion a year after we left school. She walked in and we just couldn't believe it! Fully made-up, hair dyed blonde, all done up, dressed in high-heeled shoes. Nobody had seen her, really, since she left. We were whispering to each other, "Have you seen Mary O'Brien?" It was as if she was in fancy dress!'

Dusty stunned the nuns and her old friends. She was the talking point of the evening and carried it off with the poise and style that later became her trademark. 'That beehive image didn't appeal to me,' remarks Thwaites. 'It was very tarty. So much eye make-up and it was extraordinary she had the ability to do it. You have to learn how to put all that muck on. We were all in awe of her after the change.'

Dusty had achieved the desired effect: from being just one of the girls she had become someone with the power to shock and impress. 'I just decided I wanted to become someone else ...

So I became someone else,' says Dusty. 'I had to change Mary O'Brien to become successful.'

For the next twenty-five years she left Mary far behind.

2

The Springfield Story

DUSTY'S YEARS OF pop apprenticeship began at almost the moment she left school. At first, however, she flirted briefly with acting. She often went to see plays at London's Old Vic, and had aspirations to become a Shakespearian actress. With this in mind, she enrolled for classes at Jane Campbell's acting school in Ealing. She lasted all of two weeks. 'I was miming ... my first serious try at acting. I learned I was not a good mime, that I couldn't open a window without the window being there.'

She returned to the idea of singing and decided to gain as much practical experience as she could, working in a variety of musical styles. 'I knew my chances were better, having been born with this strange little voice.' She used the 'strange little voice' in duets with Tom and spent much of her spare time with him working on songs and vocal arrangements, but still keeping the 'day jobs'. Biding her time until the big break came, Dusty worked in a laundry, a record shop and at Bentall's department store, where she sold buttons, dustbins and electric train sets. Her retail career came to an abrupt end when she blew the fuses of the store's lighting system in a demonstration.

Fortunately for Dusty, Riss Chantelle was looking for a new member for her all-girl vocal trio, the Lana Sisters. Chantelle had gained valuable experience playing guitar with the Ivy Benson Band, the leading female swing band of the day and one of the major routes in Britain for women musicians into jazz and studio work. A forthright Yorkshirewoman, Benson had high expectations of her players and made sure that they were always of top professional standard. Some of the most talented went on to form their own groups, such as Sheila Tracy's brass duo, the Tracy Sisters, or Gracie Cole's All Girl Orchestra. Having toured extensively with Benson throughout Europe and Egypt, Chantelle teamed up with a friend, Lynne Abrams, to launch her own act, then advertised in the *Stage* for a third Lana Sister.

Among the replies she received was a letter from a polite-sounding girl named Mary O'Brien. 'Dusty wrote in a way that seemed to fit. She came over as a well-educated girl, someone you could have a good conversation with,' the late Chantelle told me for the first edition of this book. 'She auditioned for us at a rehearsal room in Leicester Square, and I said yes straight away. Her voice was quite deep, and I wanted her for the bottom part of the trio. I was the middle, and Lynne was top harmony. When we sang together the sound blended perfectly. We soon developed an empathy between us.'

By then Dusty's parents were living in Brighton, so as she needed to be closer to London, Dusty moved in with Lynne's parents in Hertford. Chantelle wasted no time in booking them an audition with Southern Music Publishing. 'We went up one night at six p.m. and sang some of our numbers. We were recorded straight away.'

In 1959 they signed with Fontana, then a subsidiary of the major label Philips, which later snapped up the Springfields and Dusty as a solo star. The Lana Sisters' sweet jazzy pop slotted easily into the world of variety tours and TV shows, and promotion began in earnest. Their light vaudeville style was encouraged by their part-manager Evelyn Taylor, the legendary showbiz mother figure who also managed Adam Faith. 'She was in an office run by Joe Collins, father of Jackie and Joan – a sleazy little office doing bookings for American airbases,' Dusty said later.

One of their first bookings was for *Six-Five Special*, an early BBC pop show, whose mix of sport, comedy and music for jiving teenagers was a precursor to the legendary *Ready, Steady, Go!*. All the hip bands of the day took part, from Joe Brown and the Bruvvers to Don Lang and His Frantic Five. This early TV experience gave Dusty a taste of the burgeoning glamorous pop scene and strengthened her resolve to make it big. 'We didn't have hits but we had records,' Dusty said. 'It taught me about lighting set-ups and microphones and television techniques.'

The girls also appeared on BBC's *Drumbeat* alongside Adam Faith. They took part in a TV Christmas *Tommy Steele Spectacular* singing 'Seven Little Girls Sitting on the Back Seat' with Al Saxon, performed at charity shows and backed Nat King Cole on his London dates. ('He was smashing, a really nice man,' recalls Chantelle.)

Dusty was with the Lana Sisters for only a year, yet she packed in a wide range of experience, playing everywhere a date was offered. 'We booked it, sang it, drove it,' Chantelle said proudly. 'Denmark Street [the home of music publishing] was all raring to go in 1959. We'd get in the car, drive down there, and publishers would come rushing at you saying, "Here's a song for your next broadcast!" before you'd even got out of the car. We'd come back from town laden with acetates.'

The Lana Sisters' releases were jaunty little numbers like 'Chimes of Arcady', 'Buzzin'' and 'Tell Him No', or sentimental crooners such as 'My Mother's Eyes'. 'We did that for all the mums,' said Chantelle. 'It was hysterical. We had to sing all fast and panic-stricken – but we could also pull out the notes into some jazz-minded phrasing. We could do what we wanted to; we worked hard on our harmonies.'

Chantelle taught Dusty a lot about stagecraft. Despite the silver lurex outfits, Dusty was expected to exude sophistication. She was forbidden to whistle in the dressing room, drop cups and saucers, or fall down steps. 'Riss was very patient with me,' Dusty said. She didn't always fit in, and looked back on those days with ribald humour. 'We used to wear silver lamé pants with pale-blue tulle skirts with drawstrings, which we would pull to whip back our skirts, like flashers, halfway through the act to reveal the little lamé numbers underneath.'

Some say that Dusty's departure from the Lana Sisters was acrimonious, but Chantelle remained diplomatic. 'I think she wanted to be a solo artist, and she had to have the experience of being in a group to take her up to that point. She knew the studios, the touring, the ups and downs. A lot of people think it's going to be easy, but she saw it as a job, like an accountant or a solicitor.' Of leaving the group, Dusty said, 'I hated it when they implied that I was letting them down, but I had to move on … Sometimes you have to let people down in order to get on, particularly in show business. And when the Springfields came along, I was the only one who had set foot on a stage before. So in that way it was good tough training.'

Early in 1960 Dusty's brother Tom and his friend Tim Feild invited her to become a permanent member of their new act. Tom met Tim while playing a date at Hélène Cordet's high-society club in London. A temporary partner had fallen sick, and Tim, a singer, offered to stand in. After the show the two found that they shared the same enthusiasm for African, Latin and folk sounds. They decided to work together.

By then Tom was ready to quit daytime work and devote himself to music. 'I'd never had any lessons, but I started playing the piano by ear at a very early age, and seemed to have a feeling for harmony,' he said. 'I turned professional after having been sacked from every job I tried. I was hopeless at office work!' Tim Feild had also marched through a succession of jobs before joining the band. An Old Etonian, his first job was in the Navy. After demobilization, he tried wine-tasting, advertising, stockbroking and public relations, none of which excited him. In 1957 he packed his guitar in a rucksack and set off on a world tour. He travelled over twenty thousand miles through the USA, Japan and the Far East, busking to earn money. In Spain he even taught Elizabeth Taylor's children to waterski. The highest point for him, though, was being England's sole representative at the International Folk Festival in Lahore, West Pakistan.

'After school and the Navy, I thought I'd have a good look at the world,' Feild said. 'I had no money, so I took my guitar and decided to see how far I'd get. My father was American, so I started there. I spent a fantastic year roaming around singing for my supper.' When he returned, Feild also reached the semi-finals of the *Bid for Fame* TV series as a solo singer, before he met up with Tom.

With Feild's travelling experience and Tom's knowledge of languages, they were ready to create a robust new worldly wise folk sound. All they needed was a suitably attractive and extrovert front-person. Tom knew that his sister – with her striking hair, bright eyes and valuable experience with the Lana Sisters – would fit the bill. For her part Dusty, as the only girl in the band, would have a chance to sample the limelight as well as branching out musically. When Tom asked her to join him, she jumped at the chance.

It was an exciting start. Thirty years before Peter Gabriel combined his sensitive stadium rock with the high Senegalese vocals of Youssou N'Dour, and Sting played Latin rhythms on his crossover album *Nothing Like the Sun*, the Springfields developed their own kind of world music. Combining the influences of Latin America (Tom was a big fan of Carmen Miranda), country-and-western and pop, they forged a kind of folk internationalism within a limited and rigidly defined UK pop world.

In the late fifties the pop industry was in its infancy. 'Shake, Rattle & Roll' by Bill Haley had exploded into US charts, but the rock 'n' roll message was making little impact in Britain. While America had specialist radio stations and inspired DJs, broadcasting in Britain was restricted to the BBC's Home Service – its classical Third Programme and the Light Programme. There was a clear division between stuffy, high-brow, high-culture arts, and racy light entertainment. In the latter category, pop artists like Lonnie Donegan, Billy Fury and Cliff Richard emulated American styles. The four major record companies – EMI, Decca, Philips and Pye – dominated this market, with virtually all the hit records. They leased

American songs and, in the case of rock 'n' roll, had British artists record them in a considerably more conservative, lightweight form than in the USA.

The Springfields had adventurous tastes and from their first intensive rehearsals began creating a fresh pop sound. Legend has it that the trio hit upon a name for the band while strumming guitars one spring day in a sunny field. In 1960, with a catchy name and a strong identity, they went on a frenetic round of concerts and cabaret appearances. They were booked in at Butlin's holiday camps and spent sixteen weeks on the road in an old Volkswagen bus. Their trademark was versatility: with folk-harmony accessibility, a collection of instruments that included piano, guitar, bongos and conga drums, and songs composed by Tom that featured words in Hebrew, German, Greek, Czech and Russian, the band could play to any audience.

By 1961, the first wave of rock 'n' roll hysteria had subsided, only to be overtaken by a demand for softer, more melodic pop music, and the group was invited to audition by Johnny Franz, a down-to-earth cockney who worked for Philips. At their first informal session, the Springfields nervously played guitars and sang their version of 'Dear John', an 1860s American Civil War song. Franz was so impressed that he signed them immediately, led them into the studio, then put out 'Dear John' as their first single.

Johnny Franz's role in the success of the Springfields and in Dusty's later solo career was of crucial importance. An astute, affable man, he was one of pop's unsung heroes. His death from a heart attack in 1977, when he was in his fifties, marked the end of a particular recording tradition. 'I respected him tremendously. He was one of the old guard of house producers,' recalls Dave Shrimpton, production manager at Philips in the sixties. 'He knew what he had to do and got on with it ... extremely successfully.'

In the unsophisticated studio days of the late fifties and early sixties, there was no such thing as a producer. Instead, record labels would hire a person who, with the title of A&R manager – which, in the fifties, stood for Artists & Recording, rather than the later Artists & Repertoire – would organize and oversee recording sessions. They would sign artists, draw up contracts, authorize payment, book musicians and studios, and throw in a rudimentary critical assessment along the way.

Johnny Franz was highly organized and musically tuned in to his acts. 'In marketing meetings he'd promote his artists well,' says Dave Shrimpton. 'He had the Midas touch. He wasn't a big-timer, he didn't lay down the law, but he had a good radio and promotion team working for him.' He began his career after the war as a musician hanging around Denmark Street, London's Tin Pan Alley, which was filled with sheet-music publishing companies, buskers and musicians on the make. Until the sixties, it was the centre of the British music business.

After a stint playing piano for the singer Anne Shelton, Franz joined Philips in 1954 as A&R manager. His skill as a pianist stood him in good stead and he had perfect pitch: 'You could give him any note and he'd say straight away "A flat" or "C sharp",' Shrimpton recalls. 'It was a good party trick, but he was able to utilize that gift in the job.' Paddy Fleming, former head of press and promotion at Philips, remembers that Franz had 'brilliant ears. He would hear the contrast of artists, and when he said an artist was good, I believed him. When an unknown little girl called Shirley Bassey came down from Cardiff, he listened and said, "Yes, great singer." He saw that potential, too, in Dusty.' He worked with most of Philips's artists until the seventies; stars such as Frankie Vaughan, Marty Wilde, Shirley Bassey and the Walker Brothers benefited from his advice and expertise. In April 1961 it was the Springfields' turn. 'The three of them sat right in front of my desk and sang "Dear John",' Franz said later. 'It was a new sound, a fresh sound. I signed them on the spot.'

'Dear John' was not a hit, but it ensured that the Springfields were noticed. That year they appeared in an *NME* article as one of 'Ten Future Star Attractions'. Of the ten listed – who included Danny Williams, Anita Scott, Russ Sainty and the Krew Kats – only the Springfields achieved lasting acclaim. With their sharp instrumentation and fresh harmonies, they stood out among the balladeers, crooners and second-rate rock 'n' rollers. Having travelled the country playing myriad isolated dates, they now undertook their first major six-week tour with comedian and musician Charlie Drake. Their profile on the cabaret and variety circuit rose considerably after their second single, 'Breakaway', reached no. 31 in the British charts in July, and stayed in the listing for eight weeks.

Their quirky appeal led the Springfields to radio slots on *Parade of the Pops*, *Saturday Club* and *Easy Beat*, while TV shows like *Thank Your Lucky Stars* and *The Benny Hill Show* introduced them to a mainstream family audience. 'We got TV exposure very quickly,' Dusty told the *Observer*. 'We discovered that if you sang loud and fast everybody got terribly impressed. We were terribly cheerful. It was extremely important to be cheerful.' If they were becoming cynical behind the smiles, they took care not to let it show.

By the release of their third single, 'Bambino', the Springfields had built up a healthy cross-section of fans. Released in time for Christmas 1961, 'Bambino' was a suitably schmaltzy reworking of a centuries-old Neapolitan Christmas carol. Tom had updated and retitled it to create a huge bestseller. It reached no. 16 in the UK Top 20 and remained in the charts for three months.

With this maximum exposure, the Springfields leaped seemingly from nowhere to win Top Vocal-Instrumental Group in *Melody Maker*, and Best Vocal Group in *NME*'s end-of-year Popularity Poll. They toppled previous winners the King Brothers, and eclipsed favourites like the Mudlarks and the Dallas Boys. Afterwards Tom enthused breathlessly, 'We're amazed! ... Since we heard the news, our feet haven't touched the ground.'

The Springfields were hailed as symbols of pop's new middle class. Much was made of the fact that the boys had worked at Lloyds and that Dusty was an ex-convent girl. 'They've taken over from that armpit-scratching school whose interviews had to be severely manipulated by their trainers,' proclaimed sixties hipster magazine *Scene*. Dusty felt inhibited by her background: 'When you're middle class you always wonder what people will think and say if you do something different – like standing in front of a thousand people and singing of love and romance,' she said. 'If you're working class you don't think like that, because you're out to prove something to the world. And the upper classes can do this just as a giggle and no one questions them.'

The Springfields were ready to break on to an international level: 1962 proved a key year for their success in the US. Their next two singles, the slow mellow ballad 'Goodnight Irene' and the countrified harmony song 'Silver Threads and Golden

Needles', opened up the American market. Dusty's voice emerges on the latter with a new soulful edge, an indication of the direction she would later pursue. 'Silver Threads' shot into the US Top 20 and reached no. 1 and no. 2 in New Zealand and Australia respectively.

The Springfields were particularly pleased with their impact in America. 'You've got no idea how stunned we were when "Silver Threads" got into the US Hot 100,' Tom told *NME*. 'We recorded it for Britain and gave up hope when it didn't make the charts here. Now we're trying to adjust ourselves pretty quickly! It's surprising how an American hit can set the wheels turning. The offers have started to come in like a whirlwind.' Yet while vocal groups were popular in America – aided by the burgeoning R&B phenomenon – by mid-1962, it seemed that fans were tired of the drawling nasal style pioneered by the Everly Brothers. Sugary-sweet harmonies were being rejected in favour of a more vigorous pop beat sound.

Though charmingly idiosyncratic, the Springfields didn't always sell. The success of 'Silver Threads' was followed by a miss. 'I suspect that their rather off-beat choice of material and unusual style of interpretation deters many teenage buyers, and it is possible that a similar fate will befall their latest release, "Swahili Papa",' reported *NME* in September 1962. However, the Springfields proved their staying power – with their long-awaited debut album, *Kinda Folksy*, in 1962. A jaunty collection, it includes the crooning country song 'Black Hills of Dakota', the spaghetti-Western folk of 'Allentown Jail' and the folk standard 'Tzena Tzena Tzena'. Their style is both vigorous and homey. 'Dear Hearts and Gentle People', for instance, begins with apple-pie philosophizing about dutifully reading the Bible only to fly into a swinging-sixties guitar break halfway through.

Dusty sings folksy narratives with great, if ironic, gusto. We have Stella in 'They Took John Away', loath to settle down while she's 'making whoopee', alongside the demure heroine of 'Silver Dollar', who argues that a woman's destiny is to find a good man. Dusty is featured on the album cover sitting in front of a huge conga drum, while the two boys stand behind her, smiling, their hands resting on two acoustic guitars. It's a wholesome, ebullient picture.

Even though she sang with energy and enthusiasm, once the initial euphoria wore off Dusty found being in the Springfields a frustrating experience. As she veered more towards punchy R&B, the boys' harmonious congas and acoustic guitars felt increasingly anodyne, but she didn't have the opportunity to voice her dissatisfaction with the band, especially when their epic folk song 'Island of Dreams' became the group's biggest hit to date. Replete with finger-pickin' banjo, soothing strings and an enveloping chorus, it was in the UK charts for over six months, becoming the fourth bestselling single in 1963, only pipped by the Beatles and Roy Orbison.

However, Dusty's sense that she hadn't quite found her milieu – 'my body was wrong, my face was wrong' – was echoed by those who met her at the time. Frankie Culling was a glamorous blonde singer with Granada TV's house band, the Granadeers, who sang with all the stars of the day, including Jerry Lewis, Engelbert Humperdinck, Anita Harris ('lots of elbows') and Nat King Cole ('marvellous man. Drank dry martinis and smoked the entire time'). She remembers rehearsing with the Springfields one night in a room above the Six Bells pub opposite the TV studios in Chelsea. 'Dusty came in with lots of Liberty bags, because she loved going shopping. She was with her brother Tom, who was very laid-back, very cute. She had wild bouffant blonde hair and thick black eye make-up, and she sang "Lizzie Borden – you can't cut your mother up in Massachusetts". The thing was, though, she seemed nervous, and all her movements were very jerky, as if she wasn't sure she was doing the right thing,' recalls Culling. 'For a name – because she was a name in those days – I expected somebody much more relaxed. She was quite distant, not particularly friendly, she gave the impression she was never going to stay long, if you know what I mean?'

After rehearsal the band went over to the studios with the Granadeers and played a set. Frankie gained a different impression of Dusty: 'Although she was a bit awkward there was definitely an aura about her. She was very highly tuned, and her vocal style was raucous and punchy. She had bags of energy, definitely a goer.'

Dusty and the boys kept up a furious pace, recording the Springfields-composed 'Little Boat' theme song to the film *Just for Fun*, appearing as top billing on TV shows like *Discs-a-Go-Go*, and releasing their first Stateside album *Silver Threads and Golden Needles*. But just as 'Island of Dreams' sailed up the charts, unity within the group broke down. Success had been rapid, and the stress was taking its toll. The musical differences between Dusty and Tom, which had seemed so dynamic in the beginning, were now the cause of frequent bickering. While Tom was committed to folk and alternative rhythms, Dusty was more focused on pop. They clashed and, as brother and sister, lashed out at each other with unselfconscious intensity. Tim Feild ended up acting as a buffer between the two, often suggesting, 'Let's try it both ways and see what sounds best.'

It was Feild's warm, sunny personality that eased tension in the group, though he found the situation trying. He once complained about Dusty's stage dresses. 'They used to irritate me beyond bounds,' he said. 'She goes for exotic creations which require at least fourteen stiff petticoats. And Dusty, in true grande dame fashion, flatly refused to transport her petticoats in and out of theatres – a chore which raised my temper.' Dusty said later that he had spoken in jest, and that her skirts had become a huge joke with the group. 'They were hooped and covered in canvas and looked like those pods that drop in the ocean after a space shuttle.'

At the end of 1962 Feild's wife Rachel was taken ill, and he had to leave the group to take care of her. His young twenty-one-year-old replacement, the convivial, chatty Mike Longhurst-Pickworth, better known as Mike Hurst, was already a friend of the band. 'It was a pity Tim left,' recalls Pat Rhodes. 'Mike Hurst got on with everyone, but he was very abrasive. Compared to Tim, his manner was brash and he didn't blend in so well. When Tim left, the warmth in the music disappeared. It was no longer the Springfields, personally.'

Ever vigilant, Dusty kept up a façade of cheery enthusiasm. She had maintained contact with her old school, St Anne's in Ealing, and in autumn 1962 contributed a short essay for the old girls' section of the school magazine. 'Showbusiness is enjoyable but entails much hard work,' she wrote. 'In town, an average day begins at about 8 a.m., with a hairdressing appointment (I am writing this at the hairdresser's). After this probably a press interview, a hasty snack lunch and an afternoon rehearsal and recording session. Then another rehearsal for the evening performance.' She adds politely that many show-business people are 'interesting and charming. It is interesting to note how many Catholics there are, Max Bygraves, Joan Turner, Dickie Henderson and Anne Shelton to name a few.' She recounts a few 'on-the-road' stories – there is one about the time when the band were touring and arrived at a small town in Scotland with two dance halls. When news got around that the Springfields were in one hall the other emptied rapidly. The owners of the empty hall scooted over and fused the Springfields' microphone and lighting system, which 'left the place in complete darkness and we three cowering behind the drum kit warding off irate Scots!' Incidents like this helped to relieve the boredom of long journeys and tough schedules and eased the mounting friction within the band.

Mike Hurst made his vinyl debut with the Springfields at the 'Island of Dreams' recording session. A trainee insurance broker who played rock 'n' roll at parties, he had been selected from a rigorous round of auditions. Although keen, confident and willing to learn, he was flung in at the deep end at the height of the Springfields' success. 'Superficially everything was okay,' says Pat Rhodes, 'but deep down I don't think they really got on. There were a few more arguments when he joined. He was a lot younger and hadn't had the experience of showbiz.'

The Springfields strengthened their mainstream appeal by recording a Christmas EP on Philips for *Woman's Own* magazine. With swinging renditions of traditional carols such as 'The Twelve Days of Christmas' and 'Mary's Boy Child', they were in danger of restricting themselves to a world of bland easy-listening. All this changed at the end of 1962 when they were given the opportunity to record an album in Nashville, the home of country music.

Owner of Sun Records in Nashville in the eighties, Shelby Singleton was the man responsible for introducing the Springfields to America. As former A&R manager with Philips's offshoot Mercury, Singleton spent much of his time in the fifties and sixties scouting Europe for talent that would sell in the States. 'I brought many European acts to Nashville, like Johnny Hallyday and Nana Mouskouri. And lots of black American acts were very interested in knowing more about Europe. So in all ways we were broadening the scope of our recording wherever we could. We wanted to make international hits,' the late Singleton told me in 1988.

As Mercury sales manager for the entire American South, Singleton had practical promotion experience and the ear for an immediately commercial sound. As well as signing successful rock 'n' roll acts such as Johnny Preston and The Big Bopper, he pioneered the recording of black music in Nashville, with artists like Brook Benton and Clyde McPhatter. Fusing soul with country on such classic hits as 'Rainy Night in Georgia' and 'Lover Please', these singers signalled an early cross-fertilization of segregated 'black' and 'white' sounds.

Shelby first heard the Springfields on a trip to London, when Johnny Franz played him a recording of 'Silver Threads and Golden Needles'. 'I liked it very much,' Singleton said. 'I liked the unusual harmonies, and I wanted to release it in America.' The prospect of a group of fresh-faced Limeys coming to record down-home country music must have seemed comical, but Singleton insisted that the Nashville musicians treated the Springfields 'just like another act'. And two years of intensive touring and recording meant that the Springfields weren't fazed by lengthy Nashville recording sessions with top-notch players.

Winning the respect of what then were £400-a-week musicians was a feat in itself, and the group ensured this by recording the nineteen songs chosen for them well ahead of schedule. Tom even had time to write a couple of extra songs, one of which, 'Dance', they recorded straight away. 'All the studio helped me out with these numbers,' says Tom, 'and it was strange to see genteel lady violinists really with the beat, handclapping furiously.'

As one of the first British acts to have a US Top 20 hit, the Springfields attracted attention. DJ Ralph Emery, a local 'Grand Ole Opry' bigwig, invited them on his radio show, while WENO Nashville radio DJ Ed Hamilton contributed enthusiastic liner notes to their new album. 'It's just about as far from Yorkshire pudding to country ham as it is from London, England to Nashville, Tennessee,' he wrote. 'There's a tremendous geographical difference ... a difference narrowed completely by one common denominator ... music!'

Arranged by Bill Justis, who worked on Sun Records hits by Johnny Cash, Charlie Rich and Jerry Lee Lewis, their Nashville album *Folk Songs from the Hills* is a mixture of hillbilly and rockabilly, featuring standards like 'Greenback Dollar', 'There's a Big Wheel' and 'Mountain Boy'. Though her American accent sounds forced, Dusty was developing a soulful edge. Early on, Singleton saw Dusty's R&B potential. 'I thought she had the most unusual sound of the three people in the group,' he said. 'She was doing country-and-western, which was something she didn't want to do. She had become more "black" with her voice, and she felt restricted within the group.'

The *Folk Songs* album sleeve depicts a blonde-haired Dusty on a bale of hay in a tartan dress and woolly black tights, a camp corny image that was at odds with her interest in emerging soul sounds and hip mod style. Fired by R&B, she later recalled the immediacy of her love affair with black American music. 'I was passing a record shop in Times Square and the Exciters' "Tell Him" was blasting out. The *attack* in it! It was the most exciting thing I'd ever heard. The only black music I'd heard in England was big-band jazz and Latin music, which I loved. But this was a revelation.' She appreciated the ballsiness of it, the 'dirty, low-down voice' and the crisp, powerful production that was, as yet, unheard of in Britain. To a white convent-educated teenager, such a gritty sound came as a revelation.

The Springfields returned home from the US to find they were British Number One Vocal Group for the second year running. They undertook a successful tour of Australia and Europe, and made high-profile TV appearances in Britain, including a run on BBC TV's prime comedy programme *The Dick Emery Show*. Their next single, 'Say I Won't Be There', Tom's reworking of the traditional French song '*Au clair de la lune*', went into the charts for fifteen weeks, reaching no. 5.

Declaring themselves 'older and wiser', Dusty emphasized the importance of their trip to Nashville. 'It changed everything for us. There's no doubt it channelled us into doing country-and-western music without us knowing it.' Criticized for adopting fake hillbilly accents, Tom retorted, 'We used to sing quite a few Spanish songs – and then we couldn't sing in anything *but* a Spanish accent. You can never be authentic if you're British. It's mimicry, and if the mimicry is accurate for country music then you'll sound American.'

Constantly caught between folk and pop, the Springfields found themselves arguing over which songs would be appropriate to sing. 'One of the difficulties of being the Springfields is that there is lots of material we would like to sing, but we must be careful not to steer into an arty or poppy category,' said Dusty. 'You see, we haven't enough class for a folk concert and not enough pop background for a rock concert!'

Dubbed the International Springfields, the group's aptitude with languages and versatile reworking of traditional folk songs attracted ever wider audiences. As the band's chief arranger, Tom was the focus during interviews. Although the Springfields had a policy of 'equal publicity for all', Dusty was overlooked by journalists wishing to discuss with Tom the band's musical style, which must have rankled.

In March 1963, Dusty got her chance to shine. Appearing on prime-time BBC show *Juke Box Jury*, she talked knowledgeably about music, showing her interest in genres other than pop. She came across as bright and questioning on the TV special *Here Come the Girls*. 'Suddenly Dusty Springfield is emerging as an interesting personality, and the first to notice it are the television people,' noted *NME*.

She was developing a no-nonsense professionalism, and Mike Hurst recalls that she was tough to work with. Remembering when the group first 'went electric' at the Winter Gardens in Blackpool, he says:

We had amplifiers three feet high and we thought it was great. The impresario Harold Fielding was at our rehearsal. Suddenly his voice boomed from the auditorium: 'Those bloody things'll have to go. They ruin the look of the act.'

'No, they're staying,' said Dusty.

'They're going.'

'Up yours, they're staying.'

Then a woman [Harold's wife] piped up: 'Don't let her talk to you like that!'

'Tell that bloody cow to shut up,' was Dusty's reply.

'Right, you'll never work in one of my shows again,' said Harold.

It was hilarious. Dusty always spoke her mind.

Later Dusty told *Q* magazine that they weren't at all content with that 'happy, breezy music. And I was just doing it to get famous – I was a fairly calculating bastard.' Her strategic solo TV appearances paved the way for her final departure from the band. The Springfields had watched the Beatles play the Cavern and could see the writing on the wall for their down-home pop. Phil Spector, and the edgy, soulful girl-group sound, was now beginning to take over the charts.

The Springfields' next single, 'Come on Home', peaked at no. 31 amid rumours that the group were to disband. In October 1963, at the height of their recording career, they topped the bill on *Sunday Night at the London Palladium*. Outwardly, everything seemed to be running smoothly but, aware that she was about to leave the group and that this was the last time she would sing with her brother, Dusty burst into tears mid-song. Luckily many people assumed it was part of the act. Shortly after the show, she quit. This came as a surprise to the Springfields' fans, but to those working in the business, the group's divergent musical interests had been apparent for some time.

The strange thing was that even before the Springfields started, they had set a date to break up, and Dusty claims that she had recorded her first solo record before the split. 'Tom can't bear to be in the public eye, and he said, "Let's give it three years. If we haven't made it, never mind. If we have, we'll disband the group and go our separate ways,"' explains Pat Rhodes.

Dusty had the confidence to go solo, a direction she'd been aching to follow for months. Her mother was not so pleased. 'I'll miss seeing your name in the papers!' she wailed, before Dusty convinced her that it would be back there soon, even bigger and better than before.

Hurst, meanwhile, was happy to pursue a separate career. He opened a folk club to capitalize on the then-thriving folk scene, and performed songs for Philips, none of which, unfortunately, was a hit. He had more success in producing other artists, notably the folk-inspired Cat Stevens, with 'Matthew & Son' and 'I'm Gonna Get Me a Gun', and later the rock 'n' roll revivalists Showaddywaddy.

Tom left to form an orchestra, issuing two albums of his own and a single, 'The Moon Behind the Hill'. He went on to produce and compose for top pop acts, becoming more successful with the Seekers, a more refined pop version of the Springfields. Dusty had discovered this Australian group in 1964 when they had supported her at a Blackpool charity show soon after their arrival in Britain. Tom said, 'As soon as I heard them, I knew they could do great things with the right material.' He wrote many worldwide hits for them, including 'I'll Never Find Another You', 'Morningtown Ride' and 'Georgy Girl', before concentrating on orchestral album arrangements and songwriting for other acts.

The more Dusty attracted fortune and fame, the more reclusive her elder brother became, content to write music behind the scenes. Tim Feild pursued a career as an interior decorator, and later chose a spiritual path, becoming involved with the Islamic Sufi religion. He changed his name to Reshad Feild, moved to Zurich and published books on Sufi philosophy. Although Eastern religions are no longer considered strange or exotic, in the early sixties Reshad Feild's Sufism was thought peculiar. Hurst remembers a time shortly after Dusty launched her solo career when Feild and his spiritual friends cornered Johnny Franz backstage at the Palladium. '"Fellas all in sheets", is how Franz described them. They surrounded him and chanted for Dusty's success. Poor guy was totally confused!'

Even though the Springfields disbanded, their records kept coming. Philips released the 'posthumous' single 'If I Was Down and Out / Maracabamba' from the British film *It's All Over Town*, but it had little impact on the charts. In 1964 the company put out a hits album, *The Springfields Story*, and their songs were repackaged again and again on various compilations, showing the enduring strength of their appeal.

Dusty, however, was keen to shake off that folksy down-home image. In November 1963, immediately after the band split, she released her first solo single, 'I Only Want to Be with You'. The rapidity with which she scaled new pop heights took everyone – not least herself – completely by surprise.

3

We Call It the Vamp

'I WAS STRUGGLING TO establish something in England that hadn't been done before, to use those musical influences I could hear in my head. I then got pigeon-holed by that awful phrase "blue-eyed soul singer", a term coined in 1969 that stuck. If I could do the record business all over again, I would have mixed funky R&B with something Scottish, melodic, a real Britishness. In the sixties no one could quite *get* those sounds,' Dusty said to me in 1988, when Phonogram released her album *The Silver Collection*.

From the moment Dusty went solo, she fashioned a new style, providing the bridge between soul and the pop mainstream. An astute entertainer, she attracted a family audience as well as a cult following. And as youth mod culture grew in the sixties – with its stringent attention to fashion, Motown and TV pop programmes like *Ready Steady Go!* – Dusty Springfield, panda-eyed and urbane, emerged as queen bee.

'She was *the* soul singer. Out of all the girls – Lulu, Cilla and all of that – it was Dusty doin' it for me. She made me feel it,' remembers P. P. (Pat) Arnold, the sixties soul diva and a former 'Ikette' on the road with Ike and Tina Turner. Part of what Dusty made Arnold feel was the Vamp, a sound and a style that emerged from the US gospel scene. 'Everything from sixties R&B to house and garage in the nineties that's just gospel, that's just church, we call it the Vamp,' continues Arnold. 'In gospel music, when you sing a song you sing the verse, present the song, then move into the chorus, which is the hook, the groove. Then when you get to the end of the song, all hell breaks loose.'

There is a sense of that full-tilt energy in Dusty's debut solo single, 'I Only Want to Be with You', a joyful, clattering statement of intent, which couldn't have been further from the Springfields in its clarity and originality. It captured some of the verve she'd heard on that Exciters record blasting out in Times Square. It signalled a way out of the stifling conformism of the early sixties UK pop industry, still limited by show tunes and nostalgia.

Dusty had a rich, husky, alto sound that was perfectly suited to the R&B songs she so loved, and, according to Arnold, she spent a lot of time in the mid- to late sixties recording with singer Madeline Bell, 'so that kinda locked it down'. Dusty was also to use the 'Witches' Brew' as backing on her records, the 'Old Girl' network – a pool of talented female session singers that included such American expatriates as Arnold, Madeline Bell and the frank, flamboyant gospel singer Doris Troy.

While there is a tradition of British performers relocating to the States, little has been said about American artists who stayed here. With each US soul revue that came to Britain, there was always at least one artist who stayed behind. Madeline Bell, for instance, came over from Newark, New Jersey, with Alex Bradford's touring gospel spectacular 'Black Nativity', and never returned. 'When I came over to England in 1963 there were, to my knowledge, two or three other black singers in this country, and they sang jazz. I like to think I was one of the first, then came Doris Troy and P. P. Arnold,' Bell told me in 1995 when I was talking to her for my book *She Bop*. 'Suddenly there was this different sound. Before there had been ladies like the Ladybirds and the Breakaways and they were all very good and could read – you could put music in front of them and they'd read it *like* that.' She clicked her finger. 'Course we couldn't read, but we had a feel, because we were solo singers who went out at night and did our own thing. People would say, "What a great singer you are," and I'd say, "You can find ten like me on every street corner where I come from. Every church has a choir, every choir at least ten girl singers who could sing me off the stage."' Dusty brought that energy into pop. Five years of waiting, working and hoping paid off when, on 21 November 1963, 'I Only Want to Be with You' hit the British charts at no. 18. An instant success, it went up to no. 4, and stayed in the charts for thirteen weeks, attracting global sales of a million copies and a gold disc in the UK.

Her rapid rise to popularity was accelerated by well-thought-out management and highly organized promotion. 'Dusty always had that charismatic persona on television. When she appeared on *Sunday Night at the London Palladium* with the Springfields, it was always her and the two guys. It was a logical progression to go from a country group to a solo career,' says Dave Shrimpton, then production manager at Philips. 'Her first single was a *pop* single, so BBC's Light Programme [then the only official radio station] immediately latched on to it. It was an overnight success, launching nineteen hit singles.'

Vic Billings, Dusty's personal manager throughout the sixties, was more cautious. 'I always thought she would be a big star – but for a time it was touch and go because she'd broken from a successful group,' he told me in the late eighties. 'We put a lot of thought into it. With Johnny Franz as her recording manager we originally did nine tracks and picked "I Only Want to Be with You" from them. It became a big hit, and from then on it was merely a matter of finding the right songs at the right time.'

From the beginning of her solo career, Dusty displayed an aptitude for finding the right songs. She nearly started out with Berry Gordy's song 'Money', which the Beatles issued on an album at the same time but settled instead for 'I Only Want to Be with You', a Mike Hawker / Ivor Raymonde composition.

Ivor Raymonde died in 1990, but a year before his death he told me he wrote the song while on holiday in West Wittering, Sussex. When he came back to London, he played the melody to Dusty during a 'routining session', or production meeting. 'She loved the tune, that tempo,' he said. 'At that time there were a lot of songs about dance, like "The Twist" and "Dancing in the Street", and she wanted a song associated with dancing. I asked Mike Hawker [who'd had a hit with Helen Shapiro's "Walking Back to Happiness"] to write a lyric. He wrote it that night and read the lyrics to Dusty over the phone at seven thirty in the morning. She loved it.'

Raymonde became a major figure in creating Dusty Springfield's sound. A former student at the Trinity College of Music in London, he was an accomplished classical and jazz pianist. After stints in various bands, including one with jazz veteran Ronnie Scott, he became musical director at the BBC, arranging, and singing bass in the occasional session. From there it was a short step into recording. He joined Philips in the late fifties, to produce such artists as the Walker Brothers, Marty Wilde and, of course, the Springfields.

'Being young, lovely and a bit big-headed in those days, I tried to do something the Americans weren't doing,' said Raymonde. 'Before the sixties we used to pinch and steal things from American records. I then had good success with Marty Wilde's "Danny", a song based on Conway Twitty's "Donna". To my utter amazement, Americans began copying my arrangements absolutely note for note. Well, imitation is the sincerest form of flattery. After that I tried to write something special or unique to me for each record.' His son, Simon, inherited his father's talent, and in the eighties created surreal pop soundscapes with the Cocteau Twins.

Raymonde proved a big money-spinner for Philips, writing hits for such performers as Frankie Vaughan and Anne Shelton. In return, the record company invested more money in his sessions, and Raymonde's basic horn, trumpet and rhythm sections were augmented by strings. By a stroke of luck, Dusty arrived at this point, and was able to take full advantage of Raymonde's new studio facilities. 'For a long time, artists recorded on a basic two-track,' recalled Raymonde, 'but Dusty recorded on four-track. We thought that was the ultimate.'

As there were then no double-tracking or overlaying techniques, Raymonde would squeeze as many top orchestral musicians from the Royal Philharmonic Orchestra as he could into his Stanhope Gate studio at Marble Arch in London. Influenced ('though not slavishly') by Phil Spector's enigmatically blurred 'wall of sound' production for acts like the Chiffons and the Ronettes, he delighted in adapting that orchestral edge to his own tastes: 'We'd make the records very important-sounding with a huge band, then we'd take the recorded acetate and deliberately distort it.'

Dusty didn't find the process easy. 'Philips was an extremely dead studio ... it sounded as though someone had turned down the treble on everything and ... I couldn't get an edge,' she once said. 'There was no ambience and it was like singing in a padded cell and, you know, I'd land up feeling like I was *in* a padded cell. I had to get out of there!' More often than not, she would end up in the ladies' toilet because the acoustics were right. 'Close My Eyes and Count to Ten', for instance, was recorded at the end of the corridor. 'I'm paralysed by studios,' she said. 'I feel trapped and I feel tested.' Dusty would always add her vocals last, after the rhythm track, orchestration and overdubs. She would gather her courage together, enter the studio, have the music cranked up high in her headphones to a decibel level 'on the threshold of pain', and then sing. That is how she forced herself to perform at that level of exhilaration.

That intense pitch, coupled with Ivor Raymonde's distortion techniques, contributed to the Spectorish sound on Dusty's sixties pop hits, an overblown extravaganza that appealed to everyone. 'It wasn't only kids buying her records,' says Dave Shrimpton. 'She had a mature audience too. It meant that everybody was buying her records. Not even the Stones and the Beatles had that. The record company and management pushed like mad to get as much exposure as they could. Frankly, Philips did a good job on Dusty in the sixties.'

Immediately after her solo debut was released, promotional wheels turned. Within three weeks she had appeared on every music TV show going, from *Saturday Club* to *Parade of the Pops* to *Thank Your Lucky Stars*. The press showered her with accolades. 'A challenging, tension-packed time for Dusty, and an exciting and perhaps memorable time for the public, who may be about to witness the birth of a brilliant new star,' the *NME* gushed, while *Melody Maker* proclaimed: 'The days of tense anxiety are over. The nerves and the stage fright are momentarily eased. The decision to break up the Springfields seems to be paying off. FOR DUSTY SPRINGFIELD IS A SOLO STAR.'

'It's marvellous to be popular, but foolish to think it will last,' Dusty said pragmatically, two weeks after 'I Only Want to Be with You' hit the charts.

Vic Billings had other ideas. 'We didn't want her to become a singer who had a couple of hits, then went and did end-of-pier shows in the summer and pantomimes at Christmas, and called herself a star,' he said. 'Everything rested on the records. We had to establish her. In those days the rule of thumb was you'd consider yourself a star if the third single was a hit. We did records two by two – two ballads, two uptempos, two ballads, et cetera.'

In 1963 Billings was finding his feet as a manager. Originally from Devon, he moved to London in 1954 and became a group trainee in the Rank Organisation. He graduated to house manager in Glasgow, then to booking live shows for the New Victoria Theatre in London, ending up as assistant controller at the Victor Sylvester dance studios. However, his burning ambition was to be a pop manager. 'It was a catch-22. I was told that if I had the experience, they'd take me on. So I decided to start up on my own.'

After opening a small office in London's South Molton Street, Billings handled such acts as Eden Kane and Paul Raven (who later made his name as seventies glam-rock star Gary Glitter). He spotted Dusty when he was working for the agent Tito Burns and arranging odd bookings for the Springfields. 'I heard they were splitting up, and I thought she needed a good manager, so I phoned her up. We went out, had a cup of coffee and talked music. She said, "I'll think about it." Next thing I knew people were saying, "I hear you're going to manage Dusty Springfield." She'd told everyone already!' Billings was a polite, sensitive man with a warm, almost camp sense of humour. Although with Dusty he hit the big time quickly, he was still relatively unknown as a manager and in the beginning was knocked back by others. 'I'd had a lot of experience with live shows but wasn't in with the big agents. What hurt me was she had "I Only Want to Be with You" and wanted to do the major TV show *Sunday Night at the London Palladium*. But the Beverley Sisters turned up when she was in the charts and sang *her* song on the *Palladium*. Which, to say the least, pissed me off. It was a fight to get into the establishment.'

In a sense, Dusty and Billings learned their trade together. Eventually he got her on to various *Palladium* shows and, as her popularity grew, people advised him that she should be topping the bill. 'I thought, we'll let her top when she's ready,' Billings recalled. 'She was learning. When she first left the boys, she missed them. She'd been crammed in with them, unused to moving much onstage. It was when her personal development came as a solo singer that she topped the bill.'

Early in 1964 Dusty released her second single, 'Stay Awhile'. Another uptempo bouncy pop number, this Hawker/Raymonde composition reached no. 13 and stayed in the charts for ten weeks. Despite its obvious quality, Dusty felt despondent. 'It's terrible!' she declared. 'I don't feel in the least confident about it.' Her reaction was not unusual – she was often overcritical of her own work. 'I'm pretty good at assessing other people's discs, but when it comes to my own efforts, I'm hopeless,' she wailed.

It was in the recording studio that many of Dusty's insecurities came out. She had constructed the star persona of Dusty Springfield, but then had difficulty believing in it. She didn't trust her voice since she was riddled with self-doubt – and she was a passionate perfectionist, which often caused friction. Songwriter Clive Westlake remarked candidly to me that, 'She was a bitch in the studio.' Dusty has countered this: 'I was just blundering through it. It was called tunnel vision. I wanted it that way, so they probably went off and said, "What a cow!" To this day Clive Westlake calls me a cow because I knew what I wanted.'

According to Ivor Raymonde, 'She'd got quite a reputation for being a hard case. Vera Lynn or Anne Shelton had never spoken up. They'd just gone in the studio, recorded and walked out. Dusty took a more personal interest in a record. She was good to work with – I was absolutely knocked out when she decided to do my songs – but she was also an exacting artist. Bad musicians would annoy her, the tempo had to be just so, and before a session the key had to be set so it wasn't too high or low. She was a perfectionist, like me, so we got on well.' Simon Raymonde recalls his late father talking to him about Dusty, saying that she was painfully shy. 'My dad said she had a lot of hurdles to get over, a lot of problems with self-confidence. However, she wasn't frightened to try something new and she lobbied to get good songs. Very few people had the nerve and strength of character to hold out for that. Her voice is peerless, and that's why she's revered.'

Dusty's former lover, folk star Julie Felix recalls: 'She was such a musician. She knew exactly what she wanted. Those days women were so disrespected.' Both signed to Philips, with Felix's records released on subsidiary Fontana, the two women would sometimes go to each other's recording sessions. 'She taught me what to listen to, and got me into recording techniques,' says Felix. 'I had terrible trouble with headphones, for instance, so she taught me to sing with speakers in front of me, as if it was a performance. I learned so much from her.'

After many intensive sessions, Dusty's debut solo album, *A Girl Called Dusty*, came out in the spring of 1964. The unwieldy Springfield cravats and starched skirts were gone: twenty-five-year-old Dusty appeared on the sleeve in a casual denim shirt and jeans, projecting calm, hip assurance. Her album opened with the raw, rootsy track 'Mama Said', a cheery acknowledgement of burgeoning American soul. Also featured is a version of the Lesley Gore classic 'You Don't Own Me', plus the edgy girl group song 'When the Lovelight Starts Shining Thru His Eyes' and the jaunty teen fantasy 'Wishin' and Hopin''. Dusty was now bang up to date.

Johnny Franz was overall producer of the record in the UK, but for the US version (simply called *Dusty*) a few tracks were recorded at New York's Mira Sound Studios with Nashville arranger Jerry Kennedy and Shelby Singleton, the A&R inspiration behind the Springfields' Nashville album, *Folk Songs from the Hills*. Singleton acted as a catalyst for Dusty's soulful vision, enabling her to realize some of the sounds she heard in her head but until then hadn't been able to fix on vinyl. He recalls that after leaving the Springfields, Dusty became 'more black with her voice. She was very professional, certain that she didn't want to do country music and that she wanted to do more soul.'

The stand-out track is 'Mockingbird', formerly a big underground R&B hit for Charlie and Inez Foxx, the black brother and sister duo whose early sixties songs paved the way for Marvin Gaye and Tammi Terrell. Here, Dusty takes both parts of the duet, singing key lines with a deadpan delivery, while her raucous backing vocals act as an ironic counterpart. It's a mistress-piece, both celebratory and caustic. Like many white beat artists, she was keen to record songs that had been big in the US R&B charts – the Beatles did this with 'Twist & Shout', the Searchers with the Drifters' 'Sweets for My Sweet' and Wayne Fontana and the Mindbenders with 'Groovy Kind of Love', originally sung by Patti LaBelle. One of the most famous was the Moody Blues recording of Bessie Banks's phenomenal 'Go Now'.

A Girl Called Dusty also showed her facility with epic ballads, establishing what was to become a fruitful relationship with songwriters Burt Bacharach and Hal David. Her version of 'Twenty-four Hours from Tulsa' is racked with lust and remorse, while 'Anyone Who Had a Heart' is made all the more poignant by her almost unbearably sharp, breathy style, a technique that took hours to perfect.

Brooks Arthur, who became Dusty's producer in the seventies, worked on this session as an engineer. He had previously been with Phil Spector and was intrigued and enthralled by Dusty's approach. 'I remember her microphone technique. She worked it to the maximum, making great sounds with her vocals by moving in and out on the mike and singing sideways,' he says. 'When she sang "You Don't Own Me" she moved her hands and head as if it was a stage show. She knew the science of recording.'

A triumph of versatility and conviction, *A Girl Called Dusty* went into the Top 10, remaining in the album charts for twenty-three weeks. It turned out to be the nineteenth bestselling album of 1964, sending Dusty into the first division of UK pop. When her third single, 'I Just Don't Know What to Do with Myself', was released, it was only the Beatles and the Rolling Stones who kept her off the top spot.

That summer Dusty cemented her link with American soul when she went to play twelve days in Murray ('The K') Kaufman's shows at New York's 5,000-seater Fox Theater, in Brooklyn. Kaufman was a famous New York radio DJ who, during Beatlemania, considered himself a virtual fifth Beatle and loved all things Liverpool. The Fox was a cavernous working cinema with popular live shows, and Dusty's visit was as arduous as it was exciting, with six rowdy shows a day starting at ten in the morning. Many were packed with children singing along to the hits of the day.

This was the first time she really performed with the R&B artists she admired, doing shows with the Ronettes, the Contours, Little Anthony and the Imperials, and Motown acts such as the Supremes and the Temptations. As one of the few white acts on the bill, she at first found it daunting. Martha Reeves, lead singer with Martha and the Vandellas, remembered being summoned by Kaufman soon after the start of the season. She thought something had gone terribly wrong, but he said: 'We got a problem we think you can help us with. We've got a young lady from across the water and she's a bit unhappy, missing home.'

Reeves went to Dusty's dressing-room door, but the young UK star wouldn't let her come in. 'Dusty was having a fit, throwing teapots at the wall and cursing loudly. She was obviously upset,' recalls Reeves. Kaufman knocked on the door saying, 'Here's someone to see you.' Dusty told them to go away. Then he said, 'This is Martha Reeves at the door and she wants to talk to you.'

Inch by inch, Dusty opened the door. Kaufman pushed Reeves into the room and walked off. 'I started kicking the stuff around 'cos it sounded like fun to hear the breaking of cups and saucers,' Reeves laughs. Then Dusty confided that she had no friends and had to do shows with people she didn't know, and that Kaufman had forgotten to introduce her. 'She wasn't happy. We talked, and became closest companions for the rest of the summer.'

From then on, Dusty began to relax. She would squeeze up in the tiny dressing room with the Ronettes, swapping stories and make-up hints. 'It was hot, like 104 degrees, and all our beehives were in there – three black beehives and one white one. It was collisions constantly,' Dusty recalled. Next door were Martha and the Vandellas, and on the other side were the Supremes. Diana Ross's mother hemmed Dusty's dresses for her, while Smokey Robinson's wife, Claudette, would cook dinner for everyone on the top floor of the building.

Dusty learned a lot from this backstage sorority. She began to experiment with her vocals, taking tips from the Shirelles' lead singer, Shirley Alston, and singing backup for the Vandellas while standing in the wings. She enthused about the latter as the most exciting group she had ever seen. 'Dancing in the Street' had 'a beat like a sledgehammer', while Martha Reeves's voice 'had a richness that some of the other groups didn't have'. But it seems Dusty didn't always hit it off with the other female soul artists. Writer

David Evans alleges that Nina Simone, for instance, resented her presence on the scene, and even once threw a glass of whisky in her face. 'She called me a honky and resented me being alive!' Dusty said. 'She was having a few problems, which I thought I could solve by being nice. Huh. I was still as naive as ever.'

Dusty spent that tough, challenging American trip watching and learning. 'It was a dream come true,' she said later. 'It was priceless. I would've *paid* to do it. I was the token whitey, the token honky. They were very affectionate – if someone caused me any trouble they'd say, "Don't lean on her, she's with us." I blundered my way through Harlem not *knowing* what was around me, a beehive surrounded by pimps, hookers, addicts and pushers. I stayed at the Hotel Teresa, with broken windows, and Malcolm X was there. God protects fools and innocents. I grew up fast.'

Martha Reeves recalls Dusty coming to visit her backstage at the Harlem Apollo one night. 'There she was, she'd bravely got a taxi and come to the back door. I don't know how she did it. I said, "What are you doing here in Harlem? Aren't you afraid?" "No," she said, "I'm going where I wanna go."' That single-mindedness came to the fore again when Dusty acted as an ambassador for the Motown sound in the UK.

By the time she returned from America it had become de rigueur for any self-respecting mod to keep an eye on *Ready, Steady, Go!* Descending from the cappuccino or coffee-bar cats of the late fifties who listened to modern jazz (hence the term modernist for early mods), the mods looked with disdain on their main youth culture rivals, the greasy 'ton-up' biker boy rockers. Mods adapted a sophisticated Italian continental image, with the emphasis on detail, tailored suits for the boys and, for girls, short, sharp dresses. They rode clean scooters and claimed a devoted allegiance to three US soul labels: Stax, Atlantic and Motown. Every Friday evening *Ready, Steady, Go!* would begin with the statement 'The weekend starts here', showing resident *RSG!* faces or top mods demonstrating the latest dance steps or the latest gear. It was an important link for mods nationwide.

Among the many sixties pop shows – from *Oh Boy!* to *Wham!* and *Thank Your Lucky Stars* – *Ready, Steady, Go!* stood out because of its pioneering approach. It was raw and spontaneous, with an immediacy and a documentary feel that was not necessarily flattering to the artists, but they loved its anarchy. Dusty made frequent appearances, whether it was looking relaxed and jaunty walking down a flight of stairs to 'Every Day I Have to Cry', or throwing herself with dramatic abandon into a crowd of mods while singing a heart-wrenching ballad. While beat boys like Mick Jagger were considered less cool to the style cognoscenti, Dusty's fluid pop-soul became synonymous with a new, discriminating pop audience.

'*Ready, Steady, Go!* actually *created* the mod scene,' the late Dave Godin told me. A renowned soul writer and archivist, he was Dusty's friend and founder of the Motown Appreciation Society in Britain. 'After the health and educational opportunities created by the 1945 Beveridge Report, there was a new middle class. Mods were the cultural avant-garde and *Ready, Steady, Go!* was their showcase. They wanted to look like a million dollars on TV,' he said. White, suburban and immersed in black music, Dusty was the ultimate mod queen. Countless 'modettes' copied her eye make-up and casual style; to them she was something of a mentor.

One-time leader of the Dave Clark Five, an astute Dave Clark bought up the *RSG!* series and released highlights on video in the eighties. His enthusiasm is still unabated. 'The show was live. Everyone was crammed in a studio at Holborn – the building that became the Registrar of Births, Marriages and Deaths,' he says. '*Ready, Steady, Go!* wasn't pretentious. It had tension and excitement, it didn't matter if you were DC5 or the Beatles, you would open the show regardless of who you were. Everyone dropped in, whether it was Michael Caine, Zandra Rhodes or Mary Quant. It was a show that depicted fashion and taste, and it gave unknowns a chance. The camera didn't hide the sweat, and people answered frankly in earthy interviews. It depicted what the sixties were all about.'

Dave Godin remembered its hilarity and chaotic feel. 'Once, the soul singer Irma Thomas appeared, and she had to walk down a staircase in a tight sequin dress looking like a million dollars, while me and a crowd of male fans accompanied her, looking adoring. It wasn't rehearsed, and she was scared stiff of slipping. While miming "Time Is on My Side", she sang to us, "I can't see where I'm fuckin' goin'…" '

RSG! became a hotbed of talent and activity, a kind of sixties pop barometer. 'There was a lot of camaraderie with everybody,' recalls singer Lulu. 'We were a bit of a family, and the eyes of the world, especially with the success of the Beatles, were looking at this country.' Dusty later said animatedly, '*RSG!*, yeah, great, all that hair! You needed a spanner to cut it out! Live, the show was absolute chaos. Especially the New Year's Eve ones, because everyone had far too much to drink. They used to announce people and they weren't there. I filled in for Gene Pitney one time. Now *that* was interesting.'

Though a white middle-class Irish London girl, Dusty gained the respect of her black American peers and cemented her friendship with Martha Reeves. 'When I heard her on the radio before we met, I just assumed she was American and black,' the latter said of Dusty. 'Motown signed up nearly all the best new talent at that time, and I remember being a little surprised to find she was with a different label – and I was absolutely astounded when I finally saw her on TV.' In 1964, the year that Mary Wells's 'My Guy' became the first Motown hit in Britain, reaching no. 5, Dusty effectively became PR and champion of the Detroit soul label. She worked closely with Dave Godin, who founded the British Motown Appreciation Society while he was owner of Soul City, a London shop that specialized in soul imports.

Back in 1964 Motown needed all the publicity it could get. The previous year three Motown delegates had spent several weeks in Europe investigating international distribution. They emerged with a short-lived deal with Oriole Records, a small outlet in London unable to offer the degree of promotion necessary to break black American artists into Britain. In 1963 only one British-produced record reached the US Top 10, compared to thirty-two the following year. While Britain was doing well, though, the US suffered: American-produced hits dropped by almost 40 per cent, and while it was difficult for a major white American pop act to score UK hits, for an unknown black artist from Detroit it was almost impossible.

Already a faithful follower of soul music, Godin hatched a plan. 'I wrote to Motown boss Berry Gordy saying, "Your marvellous record thing is terribly handled over here." I got a six-page telegram back – I never knew such things existed! – saying, "Would you like to come and visit us in Detroit?" I went on the trip with a note of good wishes from Dusty and Vicki [Wickham, the associate producer of *RSG!*], and got a big reception. I was the first British person to visit Motown. I was pretty fly, even in those days.'

As no one could guarantee which Motown artist would take off first, Godin decided that it would be best to sell the corporate-label identity and sound in Britain. In preparation for the first Motown tour of the UK, the Supremes' 'Where Did Our Love Go?' was released during 1964 as a follow-up to Mary Wells's success. It was picked up by pirate stations like Radio Caroline, played to death, and consequently became a huge hit, reaching no. 2 in the UK charts. Its follow-up, 'Baby Love', then went to no. 1. Few other American releases broke the hold Britain had on its own charts between 1963 and 1965.

'Black American culture, primarily manifested in soul music, was a truly subversive culture working in American society,' Godin told me. 'Reactionary elements were very aware of it. Radio stations wouldn't play "race" records because it represented opposition to mainstream culture. Soul music had to gain a degree of respectability. This is where people like Dusty, Vicki and I were very useful. We were white people who loved the music, were on its wavelength, but because we were white and could dress up relatively bourgeois, we could open doors where a black promoter couldn't.'

Vicki Wickham worked hard to bring acts from the Tamla-Motown Revue on to *RSG!* 'The Motown Revue was sold because Dusty said, "Package me with it and my name will get it on,"' recalled Godin. 'Until that point the powers that be hadn't heard of Motown and weren't interested. Dusty had a positive enthusiasm for the music. At the same time, she didn't pretend she was the bona fide article. She acknowledged her roots, and often said that she wished she'd been born black.'

It was at this time that singer Cliff Richard affectionately, but rather crudely, called her 'the White Negress'.

In March 1965 the Revue arrived in Britain to spread the word. Dusty hosted a TV special introducing the 'fabulous' Supremes, the 'exciting' Martha and the Vandellas, the 'fantastic' Stevie Wonder, the 'amazing' Smokey Robinson and the Miracles, and the Earl Van Dyke Six. They toured the UK with guest Georgie Fame and the Blue Flames, doing a frenetic twenty-one shows in twenty-four days.

Godin remembered the opening night of the tour on 20 March at London's Astoria Theatre, Finsbury Park: 'Every soul fan in London had turned out to pack that place. I can't describe the air of celebration. Everyone was so elated they were talking to strangers. I sat talking with Dusty in the stalls and some kids came up asking for her autograph. "Any other time," she said, "but not tonight, because I'm here as a fan." She has this really noble side to her. Very noble ...' It came to the fore when Motown boss Berry Gordy began pushing the nascent Supremes at the expense of the Vandellas. 'I was supposed to be starring on this special tour, but I was pushed to the side and I'm still a little angry about that,' recalled Martha Reeves. 'I got my revenge because we were the ones to sing with Dusty on "Wishin' and Hopin'". I saw Ross in the wings eating her heart out – she didn't know Dusty well enough to get that spot so ... I won!'

Despite the elation of the first night, the rest of the Motown tour was decidedly rocky: Georgie Fame was booed off by soul fans who'd come to witness 'the real thing'; in some areas the venues were only a third full, and halfway through, bandleader Earl Van Dyke and his musicians went on strike, complaining that they were underpaid. After hasty negotiations, Berry Gordy increased their fee, and the Revue trundled on.

When asked by *Melody Maker* why the tour had been a flop, Dusty answered, 'It was too advanced. Motown audiences in the States get an enormous proportion of coloured people and, of course, there isn't such a large community here. And the majority of the acts weren't sufficiently well known here. They knew the Supremes, of course, and had just about heard of Martha, but the rest of the acts were unknown to the average customer.'

However, the press reacted favourably. Ron Boyle of the *Daily Express* in particular applauded the new label in colourful phrases: 'To counterblast the Liverpool sound along came the Detroit sound known to the "in" crowd as Tamla-Motown ... The punch of the big beat in a velvet glove.' By 1966, Motown was steadily reaping the benefits, with regular Top 20 hits and a devoted British following. 'Dusty had a lot to do with our recognition. She touted us,' Martha Reeves asserted. 'Any chance she got she'd mention Detroit and the Motown sound. Lots of things happened after that tour, so she introduced Motown to England. She can take credit for that.'

It was during the first flush of her solo success, in the middle of her campaign for Motown, that Dusty was propelled into the political arena. At the end of 1964, a seemingly insignificant clause was added to her contract before a tour of South Africa. It resulted in a furore that involved the UK Musicians Union, the entertainers' union Equity, the House of Commons and the South African government itself. She was not destined to have the smooth ride to success she so desperately wanted.

4

Dusty in South Africa

Dusty's commitment to American soul and racial integration took a darker turn at the end of 1964 when she was scheduled to play South Africa. Nearly twenty-five years later South African apartheid had become a major debate in political pop, with the spectacular Nelson Mandela 70th Birthday Tribute at Wembley Arena on 11 July 1988 surpassing Band Aid, Live Aid and the Amnesty World Tour in its sheer size and impact.

A host of major stars, including Whitney Houston, Harry Belafonte, Stevie Wonder, Miriam Makeba, Sting, Dire Straits and Simple Minds took part in the marathon eleven-hour event, which was watched by 72,000 people in the stadium and transmitted live by satellite to sixty-three countries. The underlying purpose was clear: to raise the issue of apartheid by focusing on ANC leader Nelson Mandela, who had reached his seventieth birthday after years spent as a political prisoner. The money went to British Anti-Apartheid and various aid groups in South Africa.

To Jerry Dammers, leader of the British musicians' pressure group Artists Against Apartheid and writer of the hit 'Free

Nelson Mandela', this concert crowned a decade of intensive pop campaigning. Within two years, many of the artists who performed at Wembley were back on the same stage with the recently released Mandela victoriously addressing the crowd. The long-term effects of economic sanctions against South Africa, along with initiatives by President de Klerk, were principal factors in securing Mandela's release in February 1990, but pop played its part in publicizing the plight of South Africa's most famous prisoner. In the late eighties the connection between pop music and the fight against apartheid was vitally important.

South Africa, however, was not high on pop's agenda throughout the sixties and seventies. Apart from 'Biko' by Peter Gabriel, Gil Scott-Heron's 'Johannesburg' and protest singer Ewan MacColl's *Angry Muse* album, few songs directly condemned apartheid, and artists continued to play Sun City, an entertainment complex in the 'homeland' of Bophuthatswana, dubbed the Las Vegas of South Africa.

This changed in December 1980 when the UN passed Resolution 35/206 supporting an official cultural boycott of South Africa. Six years later fierce controversy broke out over Paul Simon's naive decision to record his bestselling *Graceland* album there with South African musicians, and his concerts were picketed.

By contrast, in 1964 there was minimal support for a boycott. Dusty's manager Vic Billings went out on a reconnaissance mission to South Africa. A few months previously, he had drawn up with South African promoter Dennis Wainer a contract that contained a clause stipulating that Dusty and her backing band, the Echoes, who were all Musicians Union members, would perform only at non-segregated venues. She was the first British artist to include a 'no apartheid' clause in a South African contract. Until then performers had appeared regularly without controversy before segregated audiences, and the Musicians Union was a solitary voice in opposition. In 1957, long before equal-rights legislation had been cracked in Britain, and before any other trade union took a similar stand, the MU organized a strike at the Scala Ballroom, Wolverhampton, against a 'colour bar' imposed by the management.

The strike made British trade union legal history, with a row in the courts as to whether musicians were entitled to take such collective action. Now, of course, segregation is illegal and universally deplored, but at the time the MU was not without its critics. In 1962 their decision to place an embargo on professional work in South Africa was the beginning of a furious controversy that raged for decades until the final dismantling of apartheid.

In the sixties repression in South Africa intensified, brought on by the organization of the labour movement, the sweep of black consciousness through colleges and schools and, in 1961, the formation of the ANC's armed wing, Umkhonto we Sizwe. Detention without trial was introduced, first for ninety days, then for 180 and, under the Terrorism Act of 1966, for an indefinite period. Security police tortured detainees at will, and deaths occurred during detention.

In the UK in 1964, though, the idea of a Western cultural boycott was still in its infancy. Almost unwittingly, Dusty became a test case for this policy. Her decision to include a 'big black clause' stemmed from her love of and respect for black music, and her friendships with prominent black American singers like

Martha Reeves, Dionne Warwick and Stevie Wonder, all of whom felt strongly about the worsening situation for blacks in South Africa. To an extent it reflected what was going on in the USA, with its own growing civil rights movement.

'Dusty was anti-apartheid. Black injustice really burned her,' said her friend Dave Godin. 'There were different perspectives in the sixties ... The black issue was almost as equally focused on the USA, because there was the Montgomery bus boycott, the murder of white civil rights workers from New York, the lynchings and the assassination of Martin Luther King.'

Dusty's contemporary P. P. Arnold remembers it as a time of urgent political change. 'Before I came to England I'd never lived in a mixed society. In America everything is black and white. On the road with Ike and Tina it was the chitlin' circuit – all black clubs and theatres like the Apollo and the Howard. I was coming out of the civil rights movement. The Watts riots started right around the corner from where I lived and grew up. The struggle for integration was happening, and it was exciting to be part of the whole integrated cosmopolitan thing in England in the sixties.'

Later Dusty condemned the racism of the Ku Klux Klan: 'In a country which abhors Communism and will break anybody's neck if they say anything against the American Constitution, I don't see how this kind of thing is allowed to exist.' In a bitter irony, twenty-five years later she was adopted as a musical heroine by the crudely racist British Movement organization. In an issue of their fanzine *Vanguard* she was briefly applauded as a 'white woman expressing a white culture', on the basis of her iconic image – the sixties blonde beehive and white gown.

In sixties Britain there was a growing awareness of the

inherent evils of racism, but it was a slow process. Hippie musicians and underground rockers may have been enlightened, but many mainstream performers remained resolutely apolitical. 'Dusty was the first one who had the *guts* to stand up and make a statement,' asserts her secretary, Pat Rhodes. Prior to her South African dates Dusty made a statement that the authorities there found deeply provocative. It first appeared in *New Musical Express* on 27 November 1964: 'I've got a special clause written into the contract which stipulates that I shall play only to non-segregated audiences. That's my little bit to help the coloured people there. I think I'm the first British artist to do this. Brian Poole and the Tremeloes were supposed to do the same, but I believe that in the end they had to play some segregated concerts. If they force me into anything like that I'll be on the first plane home.' It was this statement that caused trouble for her later.

Ten days before the tour was due to start, Vic Billings flew out to South Africa. 'It was a beautiful country but as soon as I got to Johannesburg, I didn't really like it. The guy promoting it, Dennis Wainer, was a Jewish lawyer who ran a legal aid for coloured people, so the South African government weren't terribly enamoured of him. Also, it emerged afterwards that in 1965 they were going to strengthen the "Bantu" laws. We were on a sticky wicket before we went. We didn't know *what* was going on, apart from the fact that we were caught up in the middle of it.'

Initially there were no problems. Dusty's first two shows in Johannesburg were a non-segregated success. She then went on to Wittebome, ten miles outside Cape Town, for the next shows. 'Both were sold out,' recalled Billings. 'It was rather sweet. All the coloured kids and the white kids were together outside the stage door, and they all knew her records. There was no racial tension among young people.'

Government officials, however, saw this as a blatant flouting of apartheid laws. Within days of Dusty's arrival in South Africa they had been tailing the group, to present them with an ultimatum in Cape Town. Billings remembered, 'The police arrived just before our second show there, took us to the hotel, took our passports and said, "We're going to have to sort out your working permit." They came back the next day and said that the tour could continue, but only if we played to segregated audiences.'

Because Dusty had sworn before she left Britain that any alteration in the contract would result in her taking 'the first plane home', the South African authorities were clearly prepared to push her to a breach of contract or, better still, have her out of the country altogether. 'They gave us twenty-four hours to stay in South Africa, which was tantamount to deportation,' said Billings. 'It got rather nasty. Dusty was very upset. We were scared and marooned in a hotel for three days, not allowed to make calls home to London and surrounded by people opposed to us. I refused to go without the Echoes. They were in another hotel and the police hadn't bothered with them. I said I wasn't leaving Cape Town until I'd got the group with me.'

Eventually the authorities served a deportation order and transferred the party to Johannesburg, where they were offered just two seats on a plane to Rome. Billings, again, refused to go without the rest of the group. 'They had to phone up the Ministry of the Interior to allow us another twenty-four hours and get us all on to a BOAC plane home. The first class had been roped off for us, and when we got on all the other passengers got up and clapped.'

On 17 December Dusty arrived back in London to a tumultuous press reception. She was pictured on the front page of all the daily papers under such headlines as 'POP STAR IN COLOUR BAR ROW', 'DUSTY ORDERED OUT', 'DUSTY: NOW FOR A BOYCOTT?' and 'SHOWBIZ V. APARTHEID'. 'We never realized it had caused so much fuss,' said Billings. 'It was horrendous and frightening.' Amid the barrage of publicity, major South African impresario Alfred Herbert was quick to release the damning statement: 'I don't think Miss Springfield came here so much to sing as to make a name for herself as a martyr and reap a lot of publicity before she goes to America.'

Dusty retorted furiously, 'I could jump off Tower Bridge if I wanted my name in the papers. I would hardly put the whole Echoes show out of work for publicity. I have been to America four times already. I don't need this type of publicity. I did not break any laws; it was agreed I should appear before multiracial audiences.' After that statement was issued, she cried for days.

While the group had been holed up in Cape Town, Dusty's agent, then Tito Burns, was left holding the reins in London. He gave daily statements to the press in support of Dusty: 'We made it absolutely plain that Dusty would not tolerate being made to sing to segregated audiences,' he said. 'She has very strong feelings about this colour business – Dusty's a pretty deep-thinking girl. I'm fully behind her in everything she does in this matter.'

Beatle Ringo Starr then spoke up: 'Good for Dusty. I would have done the same thing. It's stupid to have segregated audiences, especially as the music came from the Negroes in the first place.'

Songwriter Mitch Murray added, 'A disappointing number of British stars have been only too eager to play to South African audiences, segregated or not. Some of them, luckily, have been stopped in their tracks by the Musicians Union.'

However, Dusty was also the target of fierce criticism from those anxious to protect show-business profit and privilege. 'I was very annoyed with people like Max Bygraves who said we did it for publicity,' says Billings. 'I'd like *him* to have gone out there and gone through what we went through. We stuck to our guns. The MU would've blacklisted Dusty if we'd played to segregated audiences. It was our principle anyway. We had coloured friends who didn't like what was going on there.'

Dusty's action hit a raw nerve with comedian and singer Max Bygraves, as he was due to visit the country a few months later as part of a £55,000 world tour, but without his MU accompanist Gladys Morgan. Her stand sparked off furious debate in the British show-business unions Equity and the Variety Artists Federation, as Dusty was a member of both. The day after her expulsion from South Africa, the assistant secretary of Equity, Peter Plouviez, announced, 'We will find it difficult to resist pressure from a large section of our members who have been calling for a boycott.' While the MU was already exercising its ban on work in South Africa, Equity and Variety Artists still allowed their members to perform there, which resulted in confusion. Many acts were split down the middle: pop singer and Equity member Adam Faith, for instance, was scheduled to fly to South Africa later that month without his group, the Roulettes, because they were in the MU.

The debate even reached the House of Commons when on 19 December fifteen MPs signed a motion applauding Dusty's action in standing against 'the obnoxious doctrine of apartheid in South Africa'. The South African Ministry of the Interior responded with a pre-prepared statement that Miss Springfield had been asked to apply for an 'alien's temporary permit', which allowed her to stay in the country for a limited time. 'It is clear, therefore, that she is not being deported as stated in the press,' read the statement, 'but that she is leaving the country because the validity of her permit expires today ... Miss Springfield came to this country with the avowed object of defying the Government's stated policy in regard to multiracial audiences ... She was on two occasions warned through her manager to observe our South African way of life in regard to entertainment and was informed that if she failed to do so, she would have to leave the country. She chose to defy the Government, and she was accordingly allowed to remain in the country for a limited time only.'

The controversy was fuelled further by accusations from a Mr Quibell, manager of Cape Town's Luxurama Theatre, where Dusty played. As the theatre was a well-known multiracial venue where unsegregated audiences had been the rule since its opening, Quibell believed that Dusty 'waved the red rag at the Government' unnecessarily in her assertion that she'd play only to mixed crowds, whatever happened. He claimed that the ensuing publicity would benefit her next tour of the States. 'As the singer who defied the South African Government ban she is likely to go down well in some places there,' he was reported as saying in *The Times*, in a dig at her support of the US civil rights movement.

By well-timed coincidence, the day that Dusty was deported, South African defence minister Mr Fouche said that South Africans should accept the principle that people of all races were entitled to equal opportunity, but in *separate spheres*. Speaking on the Day of the Covenant, a religious holiday in honour of the early pioneers, he went on, 'If we make an honest attempt not to swim against the stream of world opinion, I believe we will have the time to sell our policy to the outside world and even to certain African states.' Meanwhile, in the radical right-wing Orange Free State, leader of the opposition Sir de Villiers Graaff asserted that the whites of South Africa had the right to control their country, and 'interference from outside would not be tolerated'.

These were strategic speeches, at a time when many of the world's newspapers were focused on Dusty's deportation. Not yet as diplomatically isolated as it became in the seventies and eighties, the South African Government were keen to make apartheid seem acceptable. Dusty refuted accusations made against her but, overwhelmed by the furore, told the press, 'I'm strictly a non-political girl. I know nothing whatsoever about politics … I thought it was too easy that the clause about playing multiracial audiences went through without any questions.' Scared by the impact her action had caused, she said later, 'Whatever your personal political feelings are, if you become involved in them publicly you're bound to come out the loser. I wasn't making any major statement, I just felt better about it that way, being the naive person I was.'

She gave away her £2,000 fee for the South African tour to black South African orphan charities. 'I'm disgusted at the way I've been treated,' she said. 'I don't want a penny of my salary.' Doug Reece, of the Echoes, said that the authorities 'didn't actually tell us to go, but our feelings were so strong we thought it best to do so. It's not for us to get mixed up in politics, but the way they treat some of the coloured people is definitely wrong. We had several contracts offered us to stay. One was for a £1,000 a month each – which was a lot of money to us and very tempting. But even for that we didn't feel we could stay.'

Within the music industry there was considerable sympathy for Dusty. *Melody Maker*'s editorial said, 'Everyone in showbiz should be proud of Dusty Springfield ... Some well-meaning people say Dusty should not mix politics with business. The truth is – Dusty didn't. The South African authorities did. Dusty wanted merely to sing to people – all kinds of people, as she can do nearly anywhere else. But the powers that be in South Africa wanted to divide her audiences according to the colour of their skin. Fortunately Dusty wouldn't play ball with such nonsense.'

This debate spurred sack-loads of hate mail to *Melody Maker* that kept coming well into 1965. One such letter with a particularly virulent tone came from a Mr Jan Jordaan of Cape Town. 'If a singer comes to South Africa he must abide with the policy and rules of that country, whether he likes it or not. Frank Ifield, Russ Conway, Vera Lynn and a host of other truly great entertainers and non-"rebels" didn't create trouble while they were over here,' he wrote angrily. Jordaan criticized Dusty for calling South Africa a 'police state', saying, 'If that's the case, then Britain is a state of long-haired, third-rate entertainers with herself as undisputed queen of the mods,' which Dusty must have taken as a great compliment.

The boycott controversy widened to affect other artists. Many tours, particularly by MU bands, were called off. On 9 January 1965, another high-profile singer hit the headlines. This time it was Adam Faith. He had tried unsuccessfully for two weeks to appear before multiracial audiences in South Africa. Eventually, disgusted by the lack of unsegregated venues, he decided to cancel the rest of the tour and fly home. He was just securing his seat belt, three minutes before take-off on the 6.45 p.m. flight from Cape Town, when Sheriff Malan drove up to the airfield with a squeal of brakes, boarded the plane and placed him under arrest for breach of contract.

In the VIP lounge there were lengthy arguments, and Faith was freed when his South African record company posted a £20,000 fine in lieu of a court case scheduled for 13 January. His passport was impounded until the authorities received the money, and a dispirited Adam Faith flew home the following day. From then on, artists were wary about dealing with South Africa. Matters reached crisis point at Equity's annual general meeting in London that spring. It was a stormy gathering, at which steely-voiced actor Derek Nimmo stole the show. Addressing the meeting, he accused Dusty of being 'foolish and irresponsible' over the matter of the deportation. 'Whatever her motives may have been for making her pronouncements to the press, she certainly achieved an enormous step backwards as far as the cause of racial equality was concerned,' he fumed, claiming that she had upset the black South African community by refusing to perform before segregated audiences. He said that black people felt they were being used by her to gain personal publicity. Actor Marius Goring spoke for the union's council, saying smoothly that most members were against apartheid, as indeed was Equity. 'We are servants of the public, both black and white,' he countered. After a two-hour meeting, the union decided not to impose a boycott of South Africa on its members. But Nimmo's comments were met with angry words from Dusty's agent, Tito Burns. 'This is a ridiculous statement!' he said. 'Miss Springfield never wanted to go to South Africa. It took me six months to persuade her. She was given a virtual stormtrooper's edict there saying, "Sign this or get out!" Dusty wanted publicity like a hole in the head – she'd won every show-business award going.' Over twenty-five years later Nimmo's remarks still enraged Dusty. 'What a prat!' she snapped, during an interview with the *Guardian*'s Adam Sweeting in 1990. 'Is [Nimmo] still alive? Well, he's still a prat. I would say it to his face. That was such a prat-like thing to say.'

In 1964 the United Nations Special Committee Against Apartheid, which included speakers like the international star Miriam Makeba, called for a cultural boycott of South Africa. International pressure against apartheid began to grow, until the majority of entertainers refused to play the country as long as the apartheid system was in place.

In 1965 the *Daily Telegraph*'s Peter Simple wrote, 'If the danger increases of our being bored to death by the pontifications of actors and singers on subjects they know nothing about, there will be a good case for some form of apartheid for these over-inflated people themselves.' These 'over-inflated' people had, however naively, brought issues that were previously politically ignored to the forefront of the media. In 1986 the controversy surrounding Paul Simon's *Graceland* brought up renewed calls to clarify further the cultural boycott. Dozens of artists, including Bruce Springsteen and Bono from U2, sang on the Sun City anti-Apartheid charity record, and in 1988 hundreds performed together at Wembley. In 1964 Dusty was on her own.

5

Me and My Beehive
on the Tour Bus

THREE YEARS AFTER embarking on a solo career, Dusty was
an international star. At the peak of her sixties success she
was as influential on the pop scene in Britain as Aretha Franklin
and the Supremes were during the girl-group era in the USA.
While her unique vocal talent sent her sailing up the charts,
her image became ever more exaggerated, the wigs larger, the
gowns more elaborate, the mascara thicker. She was turning
into A Lady, a lounge diva.

But as the outward symbols of pop success became more
pronounced, inwardly Dusty felt trapped and limited by her
own creation. 'Honest to God, the bigger the hair, the blacker
the eyes, the more you can hide,' she said later. But the more
magnificent the image of the Great White Lady, the longer it
took to put together, and the less she believed in it.

'Physically it's harder for a woman, there are a lot more
expectations,' she told me. 'You can't look sloppy. A man can
look attractive and it's part of the male rock mystique, but if I
turned up like that, all scruffy ... The endurance level is much

harder for women. We have the same working conditions, the same pay and the same slog. The upkeep is the tiring part. Look at Whitney Houston, for instance, her upkeep is very demanding. Look at all those hair extensions – that's a lot of hours. No one has to do that for Sting.'

Dusty began her career in an era when women performers were expected to be big band trinkets, to dazzle. 'The fifties were a big time for clothes,' swing star Peggy Lee once said, with huge understatement. She had a penchant for coiffured hair, glistening white dresses and diamond drop earrings, but this wasn't just because she liked them: the more sensational a lady's dress, the more she was going to get noticed. At the height of her fame in the mid-fifties, Alma Cogan performed on *Sunday Night at the London Palladium* wearing a gown with an enormous powder puff skirt and 12,750 diamanté beads stitched into the bodice. She once left a theatre in a dress covered with green feathers, but by the time she had picked her way through two thousand fans they had all been plucked off.

'In those days it was the sequined gowns with a very tight waist. And these gowns were *built*,' fifties jazz singer Elaine Delmar recalls. 'You had to have someone pull you into it. Beautiful workmanship. If you bought one it could last you ten years.' Shots of Dusty in the late fifties with the Lana Sisters show her wearing the regulation diamanté, sequins and built-up bodices. According to Riss Chantelle, Dusty had to *learn* how to present herself like a lady. She undercut this, though, with an irreverent attitude, which surfaced once she went solo. As her image developed, she lost the tomboy awkwardness, but there was always a sense that she was playing a role. When fashion changed with the beat boom of the early sixties, Dusty was quick to ditch the diamanté look for the miniskirted hip young chick.

'Dusty was very serious about what she was doing. She got on with the show and then wanted to go home, no nonsense,' recalls the sixties singer Billie Davis, who often shared a dressing room with Dusty on *Ready, Steady, Go!*. 'She was also very trendy. It was important for girls not to dress in a cabaret style – flamboyant gowns, and that kind of thing. Dusty and myself were able to communicate with what kids were wearing, and the make-up. I had black leather miniskirts ... not *terribly* short, but simple. I used to like black sweaters and black trousers, sort of street style. Dusty moved on later to the designer Darnell, though, and was expected to dress in designer gowns for places like Talk of the Town.'

Davis remembers the *Ready, Steady, Go!* audience as discerning: 'They were a mod audience. There was a strict dress code. For instance, everybody had this thing about "Stan's", a shoemaker in Chelsea who could make the most pointy shoes in Britain. And all the girls were adopting Dusty's panda-eye look. At one time we used shoe polish and had great difficulty getting it off!'

Dusty, though, asserted herself by going one step further than anyone else. If girls were applying heavy paint to their eyelids, she would put on even more, making her eyelashes even thicker, her hair more outrageously peroxide blonde. Sometimes her make-up was so dark that when she appeared on TV her eyes became invisible, engulfed by two coal black circles. 'I try to be as unsexy as possible,' she said. Idolized by girls as much as boys, Dusty attracted female fans who admired her independent, sassy stance. 'Her image was very sophisticated with a slight touch of sluttishness,' her friend Dave Godin told me. 'All black eyes and long lashes. It was very well thought-out.'

Nervous about being photographed, she kept adjusting her hair and worrying about her nails, her eyes, her complexion, her figure, her good side and her bad side. At the peak of her fame in the late sixties she was also at her most anxious. She couldn't bear to be photographed from the left because that was her bad profile, and she was concerned about the laugh lines round her mouth. She covered her short hair with wigs and false pieces that obscured her features; she refused to be seen without full make-up, even at nine in the morning, and would go to endless lengths in hotels to avoid being seen by staff. If she'd ordered a meal in her room, she would hide in the bathroom until it was served. 'My body was wrong; my face was wrong. I always had a very grown-up face. I didn't look like a singer or a model,' she said.

Although she was worried about her image, Dusty was adept at coping in what was still a male world. The music industry has always been a difficult place for a woman, but in the sixties, the role of a female vocalist was far more restricted than it is today. 'This is why she clashed with male musicians – they couldn't believe that this was a woman who knew what she was talking about,' says her friend Pat Rhodes. 'God help if during a live show one of her musicians played a wrong note. She'd see him afterwards. "What happened to you"?' Dusty used her ebullient charm to deflect hostility or any attempts to belittle her, and she wasn't afraid to fight for the kind of image and production sound she wanted. Consequently she secured the affection of her peers. Glasgow belter Lulu once announced in *NME* that

Dusty was her favourite singer. 'She had this fabulous way of communicating through music and we all felt we knew her,' she recalls. 'I loved the sound of her voice; it had that husky, vulnerable quality. She was an original.'

Dusty also won people round with her goonish sense of humour. To relieve the stress of touring she indulged her love of practical jokes. 'She loved naughty jokes, she was such a clown and a terrific mimic,' says Rhodes. During one stage show the high spot of the evening came when she disappeared offstage and returned for her encore wearing a giant pair of plastic feet as a parody of Sandie Shaw, who famously went barefoot onstage 'just for a gag'. Brian Poole, who did several long international tours with Dusty, remembers her fondly as 'one of the lads'. On tours that included mostly male beat groups, from the Tremeloes to Herman's Hermits, Freddie and the Dreamers and the Searchers, Dusty was often the only female performer. She may have been The Lady on the surface, but she held her own admirably with 'the guys'.

'We were very vulgar with Dusty,' Brian Poole recalled in 1989, as he sat opposite me in the dressing room of a Walthamstow working men's club, before a Tremeloes revival gig. 'She always got back at us in a brilliantly clever way. For instance, people gave her bouquets of flowers after every night on the tour, and they never gave us a thing. Being young blokes, we thought, "We'll get this bouquet," and one night we snatched it off her in her dressing room and did horrible things to it. We stamped all over it and did other things that I won't tell you about. We were naughty! But she got us. The next theatre we did had a spiral staircase going down to the stage. She went out, bought a bag of flour, and stood at the top of the stairs with it. Just as we were about to go onstage, all smart in our black suits, she cracked it open and showered flour down on us.'

The Tremeloes appeared, severely chastened with white faces and hair. The audience loved it. Poole remembers another time on tour in Australia. 'There was a big party backstage, with all the bands on the show. We bought her a birthday cake and put the *right* amount of candles on it – well, probably a few more. And she didn't like *that*! She took the cake, saying, "I think this is absolutely lovely, absolutely beautiful," then put it on the floor and jumped all over it, stamping it out of existence! The lady was a lot of fun.' Poole remembers how Dusty would go with the lads to the movies on their afternoons off. 'She was very professional onstage, and when she was off she just wanted to have fun. She liked life and enjoyed herself. Even when she got back at us, we loved it. We'd cheer and clap her ... she seemed to have it all planned.'

Rhodes was Dusty's PA and confidante on her tours throughout the sixties. 'You can't expect a girl to go out all on her own. The tours we did were with people like Brian Poole and the Tremeloes and Gerry and the Pacemakers, and she was the only girl. She needed another female around.' Rhodes first came to Dusty's notice when she was working for the Springfields' manager Emlyn Griffiths, running the office as his booking agent. 'It was our little joke. Dusty used to say to me "When I'm big and famous I'll take you away from this office,"' Rhodes remembers. 'Then when I went on tour with her I did everything she needed – went shopping, bought cosmetics, looked after musicians and backing singers, and kept the press away, which was a helluva job at that time.'

She remembers how Dusty would release tension in riotous laughter. Before one club date in Batley, Yorkshire, Dusty was putting on her make-up in the dressing room while trumpeter Derek Andrews was warming up on a stage that was, unnoticed by everyone, slightly tilted. He leaned against the piano, and it started to move. 'I made a grab for him,' says Rhodes, 'he made a grab for the piano, his mute got stuck in his trumpet, the piano went straight out through the curtain, offstage, and landed upside down with this huge crash of notes. A note went ping at the end and there was silence. Then suddenly from backstage came a hysterical fit of laughing. Dusty didn't know what'd happened but she thought the sound was beautiful. She wore a lot of mascara and her eyes were soot – we couldn't speak for laughing, she was so infectious.' Dusty was banned from the club by an irate manager who was unimpressed by her laughter and anxious for the piano to be replaced. 'She paid for another. She said it was worth it for the sound. He should've damn well seen his stage was straight ... He kept shouting, "You could've killed someone!" even though it wasn't her fault!'

Dusty could also be comically frank. Her lighting designer and stage director, Fred Perry, recalls a rehearsal before a Royal Variety Performance at the Palladium: 'There was a technical hold-up ... Dusty looked around and saw that her [stage] background was a particularly sharp shade of lime. Forgetting the mikes were on, she murmured under her breath, "Mmm, vomit green." These words bounced off the walls of the theatre! As she was wearing a dress of pale grey and pale blue, the colours clashed horribly. During another run-through ... I was surprised to see a light-grey curtain come down, while the offending lime green one slowly, almost guiltily crept up into the overhead flies. Dusty never noticed this until I told her later. She looked stricken, and asked, "Was it something I said?" I answered, "Probably."'

Although it has been said that Dusty lost her temper easily and could be difficult to work with, Rhodes saw another side of her. 'She could face reality,' she says. 'Once, for instance, I was ironing a dress for her. She was doing the Sanremo Music Festival in Italy the next day and was hyped and nervous. I'd altered the dress and was gently pressing it, when it split and frayed at the bottom. I didn't know at the time, but there was a flaw in the material. I kept thinking, "How am I going to tell her?" I paced up and down my flat thinking, "She's going to hit the roof." She's already uptight and now I have to tell her the dress she wants to wear is in shreds. I went to the phone and told her. And, do you know, she just said, "Oh, okay, if there's nothing we can do about it, there's no point in getting annoyed. I'll find something else to wear."'

On Rhodes's wedding day, she remembers, Dusty dressed down: 'She bought an off-the-peg dark dress with little pink roses so she wouldn't outdo me, the bride. The funny thing is, Dusty could wear a headscarf and dark glasses and there was still a presence about her, you could feel it. She would do incredible things for people and put a lot of effort into friendships.' Both Rhodes and manager Vic Billings were a stable influence on Dusty throughout the sixties. Along with her recording manager, Johnny Franz, they acted as calm advisers, especially when the pressure was at its height.

Dusty's broad appeal spread from the south-east to northern cabaret clubs, where she broke box-office records. The venues she played varied from the more upmarket La Dolce Vita in Newcastle to the Greasbrough Working Men's Club in Rotherham. 'At Greasbrough I finished my forty-minute act, left the stage and started to change my clothes,' she said. 'They started banging tin trays like a prison riot. I had to get dressed again and go back onstage.' Her biggest contingent of fans came from the north of England where she attracted a large, working-class audience. She later remembered one date in Yorkshire where a young mum caught her eye: 'There she was with her scampi and chips, and I could tell she was enjoying my songs so much. Overworked as she was, swollen ankles and all, I was her big night out. That's why I used to go out and do it.'

Dusty also played to Northern soul crowds at all-nighters like Mojo's in Sheffield, a club organized by Peter Stringfellow. These clubs welcomed visiting soul stars like Ike and Tina Turner, Major Lance and Otis Redding, and spawned the fanatical following that made Dusty's 1967 single 'What's It Gonna Be' a cult Northern soul hit.

Alan LeCoyte, a former drummer backing Dusty, remembers some of those dates: 'The sort of people who'd come and see her were a smart, dancing crowd, lively, friendly and local – the tonic-blue jacket brigade we called them. You'd get people singing along, not screaming or throwing themselves on the stage. She wasn't a rock 'n' roll act, she was quite accessible with a wide appeal.' The band would begin a concert with an instrumental introduction, after which Dusty would bounce into some up-tempo numbers. Slowing down to heartfelt ballads, she ended with a medley of Motown songs, doing a spoof on artists like Little Eva. 'Sets were very short, only half an hour top whack,' recalls LeCoyte. 'Sometimes there'd be two shows, one at eight thirty and then another at eleven.'

Despite her down-to-earth tenacity, after months on the road Dusty became tired and stressed. She was on the publicity roller coaster, unable to handle it. 'The craziest times were 1964 to 1966,' she said, 'They were murderous. You had to have a lot of stamina. It was a lot of fun too, but the physical drudgery gets to you in the end.' She found the demands of constant TV promotion and touring a strain, and like many sixties artists, was expected to work the gruelling promotional round without proper time off. Whatever the situation, though, she was careful to dress the part. According to David Evans, she said: 'No matter what time we got back from the night before, I still got up in the morning and put the make-up on. Me and my beehive on the tour bus, eight o'clock in the morning, Madame Tussauds. Sitting bolt upright. The one time I was too tired to do it, I'll never forget it, the bus pulled up backstage and I had a scarf on and I hadn't done my make-up properly and I heard two people say, "Ooh, she doesn't look good, does she?" I never did it again. I always remember Joan Crawford never used to leave the studio with her make-up on from the set. She would always go to the dressing room, take it off, put a face on, a public Joan Crawford face, because fans would stop the car at the studio gate ... She'd make that effort every day. It must have been very wearying.'

Dusty found it difficult to always be punctual. Fred Perry remembers how she would sometimes pull up to the tour bus at Madame Tussauds just as it was starting to leave, and on one occasion she missed the bus altogether. 'She knew she was really late,' recalls Perry, 'so she actually got into a cab and said, "Manchester please!". The cab driver actually took her there!'

The constant travel and nervous tension had had an adverse effect on Dusty early in her career. Just three months after the success of 'I Only Want to Be with You' she had to cancel a string of engagements, as she was laid up with a combination of laryngitis and tonsillitis. 'I was completely rundown. I was so fatigued that I was liable to catch anything – and I did!' she said at the time. 'I shall have to take things at a less hectic pace in future.'

Attacks of laryngitis were a recurring problem. Stress directly affected Dusty's vocal performance, which is probably one reason why in later years she cut down so drastically on promotional work. 'I have very little technical expertise,' she said to a Canadian TV interviewer. 'Training really is breathing and using your vocal equipment properly. I am afraid that I just don't do it. I mean well when I go onstage, but I lose contact with any form of discipline. I've always gone for the end effect and to hell with the cost. I really want to please the people, and I'll do it any way I can.' In September 1964, while on a tour of the States, Dusty collapsed with exhaustion. She cancelled the rest of her dates to recuperate. She had got to the stage where she became thoroughly upset if she lost an eyelash and was living in a dreamworld. Her European tour, due to start that autumn, was postponed. Shortly afterwards she said, 'I'm all right physically but I'm still trying to adjust myself to life. My trouble is that I live totally on my nerves. My mother always said I didn't have much stamina and I've found out she was right.'

It had been a hectic year: she had made her solo debut at the London Palladium in February, played top of the bill throughout Britain, gone to Los Angeles to appear on Dick Clark's coast-to-coast *American Bandstand* show, and appeared in San Francisco and Seattle, before making it to New York for a prestigious appearance on *The Ed Sullivan Show*. All in all, her worldwide tour clocked up over fifty thousand miles. 'In Australia and New Zealand they worked us until we were really worn out: we'd have either twelve hours on a train, or three or four plane changes every day. And some of the halls in which we played were very grim. It got to such a pitch we just had to put our foot down!' she said.

It was in Australia that Dusty's irascibility had surfaced. 'She used to throw things all over the place, and you'd have to get out of the dressing room *quick*,' said Vic Billings. He remembered that when the long tour was nearing the end everyone, including Dusty, was tired and irritable. Dusty had a succession of wigs to which she had given the names of other pop stars – Sandie, Lulu and so on. This particular evening, just before a major stadium concert in Sydney, it was Cilla that got it.

'Cilla was suffering badly from the humidity and the lacquer. Dusty was getting all angry, pulling bits off Cilla, but it just wouldn't go right. I always knew when to leave her. Just as I left, she got hold of Cilla and threw it in the corner. I came back ten minutes later and Dusty was sitting with Cilla stuck on her head, all covered in fluff. There she was, hair pinned up, all in drag, the poor thing almost in tears. I died laughing, I couldn't help it. I thought she'd kill me. She gave me a glare and then started laughing too.'

Determined not to be held back for long, by the autumn Dusty had recovered enough from her collapse to re-enter the fray. She released 'Losing You', her fourth British single, a rousing throaty ballad written by Tom Springfield. A powerful showcase for her voice, it entered the charts in October, reached no. 9, and stayed in the charts for thirteen weeks. By November she had started another major tour. 'She came onstage ... in a white blouse, a stunning emerald green skirt reaching all the way to her green high-heeled shoes and whooped it up with "Dancing in The Street",' wrote *NME* reviewer Cordell Marks. 'If the fans love her for anything other than her singing it must surely be for the affinity she has to them. She looked as "switched on" as the hippest hipster.'

By the end of 1965, a new Dusty was emerging. Success in America had elevated her to a different league, and she began to behave accordingly. The Lady took precedence. As she became more established, there was less of the ribald backstage joking evident on earlier tours. 'Dusty was an extremely private person,' says Alan LeCoyte. 'She never travelled with people, she always came separately from your coach or van. She would do a few run-throughs on the numbers with the assumption that you roughly knew the backing. She wasn't an intimidating person – you didn't get things thrown at you, provided everyone knew what they were doing and it was all well-structured and organized. I never got the impression she enjoyed it a great deal.'

Dusty saved the best of herself for the performance, a full-blown drama that relied as much on the audience's response as it did on her stage persona. 'I'd love to have an easy time onstage, but it never works out that way. I really need the audience to lift me up, and they do. It's a wonderful feeling,' Dusty said. It was also where she felt most vulnerable. Talking to the *Telegraph Magazine* in 1995, she recalled how, in one single movement from one side of the stage to the other, she'd rattle herself by thinking, 'I've gained confidence, I've lost it, gained it, lost it. And it's just ... exhausting.'

Although she was successful in America, what she really craved was mega-stardom there, in the country she had idolized since childhood. Weaned on Hollywood movies, Dusty had always nursed a secret desire to live in California. And when she began her solo career it was black American artists like Ray Charles, and the emerging Motown sound, that fired her imagination. It was fortunate that her career took off at the same time as the British Invasion of the States, and her star rose accordingly.

'In 1776 England lost her American colonies. Last week the Beatles took them back,' *Life* magazine had announced in 1964. On 25 January the Beatles' 'I Want to Hold Your Hand' appeared on *Billboard*'s Top 40 chart, and two weeks later the band arrived in the States for a promotional blitz. The press campaign was carefully orchestrated, but the level of Beatlemania hysteria was unexpected and unprecedented. Previously uninterested in British pop, which had seemed a pale imitation of what was on offer at home, US teenagers feverishly embraced Merseybeat and British pop. After the national trauma of the assassination of John F. Kennedy in 1963, the youthful idealism his presidency engendered seemed to transfer itself to the Beatles. Americans fell for the whole package: the fresh sound of amplified skiffle and pop R&B welded to quirky lyrics, along with a presentation that was down-to-earth, witty and affectionately sarcastic.

By April, the Beatles occupied twelve positions on the Top 100 and *every* place in the Top 5. They played to 56,000 screaming fans at Shea Stadium and 'Can't Buy Me Love' had the largest advance sales of any record to date: 21 million. Their success paved the way for a host of UK artists such as the Dave Clark Five, the

Rolling Stones, Herman's Hermits, the Kinks, the Hollies and the Yardbirds. While the Invasion was a band-oriented phenomenon, several female solo vocalists cracked the *Billboard* charts. Petula Clark achieved two no. 1s with 'Downtown' and 'My Love'; Marianne Faithfull had a hit with 'As Tears Go By'; and Lulu spent seven weeks at no. 1 in 1967 with 'To Sir with Love', the theme tune from the film starring Sidney Poitier.

Dusty, however, was the most distinctive British beat girl. In 1964 'I Only Want to Be with You' went to no. 12 in the US, stayed in the chart for seven weeks and struck gold. 'Dusty at that time was very different from other female singers,' Mercury A&R man Shelby Singleton told me. 'She used different make-up and hair and, as with the Beatles, people were shocked.'

Until Adele and Amy Winehouse in the 2000s, pop's biggest-selling female performers were usually American. The US pop industry is geared towards mammoth distribution and profit-making, so UK acts outside their home country were already at a disadvantage before they could compete. Sometimes a wave of British artists are successfully packaged together as an 'Invasion' – as happened in 1964 with Dusty and the Beatles, or twenty years later with the rise of the eighties 'designer pop' video bands like Culture Club, Heaven 17 and ABC.

The UK charts reflected an interest in a home-grown product that bordered on fanaticism, and Dusty's success happened just as British music was beginning to compete at an international level. After her upbeat single 'Wishin' and Hopin'' became a 1964 summer hit in the US, Dusty said, 'I want to go on notching up hits in the American charts. It's a personal ambition really. No special reason, but when you see yourself in the charts over there you can tell yourself you're doing all right.'

Meanwhile, she worked hard at consolidating her popularity in Britain. Early in 1965 she released another Hawker/Raymonde composition, 'Your Hurtin' Kind of Love' as a single. Dusty's voice came across as strained rather than sweet in this boomy ballad, and the record wasn't as successful as earlier outings. The follow-up, 'In the Middle of Nowhere', had much more immediate appeal. Co-recorded with pop blues shouter Alan Price, this Bea Verdi/Buddy Kaye song had a sassy, rousing rhythm, with Dusty's earthy vibrato mixed upfront. She also brought in friends Madeline Bell and Doris Troy to provide last-minute additional vocals. 'Madeline and Doris knew the song because I'd tried it over with them before going into the studio,' said Dusty. 'It's a great help doing that rather than getting together with a chorus who've probably never seen the song before.'

With its raucous singalong swing and sense of camaraderie, 'In the Middle of Nowhere' went to no. 8 in the charts and stayed around for the next ten weeks. Since 'Your Hurtin' Kind of Love' flopped Dusty had wondered anxiously whether her career was over, but 'Nowhere''s success helped reassure her. She followed it with one of her favourite songs, 'Some of Your Lovin''. 'I'm highly chuffed … I think it's the best sound we've ever achieved,' she said. Written by Goffin and King, it was the closest she got to the deep Southern soul sound she so admired. This languid, sensual song became a major Top 10 hit, but despite Dusty's run of success the strain was beginning to show again. Ordered by her doctor to go on holiday, an exhausted Dusty cancelled her Bournemouth summer season to fly out to the Virgin Islands for three weeks. Restless and bored, she didn't last ten days, and made her way to the US. 'I went to drive-in movies and restaurants, just like other people, and I took pictures and behaved exactly like a tourist,' she said. 'It might seem trivial – but to me it was the most exhilarating experience in years.' For a short while she was able to leave behind the diva persona and regain a valuable sense of self.

She returned fresh from holiday to promote the release of her second album, *Ev'rything's Coming Up Dusty*. Packaged in a lavish gatefold presentation sleeve, complete with striking black and white portrait stills from *Thank Your Lucky Stars* and *Ready, Steady, Go!*, the album projected an image of Dusty that was not only top supper-club entertainment, but also reminiscent of wholesome Hollywood household names like Doris Day and Julie Andrews. It was a strange amalgam of styles – breathless, aspirational and markedly different from her debut album, *A Girl Called Dusty*, released just eighteen months earlier. Philips were eager to make the new album a major media event. 'They seem to have had a mad fit and gone potty,' Dusty giggled, 'wrapping my album up in a lovely book affair with lots of pictures.'

The recording of the album was a long, painful process, with many takes, discussions, arguments and tears. The arranger Ivor Raymonde recalled one afternoon's recording when Dusty became emotionally affected by the ballad she was singing. 'She was so moved that she rushed out of the studio and had a good cry. When she came back all her make-up had run and it looked like a ton of soot had fallen down her face.'

Ev'rything's Coming Up Dusty marked her move from light-hearted pop into a more mature 'adult' bracket, with emotive Bacharach and Goffin/King ballads, and tougher gospel-soul numbers. The opening track, 'Won't Be Long', is one of those uptempo shouters, featuring gospel-inspired tambourine and a rock 'n' roll delivery. It is followed by the slightly ponderous

Goffin/King ballad 'Oh No! Not My Baby', and a vigorously spirited Spanish-sung version of Richie Valens' 'La Bamba', where Dusty displays her aptitude for languages, a hangover from the Springfields days. Side one ends with the strange 'Doodlin''. Written by Horace Silver and Jon Hendricks, it charts a woman's breakdown as she compulsively telephones someone who clearly isn't interested in returning her love. Dusty puts in a spine-chillingly dry performance. Deceptively light, with out-of-kilter string production, this track reveals Dusty's quirkier, darker tastes. She also tries free-flight vocal phrasing on the soul sound of Rod Argent's 'If It Don't Work Out', while 'It Was Easier to Hurt Him' takes a leaf from Janis Joplin's book, with Dusty delivering bluesy entrails-dragging regret, remorse and catharsis in one fell swoop.

On this album Dusty had two conflicting pop personas – one singing aspirational ballads with overblown strings, while the other sang with a wild, gutsy R&B energy. The two were meant to complement each other, but they appealed to widely differing markets.

The fans, however, didn't seem to mind her different faces. They bought *Ev'rything's Coming Up Dusty* in droves. It entered the album charts in October, stayed there for twelve weeks and reached no. 6. Although it was Sandie Shaw's year in terms of the number of hit singles, Dusty was voted Top World Female Vocalist by *NME*, and became third bestselling British artist overall.

Dusty's career took another upturn with her biggest hit of the sixties. It took forty-seven takes to record, hit the charts in March 1966, stayed in for thirteen weeks, and was her first no. 1. It also reached the US charts in June, going to no. 4. It sold 250,000 copies in Britain and a global million by 1967. 'You Don't Have to Say You Love Me' was Dusty's pièce de résistance, the ultimate boomy ballad that gave her strategic bargaining power and a heightened world reputation.

The song came at an opportune time: 1966 had got off to a slow start with the release of 'Little by Little', a song written by Verdi and Kaye, the team behind 'In the Middle of Nowhere'. An attempt to repeat its upbeat swing, 'Little by Little' fell short of that, with a slow climb to no. 17. Dusty's vocals were muted and the rhythm perfunctory rather than inspired. 'It isn't meant to be a great number that would go rip-roaring ahead in the chart,' she said at the time. 'It's a sustainer, a potboiler. Everybody wanted something lively after "Some of Your Lovin'", so this is it.' But Dusty was being beaten in the hit stakes by artists like Cilla Black and Sandie Shaw, and needed to re-establish her position with a show-stopping hit.

The previous year she had come back from the Sanremo Music Festival in Italy with an obscure Italian song written by Pino Donaggio and Vito Pallavicini, originally titled '*Io Che No Vivo Senza Te*'. Curious about its potential, Dusty asked her friend and *Ready, Steady, Go!* producer Vicki Wickham to write some English lyrics. As recounted in his enthusiastic send-up of the sixties music business, *You Don't Have to Say You Love Me*, Vicki enlisted the help of epic hype merchant and pop manager Simon Napier-Bell.

After an evening of drinks and a meal at the Ad Lib, the two retired to Vicki's flat. Napier-Bell wrote:

… We sat listening to a scratchy old acetate singing at us in Italian.

I said, 'It's from Italy. The words have got to be romantic. It ought to start off "I love you."'

Vicki shuddered at the thought. 'How about, "I don't love you"?' she suggested.

I thought that was a bit extreme. 'No, it's going too far the other way. Why not: "You don't love me"?'

That was more dramatic, more Italian, but a bit accusatory. So we softened it a little: 'You don't *have* to love me.' But that didn't quite fit the melody, so we added two more words, 'You don't have to say you love me.' Great. That was it. We could do the rest in the taxi.

That supposedly throwaway evening's work proved fruitful for years to come. The song became a standard, covered by many artists, including Elvis Presley, who made it a favourite at his Las Vegas concerts.

The song was perfect for Dusty, with a simplicity that gave her space to be emotionally expressive. It is a stunning piece of melodrama that still sounds powerful today. 'I chose "You Don't Have to Say You Love Me" because it's commercial, and I've been crazy about it since I heard it first. It's good old schmaltz,' she said. Until this point, British girls tended to sing their ballads with more gusto than panache, standing stock still onstage and overcompensating for a lack of emotion with wide hand gestures. Dusty sang this song as if she had lived it.

After a dramatic horn introduction, there is a pause before Dusty launches in, her voice quiet and husky with tension, singing: 'When I said I needed you …'. Piano and strings filter in gently, building up to a climactic chorus, and then receding. Dusty gives a theatrically tragic performance, combining an air of faltering vulnerability with female bravado. It would have been easy to swamp the song in blowsy production and vocal histrionics, yet Dusty keeps that edge of dignity and defiance throughout.

'You Don't Have to Say You Love Me' stayed at no. 1 for just a week, but it gave Dusty a fresh burst of self-assurance. Although consistently voted top female singer, she had been overlooked for 1965's Royal Variety Performance at the London Palladium, which had severely shaken her confidence. In 1966 she shared the bill with Dave Clark, and other mainstream cabaret stars such as Johnny Hallyday, Sylvie Vartan, Tony Bennett, Ken Dodd and Shirley Bassey. 'That was the first time I met her,' recalls Dave Clark, 'and that was the only time I saw her nervous. She was the most underrated white singer in the UK, I don't think people appreciated how good she was. She was a white lady who should have been black. She had black mascara and a black soul ... she felt every moment and had tremendous emotional range.' But Dusty had never quite fitted in with the light-entertainment establishment. She wasn't as risqué as the Rolling Stones, but she had an unpredictable quality and an ebullience that wasn't easy to channel.

After the massive success of 'You Don't Have to Say You Love Me', anything else would seem like an anticlimax. The follow-up, however, a Carole King composition called 'Goin' Back', is just as resonant, and a favourite of many fans. Thoughtful and sensitive, the ballad marks a new maturity in Dusty's vocal delivery. Gone is the high-octane drama, to be replaced by a contemplative tone and muted piano accompaniment. Carole King was said to have been moved to tears when she first heard Dusty's version. Its subtlety made it a success. A Top 10 hit in the summer of 1966, it stayed in the charts for ten weeks.

In 1966 Dusty spent more time in the studio and less on the road. In May she began hosting her own TV show, an indication that she had finally 'made it' as a household star. Entitled simply *Dusty*, her first BBC series was a summer variety package of half-hour shows, with Dusty singing unknown numbers as well as her hits. Guests included everyone from comedian Dudley Moore to *Till Death Us Do Part* actor Warren Mitchell, mainstream acts like Tom Jones, Scott Walker and Manfred Mann, and counterculture rockers the Jimi Hendrix Experience. Here, at the height of her popularity, her first *Golden Hits* album shot to no. 2, staying in the charts for a total of thirty-six weeks.

By 1966 Dusty's family audience was firmly established, and anything threatening to compromise her image was quickly squashed. When James Lawrence Isherwood, a forty-nine-year-old artist from Wigan, painted a picture of Dusty naked from the waist up and displayed it in the Talbot Hotel in Winchester, Dusty tried to get her lawyers to ban it. 'She hadn't posed for the picture, and she has a family following,' said Vic Billings indignantly. The ban was waived when Isherwood offered to cover the offending part with a duster. 'I wanted to immortalize this girl,' he complained. 'She should be flattered.' The portrait was snapped up for seventy-five guineas by Victor Rawlings, a Winchester pig-keeper. Dusty was not amused.

Humour became a valuable weapon, though, when recording a chaotic TV date in France. A rowdy, irreverent audience were, for some reason, throwing coins on to the stage. Dusty kept her cool. 'I wasn't sure if it was an insult or some old French custom,' she said. 'I thought that if I stormed off I could have made things twice as bad, so I picked all the money up, naturally. I made a fortune – about ten bob for two minutes' work!' Behind the scenes Dusty was still working off tension with compulsive crockery-throwing. Pat Rhodes recalls many times on tour when Dusty vented her frustration by hurling plates out of a window, or teamed up with brother Tom to toss china against a wall 'just to hear what it sounded like'. It was rumoured that she had even thrown food at someone in a restaurant. The missile was reported first as a benign doughnut but grew into an entire plate of spaghetti bolognese. 'It was actually a bread roll,' sighs Rhodes. 'The press is always sensationalizing trivia. What happened was, someone shouted something rude to her across a restaurant and she went "Oh, shut up!" and threw a bread roll. Just one.' There was also the time at a Poll Awards ceremony in London's Post Office tower restaurant when, annoyed with the way in which the manager was ordering around his waiters, Dusty threw a pie at the back of his neck. When he tried to shake her hand goodbye, she squashed another into his palm.

But most notorious were the parties in her Baker Street flat. Dusty and her brother Tom would make sure that their guests had plenty of food and drink, and once enough alcohol had been consumed, they would start to lob food. It might start with a sardine tossed down the front of woman's dress, or cold meat slapped on the back of someone's neck, or a game of tennis with poached eggs. 'I remember Martha and the Vandellas cowering behind the couch because there was everything flying in the air. Once they got used to it they came out swinging with these huge long French loaves,' recalled Dusty. 'Even better was standing at the top of an old theatre staircase and getting a gross of cups and saucers and teaspoons and ... if you tip it from about eight floors up and record it, then put it in slow motion, it's one of the best sounds I've ever heard.' While her rock peers were throwing TV sets into hotel swimming pools, Dusty was engaged in a more genteel version of pop star abandon – but she was always careful to tidy afterwards. 'I never expected anyone else to clean it up.'

These noisy pranks covered a deep frustration with the way her career was going. To Dusty, the American music industry seemed much more alert than in Britain, with greater versatility and more room to experiment. Sustained chart success in the US was elusive, but this hardened her resolve to make it there. Her break came at the end of 1966 when she played her biggest American concerts to date at New York's prestigious jazz emporium Basin Street East, on the same bill as drummer and bandleader Buddy Rich. Before she went, Dusty admitted to being plagued by self-doubt. 'I'm terrified. So many great people have sung there and thousands more who could do it better if I tried to compete.' She was booked for a fortnight, playing two shows a night and three at weekends. She flew over two weeks early to rehearse with Rich and her arranger. Soon after her arrival, rumours began to float back to Britain that things were tense.

'Mr Rich is a little difficult to get on with – and that's the British understatement of 1966,' she wailed politely. Speaking about it over twenty years later to Q magazine, she was less restrained. 'What a *bastard*! He was the arsehole of the world. I went to ask him if I could have his band for an hour's rehearsal because I was headlining and I was expected to sing my hits like "Wishin' And Hopin'" that his band had never even *heard*. He had his legs up on the desk and he said, "You fucking broad! Who do you think you fucking *are*, bitch?"' She gave him 'a 1940s, 20th Century Fox chorus girl slap' which sent his toupee flying. He responded by threatening to sue her for assault.

Under headlines such as 'DUSTY HAS FOUR-LETTER WORD FOR BUDDY!' and 'DUSTY SLAMS US STAR!', she told the press how Rich had refused to let her rehearse until the afternoon before the show, and even though she had sixteen numbers to run through he spent an hour setting up a special drum rostrum for himself. He objected to her taking top billing, and when she suggested she go on before him on the second night, he said that his musicians would be tired after playing for her. 'His whole attitude has been so unprofessional,' she cried, saying that the jazzer's behaviour was worse than that of an obnoxious rock 'n' roll band.

Vic Billings recalled how Rich's manager ('a woman built like a Sherman tank') approached him before the opening night and said, 'Buddy's gotta top.'

'Dusty's supposed to be topping,' retorted Billings.

After fierce argument, they came to a compromise. 'On Tuesday, Wednesday and Thursday his name was above Dusty's on the canopy, and on Friday and Saturday it was reversed. It made me laugh to see men getting up every day having to change names on the canopy,' Billings said.

The real battle commenced on the first night. 'They allowed her to top, but Rich had all his old friends in there – Johnny Carson and all that mob. Rich did an hour and a half, Carson about another three hours, and finally Dusty got on. She went down great, but there were big punch-ups going on. He'd announce her saying, "She's supposed to be a great singer, but I've seen better." And she'd insult him. To a certain extent it helped the box office because they were reporting all this in the press.'

Dusty had sympathy on her side. New York critic Frank Farrell expostulated, 'What happened to Dusty shouldn't have happened to the British ambassador. When her spot was about to begin, much of the impact was taken away by a long, long list of introductions of stars in the audience ... The facts seem to indicate that some sort of cold war was going on backstage.' Claude Hall from *Billboard* magazine questioned who was supposed to be headlining: 'Buddy Rich, of World Pacific Records, took over the stage and, with assistance from friends, almost didn't let go. Actually the spotlight should have been on Dusty Springfield, the British star. It must be said that, in spite of the shoving and an attempted verbal put-down by Rich, she presented an enjoyable evening.'

Dusty's fiasco with Rich was indicative of a cold war that had spread throughout American show business. Since the British Invasion two years before, many established US musicians were peeved at British success. 'I think they were annoyed about the amount of money going out of the States in royalties,' says Billings. 'With the success of Dusty, the Beatles, Freddie and the Dreamers et cetera, musicians were asking, "What do they know about it?" Until then America had led the record business.'

The war between Dusty and Rich represented a clash between two schools of music: pop and jazz. 'He was of the Count Basie era. There wouldn't have been half as much fuss if, for instance, Ella Fitzgerald were singing. Or maybe he'd have accepted Cleo Laine.' As the fortnight rumbled on, the audience became packed out with supporters, some for Buddy and many more rooting for Dusty. Tony Bennett told Billings, 'She's great. I know what you're trying to do. Just forget all this crap, it goes on all the time.' Burt Bacharach, Dionne Warwick, Esther

Phillips, Dave Clark, the Lovin' Spoonful and Benny Goodman also dropped in to show their support for her. Each night, Dusty won over the crowd, with a gutsy rendition of 'Kansas City', a whimsical 'England Swings', a brave version of 'God Bless the Child' and, of course, 'You Don't Have to Say You Love Me'. By the end of the residency, even the band were on her side and as a mark of appreciation they gave her a pair of bright-red boxing gloves, dedicated to 'Slugger Springfield'.

With her combative spirit, Dusty was equally hard on musicians she felt didn't come up to scratch. She has spoken of the 'blind conceit' of her enthusiasm, how if she sensed any resentment on the part of a musician she would weed him out. At that time women were not expected to be assertive. 'I kept the ones I felt wanted genuinely to help me,' she said, 'those who would play for me standing up if they had piles, which is what a drummer did for a week at the Talk of the Town – and he drummed beautifully.'

She knew how to keep good musicians. Derek Wadsworth, for instance, trombonist/arranger with the Echoes, says: 'The money that Dusty offered me for one concert at a time was more than I had previously been getting *each week* at a top venue. I was the envy of all, particularly as we (that is, Wadsworth, leader Doug Reece, Vic Briggs, Gary Boyle and Ian Fenby) were accompanying *the* big female star of the time, and we were playing to adoring audiences at all the key venues of the day.'

Dusty's next major residency after Basin Street East was a nine-week pantomime run at the Liverpool Empire in 1967. She had always disliked pantomime: for rivals Lulu and Cilla Black, pantomime was part of a specific British light-entertainment tradition, but Dusty was inclined to send it up. However, the idea of it became more agreeable to her after she saw camp impressionist Danny La Rue performing a skit on her act: 'He was dressed up in a long gown with sequins and he sang a couple of my hits. I wasn't offended. I really enjoyed it – it was a good plug!'

Her own image was becoming more exaggerated. In building the image of The Lady, she took tips from male drag queens on which mascara lasted longest and how to apply the heavy eye-shadow. 'Basically I'm a drag queen myself,' she admitted later. Yet it was this glitzy image that established her on the upmarket cabaret circuit. For her 1967 Talk of the Town debut in London, she earned £2,500 a week and attracted the attention of a more moneyed, mainstream audience. Even Prime Minister Harold Wilson named her as his favourite singer.

Her evening gowns had become such a trademark that when Dusty took part in the *NME* poll-winners concert at Wembley Pool that year wearing a short dress, the crowd were shocked. 'Dazzling Dusty Springfield bubbled on in the most stunning, sparkling (and shortest) dress I have ever seen her wear,' *NME*'s Keith Altham wrote. 'Talk about miniskirts – this was more like a long blouse!'

Although Dusty was still a hit in live performance, her chart success was on the wane. Her song 'Give Me Time', for instance, peaked at no. 24 that year. A dramatic Continental ballad, this was an attempt to repeat the emotional pinnacle of 'You Don't Have to Say You Love Me'. Unfortunately it sounded ponderous, with Dusty's vocals straining against the overblown orchestral backing.

Success often comes in unlikely quarters. Although her next single 'What's It Gonna Be', an uptempo orchestral soul number that foreshadowed the Three Degrees, flopped, it was picked up by collectors on the Northern soul scene and disguised as an imported soul cut by 'Patti Austin'. It became a northern cult hit, featured regularly on the playlist at Britain's top all-nighter, the Torch in Stoke-on-Trent. Due to its unavailability, 'What's It Gonna Be' was heavily bootlegged until Philips reissued it in 1974 when the Northern soul scene was briefly the toast of the London media.

Dusty was adept at moving from one end of the pop spectrum to the other. As well as making cult soul hits, she was also heard on mainstream movie soundtracks. In America, for instance, she released the evocative, laid-back Bacharach composition 'The Look of Love' for the soundtrack to spoof Bond movie *Casino Royale*. When it was released, 'The Look of Love' was a US hit and has since become one of her most popular and oft-played songs.

Dusty was entering the territory of what sultry fifties chanteuse Eartha Kitt calls 'the rich man's entertainer, the crème de la crème of café society. You'd play hotel rooms, places where people would come according to what their pocket could stand.' She had left the mod hipster far behind, but although she was earning good money, her work at top nightclubs like New York's Copacabana and Checkers in Sydney left her feeling unsatisfied. 'I am at the crossroads,' she told David Wigg at the London *Evening News*. 'It's rather difficult to know in which direction to go. I wouldn't like to be working in this business in twenty years' time doing what I am doing now ... I'd be forty-seven and who wants to be singing at forty-seven? By then I hope I will have a settled mind.'

She had been looking at film roles, still nursing her ambition to be an actress, but most of the parts offered were 'crummy', requiring her to play a brainless pop singer. Her press interviews were becoming more introspective and wistful. In September 1967 Dusty gave her longest, most thoughtful interview yet to Penny Valentine at *Disc*. At this point she introduced her infamous teddy bear mascot, Einstein, a symbol of her childlike need for security. Old and moth-eaten, with a manic teddy-bear smile, Einstein served as Dusty's secure alter ego, a manifestation of the shy, self-protective Mary O'Brien. To Valentine, Dusty disclosed that she was easily hurt, overgenerous to people she liked and surprisingly abrupt to those she didn't. Her confusion was evident. 'What upsets me most at the moment in this business is that I'm moving into a cabaret bag. It's nice, but the cabaret league isn't for me. What direction can I go in? I always wanted to be an actress but it's pretty unlucrative unless you can break into films. I'm just groping and wandering. All I know is that I have a distinctive voice I don't particularly like listening to.'

Dusty spoke about her fear of dying as an 'aged teenybopper', and her practical, yet off-the-wall attitude to money. 'I need money because when you care terribly about things, as I do, you have to have something you *don't* care about.' She was proud that apart from a wardrobe of clothes, her only possessions included a piece of sculpture, a half-eaten Easter egg, six cups, a carpet and an exercise bicycle.

It was also the first time that she spoke frankly about marriage. Rumours had been growing about her single status, as to whether or not she was gay. She deftly fended them off with vague statements like, 'I think marriage, if it happens, is the most desirable state to be in. But there are, to be honest, no men I know that I could live with for ever.' Her name was linked romantically with various stars, from Eden Kane to Peter Sarstedt, and Burt Bacharach, with whom she had a particularly special musical rapport. Pat Rhodes explains, 'Had the time been right, they would have had a relationship. Burt was married to Angie and Dusty would never have broken up somebody's relationship. Then when Angie and Burt split up, Dusty and Burt were on the other side of the world from each other. It's a pity because I thought there really could've been something there, they were so musically tuned.'

Despite speculation, Dusty kept her love life determinedly private, which spurred the interest of the press. Stories about mysterious tall, dark, handsome men were put out to throw them off the scent. Constrained by the stringent morality of her Catholic upbringing, Dusty kept her sexuality to herself.

At the end of 1967 Dusty's third, aptly titled album, *Where Am I Going*, was released. The cover featured a picture of Dusty in a short dress and large hat, clutching her face and laughing, the album title above her in a huge psychedelic balloon, while the wacky, stream-of-consciousness sleeve notes conveyed a barely suppressed sense of hysteria.

Produced by Johnny Franz, with guest arrangers Ivor Raymonde, Wally Stott and Peter Knight, the album moves from Latin rhythms to the soulful class of tracks such as 'Don't Let Me Lose This Dream' to standards 'Sunny', Brel ballad 'If You Go Away' and the Bacharach/David song 'They Long to Be Close to You'. It is an eclectic mix. Dusty even includes protest song 'Broken Blossoms', an anti-war tune written by Tom Springfield. The song that most conveyed Dusty's state of mind was the title track. Directed by Wally Stott, this Dorothy Fields/Cy Coleman song sounds like the theme tune to an epic Sondheim musical, with Dusty performing a dramatic orchestrated rendition of her own life story. By turns forlorn and strident, Dusty asks herself, what is the point in aimless love affairs, why is she left alone 'on the shelf', and where is she heading in her life?

The song ends with a flourish, yet a question hangs in the air. At twenty-eight, Dusty was profoundly questioning her direction and her desires. She was feeling cut off from an intrinsic part of herself: the shadowy little Mary O'Brien she had so purposefully left behind many years before. Now, when she was ready to change, she was unsure that she had the inner resources to do so.

This instability was shown in stark relief with a court case. In true eccentric film-star fashion, Dusty had been wearing a pair of sunglasses at night while driving her sports car and crashed into elderly shop-owner Ida Judith Metzger, who was crossing the road. Sobbing hysterically, Dusty flung open the door and ran over to the old woman, crying, 'It wasn't your fault!' According to Mrs Metzger, 'I saw she wore dark glasses, was very pretty and very hysterical. She was taken into the ambulance because she was so hysterical.' Although she was not severely injured, for a while afterwards the old lady had difficulty in walking and her business suffered. In summing up the case Mr Justice Phillimore announced, 'I have no doubt that Miss Springfield was driving much too fast and I don't suppose her ability to keep a proper lookout was enhanced by wearing dark glasses. It seems an extraordinary thing to do when driving a car at night.' He ruled that she should pay Mrs Metzger £1,900 in damages. Once again, the 'blonde bombshell pop singer' hit the headlines. Dusty was skidding out of control. 'A pop singer should not hit an old lady,' she said. 'Suddenly I was this unstable person, this irresponsible, dirty pop singer.'

Although Dusty ended 1967 as overall bestselling female LP artist, *Where Am I Going* was released to stunning indifference. It reached no. 40 in the album charts and stayed there for a week. Dusty was disappointed with its performance: 'That's really upset me, because I'd worked hard on it. You can't keep thinking of chart success, you get past that. Of course it's important to have records in the chart as long as you can – it's very good for morale for one thing. But you can't make it the centre of everything.'

The record failed to ignite the public because it featured none of her hit singles and the tone, like the cover, was underplayed and uncertain. But the slow sales galvanized Dusty, who threw herself into work, alternating between big band cabaret shows and grittier presentations with the Echoes. One week she was playing the Batley Variety Club in Britain, the next she was in the US doing a month-long promotional tour as guest of top TV show hosts like Jonathan Winters, Pat Boone and Dick Clark.

The frenzied promotion paid off. In July 1968 Dusty had her first major hit for over a year with 'I Close My Eyes and Count to Ten'. Written by Clive Westlake, this remonstrative uptempo ballad showed Dusty back on form, singing with immaculate phrasing and uninhibited pathos. 'Clive Westlake wrote it with me in mind,' she said. 'He did a very beautiful demo, which completely sold it to me.'

The 'beautiful demo' had been recorded with a forty-piece orchestra. Struck with the success of 'All I See Is You', Westlake's earlier hit for Dusty, Vic Billings asked for 'I Close My Eyes and Count to Ten' before he had even finished writing it. 'That's it, a big smash hit,' Billings told him. Westlake put together the demo and gave it to Johnny Franz, Dusty's producer. 'Little did I know, Vic was secretly holding it for Kiki Dee,' said Westlake, when I spoke to him at his home in Nashville. 'He still had her management, but he was losing Dusty with the American deal. Dusty then rang and said, "I'll take that one. Don't give it away."'

There was a tussle for the song, but Dusty secured it. Along with Ivor Raymonde and Mike Hawker, Clive Westlake was one of her strongest British songwriters. Born in Newport, South Wales, the down-to-earth Westlake became a music teacher and head of drama at London's Trinity College of Music before he entered the business. A stalwart of music publishing, he wrote for 'every Tom, Dick and Harry' including Vera Lynn, the Hollies, Anita Harris and Cliff Richard. 'A funny old situation with Dusty,' he said. 'One could say we were friends from a distance. I was in love with her singing. She was very shy, though, when she came up against a person, and I was a bit of a raver.'

The success of 'I Close My Eyes' came at a strategically good time, as her latest TV series, *It Must Be Dusty* for the commercial channel ATV, had been slated by critics for sloppy production and uninspired billing. 'I didn't produce it and all I can say is I tried my best,' she said. 'But there are certain systems that I can't fight. There was a total lack of imagination about the whole series and, although I don't like to bring politics into it, I hope to be doing the next series back with the old firm.' Constantly preoccupied with perfection, by 1968 Dusty was filming again with the BBC.

This coincided with a highly acclaimed season at Talk of the Town, where she did a surprise spoof on Shirley Temple, singing

'On the Good Ship Lollipop'. She tapdanced with four sailors, wearing a little-girl dress covered in large red blobs and a big bow tied in her curly hair. Here her gift for comedy came to the fore, along with her penchant for imitating old movie icons. 'I saw Shirley once ... and she was definitely cute with a capital K,' she said. 'I liked the way she would look aside to see if the cameras were on her or not. It took guts to do what she did.' All blonde wigs, bolero jackets, diamanté and Peggy Lee songs, the show was hailed as one of the best cabaret acts Dusty had ever done.

By September she was back on the American cabaret circuit. In some ways her career had followed the upwardly mobile Supremes, in that while her heart lay in earthy R&B her stage show was becoming more theatrical and extravagant. She said candidly that there were only about six clubs in Britain, including the Talk of the Town, that were financially and professionally rewarding. 'At most there is about three months' work for me in Britain and that's why I have to look elsewhere.'

Her next British album release reflected this glitzy lifestyle. *Dusty ... Definitely* was a Johnny Franz tour de force production. Dusty appeared on the cover in a long yellow gown lavishly studded with sequins and diamanté, topping it off with a puffed-out blonde bouffant wig, knee-deep mascara and a simpering smile. A masterfully camp extravaganza, the album sounds richly confident, without a trace of the introspective uncertainty of *Where Am I Going*. The sound veers smoothly between the gritty gospel soul of tracks like the riotous 'Love Power' and the blowsy balladry of 'Mr Dream Merchant' or Charles Aznavour's 'Who'. Dusty concludes the set with the syrupy Hollywood strings of 'Second Time Around', a track that almost lapses into gooey hotel-foyer muzak – until it finishes with a startling crash of smashing crockery and jangling cans. At the end of an album of controlled perfection, the finale comes as a hilarious release. But the confidence of *Dusty ... Definitely* was reflected only moderately in sales. Released in time for Christmas, it went to no. 30, and stayed in the charts for only six weeks.

It was at this point that Dusty turned to Memphis and another record label for a radical change in style. Although she started negotiations in 1966, it wasn't until 1968 that she made *Dusty in Memphis*, her first recording for Atlantic, which has since become a classic. And Memphis itself opened up to her an overwhelming new world.

6

Dusty in Memphis

I N THE SIXTIES Memphis was the music capital of the world. Situated over three hundred miles upriver from the Gulf of Mexico at the junction of three states, this small, funky Southern city, the cotton-trading capital of the Mississippi Delta, was the home of musical legend. It boasted Beale Street and W. C. Handy, the city's favourite son and creator of the blues. Up on Union Avenue there was Sun Records, the place where, one afternoon in 1954, Elvis Presley recorded 'Blue Moon of Kentucky' and owner Sam Phillips said as the last note faded, 'Fine, man. That's different. That's a pop song now, everybody.' Later the King set up home there at Graceland, a majestic monument to seventies kitsch, a short bus ride from downtown.

Memphis was the centre of musical integration, where black gospel and blues singers would team up with white country session men to create a new kind of R&B. Otis Redding recorded there, as did Carla Thomas, Sam and Dave, and Wilson Pickett. Memphis musical history included the dark soul austerity of the Stax sound, as well as Atlantic Records' finest moments with Aretha Franklin.

It had been Atlantic producer Jerry Wexler who first understood Franklin's power. She had been an 'underground scam' in their studios for three or four years. 'I'd been watching her on Columbia, and when she came to Atlantic I said, "Let this sound emerge and be heard and not make it palatable,"' he told me. Although a gospel princess and the daughter of a Baptist minister, Franklin's voice had a raw, gutsy quality that was buried at the beginning of her career under directionless show tunes and jazz pop. When she arrived at Atlantic in 1966 the conditions were ideal for her to emerge, unfettered, as a star, letting rip with such classics as 'I Ain't Never Loved a Man' and 'Respect'. She was the sound of girl groups growing up.

Franklin was a tough act to follow, but just as Wexler had enabled her to open up to her full potential, so he encouraged Dusty to let go of theatrical pop artifice so that the warmth of her soul vibrato could come through. It was here, at a turning point in her career in 1968, that Dusty came to record *Dusty in Memphis*, a deceptively subtle album that captured her essence. She had been itching for years to finalize the details of her Atlantic contract in the States, and mid-1967 was a period of intensive work and psychological transition: her initial five-year solo contract with Philips had come up for renewal, and the company was anxious to keep her. Philips's managing director, a big, round-faced Australian called Leslie Gould, went to see Dusty at Talk of the Town and afterwards approached Vic Billings. 'She's marvellous. We should talk about a new contract,' he said.

'You can wait for *me* now,' was Billings's candid answer. He had been smouldering with dissatisfaction for some time over Dusty's deal with her record company. 'She'd had her first hit in 1963. He was the MD, and 1967 was the first time he went to see her,' recalled Billings. 'By then he knew he had a great-selling artist who made him look good in Amsterdam [the base for Philips Records]. Because we were working so hard, it took a while to realize how big she was becoming. There was one time when Dusty and I were on tour in America, we came back to find her hotel room was full of flowers and great bottles of champagne. Doris Troy, one of Dusty's backing singers, came in ten minutes later and we were enthusing, "Look what the record company gave us!" "I should fucking think so too," she said. "She's an international star."'

By now many fans were expressing dismay at the amount of time Dusty spent in America. In interviews she was careful to stress that she had just bought a new house in Kensington, West London, and had no intention of relocating wholesale to the US. 'Really, I'm terribly upset if people think I am neglecting them. If it gets printed that you're going to the States for a few weeks then people think you're going for ever, but it's just not true. I want to divide my time to please everybody,' she said.

She had already appeared on every major TV chat show in the States, including *The Ed Sullivan Show* in New York and Hollywood's *Lloyd Thaxton Show*, and yet still felt she had yet to break America. The Royal Variety Performance at the end of the previous year signalled a pinnacle in her British recording career, and she was anxious to move on. 'Things are very dull for me in America,' she said at the time. 'I don't agree with the way my career is being handled in the States. I think they are issuing the wrong stuff and I don't think I was given the right material when I recorded there.'

The chart-topping success of 'You Don't Have to Say You Love Me' had given her the impetus to demand more from her record company, and she became determined to leave Philips in America for the strong, soul-identified Atlantic. She said, 'I have no real quarrel with the company in Britain, but in the US they have done virtually nothing to promote me or my records. Most of the kids there seem to have no idea when I have a disc on release – in fact, they write telling me how badly I am being promoted in America!' She refused to record again until something was done. 'Some people might say my attitude is unfair to my fans in Britain. But the present situation is unfair to the fans in the States, too, and I have to think of them as well.' US Philips president Irving Green rushed into London for consultation with Dusty and Vic Billings, but the disenchantment had festered for too long. 'It was a never-ending battle with Philips,' recalled Billings. 'You really had to fight. As you got bigger and bigger the only thing you could do was be terribly unprofessional and refuse to do something – a kind of eleventh-hour brinkmanship.'

Dusty was perturbed that many of her American releases were heavily edited without her control. 'US DJs might want two minutes forty-five, and if you had a three-minute record, a fifteen-second chunk would come out,' said Billings. He was also unhappy with her contract. 'In those days if you got a penny per record sold you thought it was great. Percentages weren't heard of. Dusty started on a five-year contract with threepence a record. I was also handling Kiki Dee, who had begun on three farthings and then a penny so by comparison Dusty was doing well. We gradually pushed it up as she got more powerful, to the dizzy heights of sixpence a record.'

Her overseas contract was even more stringent, with royalties cut by half, even though Dusty spent weeks in the recording studio rerecording tracks for the European market, singing phonetically in German, Italian, French and Spanish. Record-company policy in the sixties was not favourable towards the artist. Dusty had to cover most of her considerable promotional costs from her own royalties, which was a financial strain on even a successful star. The situation had come to a head after the Royal Variety Performance in which Dusty starred with Johnny Hallyday and Sylvie Vartan.

'We had to fly back from New York specially to do it,' said Billings. 'We had to pay for the orchestration, the flights back, and the dress, which was £700. Philips phoned us, saying, "Will you come in half and half with us for an advert on the programme?" I said, "No way." He said, "It's for charity." I said: "I know it's for charity, but we've given enough ... Think of all she's done for you – it's a bit bloody shameful that you can take an advert out and expect her to pay for it!" In the end, in the official programme, right cheapskates, they put Mercury Philips: Johnny Hallyday, Sylvie Vartan and Dusty Springfield at the bottom. Things like that made me really angry. In those days there were no big advances. We didn't want to rip the arse out of the record company, we just wanted them to work *with* us.'

Dusty got a new agent, Harold Davison, along with a strong business lawyer in the States, to fine-tune the Atlantic deal. There were reservations in the Philips stable about Dusty signing to Atlantic in the US. Davison was unsure whether she could fulfil the product commitment on two separate deals, and it would be difficult to combine promotional schedules. Yet Dusty's heart was set on Atlantic. To her it was a vision of America that suited her temperament and her love of soul music. Set up in 1947 by Herb Abramson and Ahmet Ertegun, with the help of a $10,000 loan from the latter's dentist, Atlantic Records existed originally as an independent national outfit for rough-house, danceable blues and swing. During the fifties, it embraced R&B and rock 'n' roll with such artists as Jesse Stone, the Drifters and Clyde McPhatter, and opened out in the sixties to a more eclectic base, signing up artists as varied as Wilson Pickett, Buffalo Springfield and Led Zeppelin. Dusty fitted into their 'blue-eyed soul' category, along with white performers like the Rascals and Sonny and Cher. She appreciated the live, spontaneous feel of Atlantic tracks, and its commitment to deep Southern soul on the offshoot Stax label.

She was also aware of Atlantic's line of illustrious women, who included Ruth Brown, LaVern Baker and Aretha Franklin. They symbolized a soul sorority that was sassy, sophisticated and in control of its own material. That was attractive to Dusty at a time when, despite being christened by her record company as 'the first lady of song in the hit parade', she was not having much luck with her singles. Her September 1968 offering, written by Clive Westlake and called 'I Will Come to You', failed to chart. Westlake was not impressed with her delivery of the song: 'She played around and I think she missed the point,' he told me. 'She wanted to do some soul on it, and that wasn't what I intended. She threw her voice around a bit.' Westlake hinted that 'heavy music-business politics' hampered the course of Dusty's hits. The more she pursued a US deal, the less keen Philips were to promote her UK material. She eventually renewed her contract with Philips for the UK and Europe and decided on a separate one with Atlantic for the US. It was at this point that Billings and Dusty split. 'I'd spent a lot of time in America with her, but I never wanted to settle there,' he says. The parting was amicable, but it left Dusty without a personal manager. The New York-based label worked out an uneasy alliance with Philips, whereby Dusty would record in both countries and each label would take the other's recordings. 'I'd like to make it clear that I'm not dissatisfied with things here, only with Philips in America,' said Dusty. 'The Atlantic deal is no reflection at all on Johnny Franz or any other people at Philips in Britain.'

The switch to Atlantic did not go smoothly. Clive Westlake recalls, 'After she signed with Atlantic she had two record labels really. She was making American-style records like "Son of a Preacher Man" and American politics meant that they weren't interested in Philips material. It clouded her British career at that moment – "Son of a Preacher Man" got lost in Britain and "I Close My Eyes" got dwarfed by "Son of a Preacher Man" in America. In the US it was a different ball game. Atlantic were hot, and Americans didn't want to push what came over from Britain.'

'Son of a Preacher Man', the first single from the forthcoming Memphis Atlantic album and widely held to be a classic, entered the British charts in December and climbed painfully slowly to no. 9. It was a respectable Top 10 hit, but Dusty was astounded that it didn't go higher. 'This really chokes me,' she said, 'because I know sales are high, a lot more than other tunes which have got higher. Perhaps it's the Christmas boom. It went in quickly but seems to be making no progress. Everyone was so bowled over by "Preacher Man". They kept telling me how good it was, and I think they convinced me.'

'Preacher Man' was also a Top 10 hit in the US: an uptempo ballad, with a Southern soul edge, it was an unusual cultural context for Dusty, as a white British Catholic girl. The song was offered first to Aretha Franklin, as it was more immediately suited to her background as a gospel-soul singer from a Baptist church in Detroit. Initially the Lady of Soul refused, but after Dusty's hit she was keen to record it.

Dusty sells the song with vocals that are subtle and understated, complemented by Tommy Cogbill's basslines. An accomplished jazz musician, Cogbill – who died in the mid-eighties – plays the bass as if it were a lead instrument, making the overall melody dark and slightly moody. 'The fact that Dusty was a white British girl gave it the extra little spice,' says Bobby Emmons, who played Wurlitzer piano on the track. 'The sound of the song, with low chords that rang, made it dark and mysterious.'

It was the prospect of teaming her unusual husky pop voice with the cream of Stax session musicians that made Jerry Wexler determined to bring Dusty to Memphis. In 1968 he was vice president of Atlantic, working with innovative and influential white artists, as well as strong black soul performers such as Aretha and Otis Redding. He had been keeping an eye on Dusty since 1965 when she brought out 'Some of Your Lovin'', a lazy ballad with flowing Southern soul delivery. 'When it became known Dusty might be available for Atlantic, I put in a bid for her,' Wexler told me in 1989, from his Florida home. 'She seemed particularly set on Atlantic Records and stipulated in her contract that I be her producer. I was a big fan of hers. In preparation I worked diligently assembling an inventory of songs. She had some suggestions, but she was looking to me to provide her with choices.'

Dusty flew to the States and spent a long weekend with Wexler at his house on Long Island, laboriously going through nearly a hundred songs. 'She liked exactly none,' he says. 'It was disheartening. I'd worked hard to find songs to suit her, but she was too much of a perfectionist in her image of herself. Very unhappily we closed shop and she went back. But we had a contractual arrangement, so she had to return. I culled twenty of the original songs, and she was totally mad for them. I don't think there was a better selection of material, it was flawless.'

In April *Dusty in Memphis* was released to critical acclaim. It was widely considered her best record, and a sixties classic. She was the first established British artist to record in Memphis with Memphis musicians, a combination that brought out her own creativity and a more sophisticated delivery. Initially Wexler was keen for Dusty to record at Muscle Shoals studios in Alabama. She considered that too countrified, though, and plumped instead for the Southern soul musicians of American Studios in North Memphis. A beat-up building in a rundown black neighbourhood, near the Hertz Village ghetto area and round the corner from Sun, American Studios became the gritty manifestation of Dusty's white soul dream. It was here that Aretha had belted out 'Natural Woman' to the accompaniment of rats scratching in the eaves, and here that Elvis Presley stopped short in shock before a recording session when a dead rat fell from the rafters to his feet.

Despite the dilapidated surroundings, Dusty carried herself like a star. 'She was a very magazine lady. She had her hairdresser John Adams with her, and she'd have her hair blown, dried and cut every day. She had a Memphis beehive and looked like the queen of the Southern contingent. People were flabbergasted when she opened her mouth and it wasn't a Southern drawl,' engineer and co-producer Tom Dowd told me.

'She came on like she was grooming herself for court,' Wexler adds drily. As she was somewhat overawed, it took a while for Dusty to muster up the courage to sing. 'She'd walk around saying, "Fine, aren't all these boys good at playing,"' says Wexler. 'And I'd be, "But, Dusty, I need you to be at the microphone."' Having previously been accustomed to walking into studios and singing to fit over prearranged backings, Dusty was surprised at the free-form nature of the Memphis sessions. Working with the dynamic triumvirate of Jerry Wexler, Arif Mardin and Tom Dowd was demanding: they pushed her to express a complex range of feeling, to create her own sound.

At that time the Atlantic producers had a unique approach to recording, pooling their efforts equally with different projects. This meant that if one artist discarded a song, it was rescued by another and its potential religiously nurtured. By the mid-sixties, the trio had a healthy reputation for *caring* about music and the artists they used. 'There had been a tendency with star singers to record the tracks first, and then the singer would come and lay their tile in the picture,' says Wexler. 'I abhorred that, as the artist would have no part of the creative process. I wanted the interplay of singer with rhythm section, with the musicians taking cues from the vocalist.'

To performers accustomed to star treatment, this could be distressing. Piano-player Bobby Woods recalls how Petula Clark spent her first few days there in tears. 'She was used to having an arranged session with all her cheerleaders around. In Memphis, though, it was so laid-back it was three days before we even hit a lick. She kinda took that personally, until she moulded into what we were doing. We would *wait* for a good song to come through. When she left she was crying for joy.'

Although Dusty began recording feeling nervous and vulnerable, she soon opened up. 'It's really great here, so relaxed and calm!' she said at first. 'There's an attitude of communication between the singer and the musician. You can take your time and get it just right, unlike everything in Europe where it's so clinical – someone looking at meters every second.'

Communication between her and Wexler, though, was fraught. 'When it came to the final vocals,' says Wexler, 'it was the most excruciating experience I encountered. During playback we feed the track back to the singer through headphones, and she sings vocal overdubs into the mike. There's a judgement point about how loud to feed the track back, and I've always gone for the minimum possible amount. There's usually a little warfare between producer and singer at this point, the latter calling for more. The less voice you feed back on the phones, the harder the singer will project, it's a physiological fact. With Dusty, she insisted we crank up the track so loud it was physically painful. There was no way she could hear herself – it was like she was singing into a void, projecting an interior monologue. Like she was totally deaf and asked to sing from aural memory. The thing was – and this shows what a gifted, idiosyncratic artist she was – she sang perfectly in tune. Her pitch was miraculous. I am fixated on pitch, and there's a lot of rock 'n' roll I wouldn't give house room to. For intonation, there's not a better singer than Dusty, black or white.'

Such strenuous technique inevitably created conflict. 'I was very persistent. Many times she gave me good cause to throw in the towel,' says Wexler. 'One time she shoved an ashtray at me in the control room. She had a terrible argument with Tom Dowd and called him a prima donna. Now, Tom's my friend, and a very gentle person – I wouldn't have anyone call him a prima donna in my presence. I was very angry. "There's only one prima donna in the room at the moment!" I said to Dusty. She had an inferiority complex and a lot of self-doubt.'

Dowd remembered the session more light-heartedly. When reminded of the prima donna episode, he roared with laughter. 'She was a tough, tough, tough taskmaster on her own vocals. If it didn't come back how she thought she'd sung it she wanted to nix it. I could never comprehend her thought on any given song. I had to throw my preconceptions out the window and let her get on with it.'

He had done his homework beforehand, studying the keys and range of her albums, and come up with some startling conclusions. 'I recognized in her a deep jazz root. She was a European person who had a devotion to folk roots with the Springfields, and also a sensitivity to time and harmonic intervals. She had at least two cultures going for her. When she sang ballads she wouldn't just recite an Elizabethan poem, she'd borrow four or five different cultures before she got to the chorus. She was a fanatical jazz impressionist. When she told me Blossom Dearie was one of her heroines, I realized that she had obscure avant-garde genius as her goal. She looked up to people who were never popular in a certain way, and it disturbed her that she was popular for less.'

Dusty later spoke on BBC Radio One's *Atlantic Story* about the fear she felt at the Memphis sessions: 'Jerry's gone in print saying I was the most insecure singer he has come across. What he didn't realize is how intimidated I was. Because they were telling stories and talking about Aretha, and I'm going, "What am I doing on this label? Why are they recording me?" and that showed in the time it took to get vocal performances out of me. Because if there's one thing that inhibits good singing it's fear, or allowing the natural critic in me to criticize a note before it even left my throat, which destroys the flow of anything. I don't think they understood how intimidated I was, so it probably came out as scowls and fear and grumbling ...'

She felt a sham, her self-doubt making her imagine that Wexler and the boys would 'find her out'. Under this self-imposed stress she developed laryngitis again, hence the special husky quality of her vocals on the album. Wexler himself was quite a hard taskmaster, as Lulu also discovered: 'I recorded two albums with him. I found him to be a perfectionist and difficult to work with. I think he was going through a difficult time himself when Dusty and I worked with him.'

Dusty still admired Wexler's high standards. 'He is very patient and thoughtful, he doesn't mess around,' she said. One of her major problems was in comparing herself to Aretha Franklin. 'Bette Midler used to say, "You'll probably hate me because I'm white,"' says Wexler. 'It was a common failing among white female singers to set up Aretha as their benchmark. With Dusty there were no traces of black in her singing, she's not mimetic. Whatever she gets from black is transmogrified with her own sensibility. She has a pure silvery stream, she's a genuine original.' Dowd does make one comparison with Aretha Franklin. 'Aretha would call and say, "I wanna repair one line." Then she'd come in, do it, and five minutes later it *was* better. Dusty had that aspiration, but she wasn't as quick as Aretha. She'd do it, then say, "Try again," even though she'd done it.' Again, Dusty's self-doubt got in the way of her making an uninhibited recording.

While Wexler worked as visionary overseer, Dowd engineered the nuts and bolts of the project alongside his studio musicians. He even built a special piece of equipment, the Ampex 5258 console, which has now become a prized piece of vintage hardware. Arif Mardin injected the intellectual trimmings and arrangements. 'Some products have an aura, like a blessing from above,' Mardin told me. 'Whatever it was, it worked. After we did the tracks we added the Memphis horns down South and up in New York I arranged the strings and woodwind. Somehow the combination worked. The strings and woodwind with the Memphis horns at the back gave a kind of echo, a wonderful lush, tough sound. It wasn't schmaltzy at all. It had the essence of Memphis with a symphonic overlay.' Mardin recalled long nights in Atlantic laying down tracks. 'With "In the Land of Make Believe" Tom and I thought we were making an art song reminiscent of a Ravel string quartet. And we took turns sleeping on the floor when we were doing "The Windmills of Your Mind", as it was such a complicated, inventive rhythm.'

The six-strong 827 Thomas Street Band – named after the American Studios address – provided a superlative rhythm section. 'We were a unified bunch,' says drummer Gene Chrisman, 'and we still stick together.' These Memphis boys included Chrisman, Bobby Emmons, Bobby Woods, Tommy Cogbill and guitar/sitar player Reggie Young, and they worked together in the Nashville music industry for many years. They remembered Dusty with affection. 'You had a respect for her presence. She set an atmosphere,' says Emmons. 'You knew if you weren't tryin' your hardest, well … We were armed and dangerous with someone of her calibre there. We were first there to complement Dusty. It wasn't our show.'

'She sure knocked everybody out,' says Bobby Woods. 'We were used to the Wilson Picketts and Aretha Franklins. She fell right in, creating a groove for everybody to work off, just as black as the next one. We were being as creative, funky and soulful as we could be.' He remembers working round the clock on that session. 'One night in particular I was sittin' at the piano and my spirit came loose from my body. I actually saw myself sitting there. It was *long* hours.'

The result of this critical tension was an outstanding album and a consolidation of Dusty's vocal talents. Jerry Wexler christened her 'the Great White Lady'. 'I felt very tight about it ... exposed all of a sudden. But I sort of grew up as the album progressed,' Dusty said. 'Working this way forces you to be creative.' The album opens with 'Just a Little Lovin'', an upbeat Barry Mann/Cynthia Weil song with a sparser, cleaner sound than her usual elaborate orchestral arrangements. It moves into a Carole King ballad, 'So Much Love', with Dusty giving it a soft gospel treatment, and backing from the Sweet Inspirations singers. As usual, Dusty is surrounded by superlative black vocalists, in her eyes 'the real thing'. With Whitney Houston's mother Cissy, Myrna Smith, Sylvia Shemwell and Estelle Brown, the Sweet Inspirations added their polished gospel-soul to much of the Atlantic sound.

The feel of *Dusty in Memphis* was of taste and restraint, with low-key Randy Newman ballads such as 'I Don't Want to Hear It Anymore' and the light touch of Bacharach's 'In the Land of Make Believe'. Carole King's pop sound is also given a new twist on tracks like 'Don't Forget About Me', where Reggie Young's electric sitar forges an effective fuzzy melody alongside an inspirational chorus. There is a reference to late sixties psychedelia in the revolving rhythm and powerful moodiness of 'Windmills of Your Mind', and a poignant rocksteady beat on the Eddie Hinton song 'Breakfast in Bed', one of Dusty's finest and most vulnerable moments.

After the album was completed Wexler threw a farewell party at the nearby Rivermont Motel for Dusty, the musicians and the producers. By then everyone had become close – 'like a family'. There was a mood of elation, with corks popping and people spurting champagne over each other. 'It was like the locker room after the world series,' says Dowd.

The record became an inside music-business legend. 'Everybody loved it except the damn public,' said Wexler. 'It sold only a hundred thousand copies in America before Nesuhi Ertegun deleted it. Maybe he did us a favour in terms of our reputation, giving the record a rare status. People didn't expect to hear such a polished sound. They were used to raggedy-arse Bob Dylan records with everyone plunking away ... Ours was a masterful interweaving of voices and instruments, not just a bunch of chords. It was like an intricate well-worn tweed.'

Jerry Greenburg, then head of promotion, and later Atlantic's president, remembered *Dusty in Memphis* as being *the* album that writers wanted to review. 'It wasn't hard to promote her, she was well received at Top 40 radio stations, but a couple of Dusty tours would have helped promote the album. It's a shame the record wasn't more of a hit because I remember what a fantastic singer she was and how excited Jerry was to take her to Memphis.' The record enhanced Dusty's reputation, establishing her in America as a singer of hip taste. Cult *Rolling Stone* writer Greil Marcus reviewed the album in 1969, as part of a feature on special lady singers:

With the single 'The Look of Love' Dusty seemed destined to join that crowd of big-bosomed, low-necked lady singers that play what Lenny Bruce called 'the class rooms' and always encore with 'Born Free'. It didn't happen, and *Dusty in Memphis* is the reason why ... Dusty is not a soul singer, and she makes no effort to 'sound black' – rather, she is singing songs that ordinarily would have been offered by their writers to black vocalists. Most of the songs have a great deal of depth while presenting extremely direct and simple statements about love.

Dusty in Memphis was released in the US in March 1969, and in Britain the following month. It did not figure highly in either chart, going no further than no. 99 in America. Ironically, fifty years later it had mythological status, and was the inspiration for the Hollywood film *So Much Love*. Music critic Robert Christgau called it 'the all-time rock-era torch record'. For Dusty, it was her creative and artistic triumph.

By the end of the sixties, Dusty had everything going for her. She had successfully negotiated a turning point in her career with *Dusty in Memphis*, and although when it first came out the perfectionist in her was dissatisfied with the record, it was a stepping stone towards consolidating her American career. She had one Atlantic recording under her belt and was due contractually for two more. America was clearly her main goal.

It was a productive, exciting time of expanding horizons and experimental directions. Wexler, Mardin and Dowd were her winning triumvirate but, unable to rest on her laurels, Dusty became anxious yet again to move on to something fresh.

The tension began to show soon after the release of 'Son of

a Preacher Man': 'We'd forged ahead and put out the track as a single,' said Dowd, 'and Dusty was livid because she hadn't been given an opportunity to re-sing one vocal she didn't like. She went into a tizzy. In the meantime, she had a hit record!' She also had a hit with another track from the album, 'Windmills of Your Mind'. Not released in Britain, the song reached the US Top 40 in May 1969 and stayed in the charts for eight weeks. Excited by its success, Mardin and Dowd industriously prepared for the next Atlantic session with Dusty. 'When we presented her with songs for the follow-up album, she wasn't that enthralled with what we were suggesting,' says Dowd. 'Talks were amicable, but broke down. I figured we'd been dismissed. Whatever the breakdown in business communication, I have seen Dusty since, and we remained cordial.'

'I don't think she realized that *Dusty in Memphis* was going to be a classic,' added Mardin. 'She didn't want to work with the same musicians in the same town.'

Wexler decided to let her go to Kenny Gamble and Leon Huff, two Philadelphia producers he had signed on a freelance basis for the next record. 'Then they were at their height and would be a continuation of giving her an R&B matrix for her pop music.'

Wexler's interpretation was generous, for in 1969, two years before the rise of their famous Philadelphia International label, Gamble and Huff were still outside producers for Atlantic and Mercury. They were more of a cult phenomenon, making hits on their own Gamble label for the Intruders. They had been together since 1964, though Huff had established a reputation before that as a top R&B session pianist, working with Leiber and Stoller in New York, and Gamble had developed skills as a singer-songwriter. They achieved major success in the seventies with the lavishly orchestrated Philly soul sound, recording such artists as Harold Melvin and the Blue Notes, the O'Jays, the Three Degrees and Billy Paul. When Dusty joined them in Philadelphia's Sigma Sound Studios, the duo were relatively unknown and exceedingly hip. Throughout her career, Dusty had the knack of picking powerful, top-line producers at exactly the right moment. It is also interesting that she chose to work with Gamble and Huff at the same time as they were producing her friend Vicki Wickham's outrageous all-girl glam funk band Labelle. Originally a run-of-the-mill supper-club soul outfit called the Bluebells, Nona Hendryx, Sarah Dash and Patti LaBelle were transformed under Wickham's management into futuristic Philly, with an image that incorporated strutting sexuality and earthy, socially significant material. Dusty's Philly liaison was a fruitful learning experience.

At the beginning of 1970, her second Atlantic album, *A Brand New Me*, was released in the US. The title song, a bright, quirky number arranged by Thom Bell, combined her love of orchestration with an optimistic R&B soul delivery. It was a Top 20 US hit, conveniently flagging the new album – 'We had a ball working with that lady,' recalls Bell. Kenny Gamble wrote all ten tracks on the album, collaborating mainly with Leon Huff, Ugene Dozier and Roland Chambers.

It was a new direction for Dusty in that she had never before relied so much on one songwriter – hence the criticism that all the songs sound similar. There were none of her customary Bacharach ballads and tub-thumping orchestrations and she projected a laid-back persona that suits the material. 'The Star of My Show', for instance, elicits from her a fine funky

Dusty in the fourth form at St. Anne's Convent School, Ealing, circa 1950. Dusty is circled in the second row from back.

Above and right: Dusty before her transformation, as Mary O'Brien, 1954. She created a girl called Dusty from her bedroom in north London.

Above and below: Dusty Springfield, left, in the Lana Sisters, 1959. The band was formed by Riss Chantelle, along with Lynne Abrams. They put an advert in *The Stage* which Dusty replied to.

The Lana Sisters' sweet jazzy pop slotted easily into the world of variety tours and TV shows.

Left: Dusty in the original line-up of The Springfields, with Tim Feild (left) and her brother Tom Springfield (right) winning the NME Top Vocal Award, 1962. *Right:* with Mike Hurst (left) and brother Tom (right) in Australia, 1963.

Left: Recording 'I Only Want to Be With You' at Olympic Studios, Barnes, October 1963. *Below*: Dusty with her long-term secretary, Pat Rhodes, after a show in the 1970s.

Dusty on her way
to New York City
to launch her solo
career, 1965.

With her voice coach,
New York City, 1965.

One of her many
appearances on *Ready,
Steady, Go!*, 1965.

Performing at the NME Poll Winners Concert, 1967.

Dusty with legendary music engineer, Tom Dowd.

Performing with Tom Jones on his show, *Tom Jones and Special Friends*, 1970.

Performing on Lulu's show, *It's Lulu*,
London, September 1970.

Above: Dusty's love of
tennis lasted for her
entire life. Arriving
at London Heathrow
airport, ready to start
recording again, 1970.
Left: Having a break
in LA at the Bel Air
Hotel, with Phyllis
Diller and Cleo
Laine, 1976.

Performing with Neil Tennant of the Pet Shop Boys at the Brit Awards, 1988. Dusty enjoyed renewed success with their duet, 'What Have I Done to Deserve This?'.

With Alison Moyet, Sinead O'Connor and Jools Holland, June 1995. Alison and Sinead sang back-up for Dusty on 'Where Is a Woman to Go?'.

To the Greatest With Our Love Elton and David

Dusty was laid to rest in Henley-upon-Thames on 12 March 1999. Lulu said at the ceremony, 'Dusty was the first one to demonstrate girl power'. Condolences from Elton John and David Furnish (right) were among hundreds of messages from her fellow artists and fans.

THE HERITAGE FOUNDATION

DUSTY SPRINGFIELD O.B.E. 1939-1999 Singer Lived here 1968-1972

Pat Rhodes (far left) with Madeline Bell, Robin Gibb and Simon Bell at the unveiling of her blue plaque, Aubrey Walk, London, 8 May 2011.

performance, with an abrupt, orchestrated riff punctuating each refrain. 'Let Me Get in Your Way' finds her muted and ironic, adding a languid shading and toning to the fluty soul-girl backing chorus, while 'Never Love Again' is a reflective ballad with plangent Gamble and Huff basslines and an emotive crescendo.

Interviewed during her recording sessions in October 1969, Dusty sounded excited with Gamble and Huff's 'melodic R&B'. She was also impressed that the drummer Earl Young had just spent two years touring with Marvin Gaye. 'The rhythm section are the best I've worked with,' she said (maybe, after *Dusty in Memphis*, a little undiplomatically). 'They work as a unit, very tight. And they play so loud, which I like.' This was the rhythm section that developed Philly's unique hybrid of R&B and Italian orchestration. Made up of black session men and white Italian orchestral musicians from Philadelphia, the Mother Father Sister Brother (MFSB) section later released their own albums, such as *Love Is the Message* and *TSOP*, which heralded the arrival of disco. 'Mother Fuckin' Sonava Bitch' was how they were affectionately known in the studio.

After some delay, *A Brand New Me* was released in Britain towards the end of 1970 under the title *From Dusty ... with Love*. It was a moderate success, going into the album charts at no. 35, but, like *Dusty in Memphis*, wasn't a bestseller. Her last album with Johnny Franz, the reflective *See All Her Faces*, was released in 1972, but Dusty's UK career had begun to wind down long before that.

As her British market receded, Dusty hinted at a new life in America, saying that she had 'hundreds' of friends on the West Coast. 'There's something about America which seems to fit me.

Things like waking up in the middle of the night and knowing you can walk round the block and buy food in a supermarket.' The more time she spent recording in the States, the less her records were promoted at home. In 1969 she made a brief yet acclaimed appearance at the Singing Europe '69 festival in Holland, while September of that year saw a minor hit with 'Am I the Same Girl'. Her next UK single, an acoustic duet with her brother Tom entitled 'Morning Please Don't Come', was a nostalgic nod to the Springfields, but it didn't make much impact on the charts.

While Dusty colonized the pop and soul market, Tom forged a career as a producer/composer, exploring folk and Latin sounds. After writing hits for the Seekers, he worked with Puerto Rican star José Feliciano, acting as recording manager on his early material. 'I wish I had been working with him at the time of "Light My Fire",' he said ruefully in 1969, 'but I'm glad he's been recognized at last.' Tom also recorded an album of his own Latin-inspired *Sun Songs*, long before the ascent of 'world music' and eighties compilations like David Byrne's *Beleza Tropical*. It was evident that brother and sister were digging deep into their respective musical influences.

'Morning Please Don't Come' was the last time that Dusty recorded with Tom. She moved quickly back to her solo career and had some success with the husky ballad 'How Can I Be Sure' (originally a US hit for the Rascals and later immortalized by David Cassidy) when it reached the lower reaches of the Top 40. At this point she decided to move to America to launch a new career. 'My feeling was I had run out of things to do in Britain,' she told me. 'I didn't want to get bored or be pinned down to summer seasons or the cabaret circuit. The Springfields got out before people got tired of it. I could sense the rot setting in.' While compatriots like the Beatles and the Rolling Stones were experimenting with psychedelia and the concept album, Dusty was happiest in the pop sphere – but this was a space where she had less and less room to manoeuvre.

As her career slowed down, the press started asking awkward questions about her private life. Then, in a shock move, amid growing speculation about her sexuality, she fled. 'We were disappointed when Dusty vanished to America,' recalls Paddy Fleming, former head of promotions for Philips radio and press. 'She was one of our top artists and a very good performer. We were losing a lovely person. She just literally vanished.' At the age of thirty-one Dusty went to Los Angeles and very nearly didn't make it back.

7

Lady of the Canyon

SPRAWLED ACROSS A thousand square miles of a large desert basin, intersected by freeways and studded with shopping malls, palm trees, orange groves and swimming pools, LA symbolizes the American Dream. With Disneyland at one end and Hollywood at the other, it is a magnet for thousands of 'transplants', people who have moved from all over the world to 'make it'. To Dusty, a home counties girl keen to escape the stultifying mores of suburbia and the limitations of a showbiz scene dominated by variety and panto, LA was a fresh start.

With the Wild West and the madness of the Gold Rush, California has always been a focus for freewheeling speculators, and was a prime place for the young film industry. Ever since the first movie studio opened in 1911, and the director Cecil B. DeMille shared his barn-converted office space with a horse, Hollywood has been the repository of dream and fantasy. This was combined with radical political groups and countercultural movements like the Beats in the fifties and the hippies in the sixties. The erotic writer Anaïs Nin lived there, as did the underground film-maker Kenneth Anger. They formed their own artistic subculture based on free spirits, free sex and self-expression. California had created a heady, progressive society, and in the seventies, it was on a high.

'Everything was wide. In terms of psychological space everyone had a front yard. The Californian architecture style was ranch – the house and a huge amount of land,' recalls Wendy Fonarow, a teaching fellow in cultural anthropology at UCLA. To Dusty, the endlessly sunny skies of LA after the British chill, along with relaxed West Coast attitudes to homosexuality and alternative lifestyles, must have felt like liberation.

By mid-1970 Dusty was packing up the Kensington residence she had shared for several years with the artist and songwriter Norma Tanega. Rumours about her relocating to the States were rife, and one newspaper interview around this time hastened her departure. Ray Connolly of London's *Evening Standard* was a notoriously tough interviewer – analytical, blunt and unwavering. After all her cheery, family-friendly statements to the press throughout the sixties, it seems that Dusty decided to reveal to him a more controversial side of her personality. She wanted to grow up in public, to debunk once and for all the 'naive sweet girl' myth that existed as a hangover from the Springfield days. Until the *Standard* interview, Dusty had come across as an asexual, slightly awkward ex-convent girl, who joked with the lads but didn't have a sex life.

'I burp like everyone else and I'm promiscuous. My affections are easily swayed and I can be very unfaithful,' she said, in a fit of frankness. With almost self-destructive enthusiasm she then declared: 'A lot of people say I'm bent, and I've heard it so many times that I've almost learned to accept it … I couldn't stand to be thought of as a big butch lady. But I know that I'm as perfectly capable of being swayed by a girl as by a boy. More and more people feel that way and I don't see why I shouldn't.'

In 1970 the word lesbian was synonymous with 'butch' and 'masculine'. For a woman in pop, an admission of anything other than straight heterosexuality was commercial suicide. Dusty was showing a rebellious streak and risking a great deal with her open revelation. In that Ray Connolly interview she criticized the music business for making her feel 'unwomanly' and then, having admitted to bisexuality, hastily diluted its effect by adding the confusing statement, 'Being a woman is very precious to me, and that's probably why I could never get mixed up in a gay scene because it would be bound to undermine my sense of being a woman.' She went on to say that her flat had been raided by the police looking for drugs, that she suspected they had been tipped off by a crazy woman who fancied her, and that she doubted whether she'd have children – 'I probably wouldn't be a terribly good mother.' The former Catholic girl then admitted that she no longer went to Mass. 'I still think that because I don't I'm going to hell ... But I don't want to go to hell because I haven't really done anything evil. I'm just lazy and self-indulgent.'

At the age of thirty-one, Dusty had started her teen rebellion. As she walked through the doors at Philips Records after the interview, she laughed heartily at the journalist. 'D'you realize that what I've just said could put the final straw to my doom. I don't know, though. I might attract a whole new audience.' The interview, as she had intended, created a storm of controversy.

It upset her family, excited reporters and sent a shiver through the music business, particularly at Philips Records. As her world in Britain closed behind her, Dusty set up house in LA with a headful of dreams. It was heaven to walk along the star-studded Hollywood Boulevard, her spiritual home. June Haver, Judy Garland, Greta Garbo had all inspired her. Many of the actors in the films she had seen as a kid had shopped in the same shops and walked the same streets. 'Old Hollywood stars are really open for interaction. They're *there*,' says Fonarow. 'All the stuff you see is there. The backdrops you see from those films are there, the movie studios are there. Motor Street, for instance, in West LA, starts at Fox and ends at MGM, with all the studios in between.'

Situated in Laurel Canyon in the Hollywood Hills, Dusty automatically became part of LA's music community. In the seventies, many successful artists and producers were buying up huge estates that became available as old movie-stars, like Errol Flynn and Betty Grable, passed away. Fifteen minutes north of Sunset Strip, Laurel Canyon was a primary site. Now it is mainly the province of wealthy record executives, but in the seventies it still had an air of organic hipness – songwriters and musicians such as Frank Zappa, Fleetwood Mac and Chris Hillman of the Byrds lived there, and it had been immortalized by Joni Mitchell in her satirical song 'Ladies of the Canyon', a warm look at the hippie sorority of Los Angeles.

After years of gruelling promotion, travelling on the road on grubby tour buses, America became Dusty's playground. She took an unofficial sabbatical. 'She got involved with the tennis circuit and became great friends with Billie Jean King and Rosemary Casals. She wanted to follow the tennis tour round the world,' recalls former Philips head of promotion, Paddy Fleming.

In the early seventies arguments about women's liberation were attracting media headlines, and female tennis players were at the forefront of the debate. Tennis had just begun to go professional, and in the division of men's and women's tours Billie Jean King led the fight for equal pay. Women were taking control of the circuit, and in 1971, the first year of the new Virginia Slims women's pro tournament, King won $117,400 in prize money. It might have been a large sum then, but it was still less than half the prize money the male champion Rod Laver made that year. By 1973 King and others had formed the Women's Tennis Association, a dynamic, PR-conscious players' union that achieved pay parity between the sexes two years later at the US Open. One of its biggest public victories came in 1983: that year Martina Navratilova made over £6 million, the highest annual sum ever for a tennis pro of either sex.

It was an exciting era for women's tennis, and Dusty followed it avidly, often to the detriment of her own career. The tennis world offered a different lifestyle from the one to which she had become accustomed in Britain – warm, sunny, outdoors and, after many years of the promotional grind, relaxing. Tennis also provided high-profile entertainment with its own star system. A good tennis match is pure theatre, taking place in a highly regimented, enclosed space, fired by an enormous amount of controlled energy. The women's tour had a glamorous image of sexual intrigue and ambiguity. Although the female players had to look young, straight and sexy to get sponsorship deals, rumours abounded of 'lesbians in the locker room'.

The elite women's tour, which separated girls from boys, led to some controversial off-court liaisons, which later became public. In 1979 the press played up Navratilova's purchase of a Virginia mansion with lesbian novelist Rita Mae Brown; and two years later Billie Jean King's former lover, Marilyn Barnett, sued King for 'galimony'. Dusty was good friends with players like King and Rosie Casals, and once when she was still living in London she invited half of Wimbledon home to her flat. Although she wasn't keen on playing the game herself, she loved the social life that whirled around it.

Dusty did not get back to recording for two years. She dismisses her time away as being one of 'travelling around the world, having fun in an open-topped car and lazing by the pool'. In reality she had begun to fight some severe demons. The intense achievement of her twenties gave way in her early thirties to doubt and introspection. The secret self of Mary O'Brien, whom she had packed away at the age of seventeen, was demanding attention and nurture. For so long she had embraced the outward flamboyant persona of Dusty Springfield, while keeping her shy self sturdily locked inside. This led to the creation of two conflicting characters.

Like many people who move to LA, Dusty found herself in a place where no one knew the awkward, uptight suburban teenager she had once been. LA creates the opportunity for superb reinvention of self: Tallulah Bankhead did it in the twenties and thirties when she left her staid Alabama origins to become the movie actress with the rich laugh and harsh drawl; Marilyn Monroe had done it in the fifties when she dyed her hair blonde and cultivated a sexy walk. Many years later Madonna did it when she escaped suburban Michigan to take on the world. But in the same way that Dorothy had yearned for home when she was in the Land of Oz, and longed for Oz when she was in Kansas, Dusty could not shake off her roots, or her other self.

The first inkling of this for Dusty came out after a 1968 Talk of the Town appearance when she said, 'I feel like two separate people. I was coming here tonight and I saw my name up in lights. People say, "It must give you a kick, seeing your name up there," but it doesn't. It doesn't give me a thrill. Not because I'm ungrateful … it's just that it seems like a separate person. When I hear my name announced, it also feels to me like it's someone else!'

Later she admitted, 'I had no trouble with my singing or career, it was Mary O'Brien I had trouble with. To this day when they announce me as Dusty Springfield, I stand backstage and think myself into her personality.' The invention of a star persona can help an artist at the beginning of their career, but as time goes on it gets harder and harder to live with two separate personalities, and the conflict between their public and private world. David Bowie carried it off for a while in the seventies with his glam-rock hero Ziggy Stardust. However, the Ziggy character began to obscure Bowie's sense of reality and led to a near nervous breakdown.

Dusty, likewise, had trouble integrating her public and private personas. She was uneasy with fame on a day-to-day level. She hated having her picture taken, and a photo session made her anxious. It was all right when she could 'loon around' being Dusty Springfield, the performer. 'But in a shop … oh, that's the worst; or in a café on the M1 with people staring. Or in a supermarket. I can't wait to get out. I feel uncomfortable because I can't be *me* … I've got to be Dusty Springfield.' At such times Mary O'Brien was at war with Dusty Springfield, as if the latter were a bossy older sister. 'I hate to see someone who inhibits herself so much,' said her girlfriend, the artist Norma Tanega.

Once Dusty had moved to the States – to unfamiliar surroundings with people she didn't know well – the shy, diffident Mary surfaced. She felt intimidated and alone, and her career lost its momentum. 'The loss of conviction, it's not an overnight thing,' she said, with hindsight. 'It's that so much of my success had been in Europe ... I had never played in the States for any length of time. I would come over and do guest spots on *The Ed Sullivan Show* and it was always the image of whatever single I had out at that time ... so much of my image had been intermittent with these singles.

'You know, a little bit of "Wishin' and Hopin'" here, a little bit of "You Don't Have to Say You Love Me" there. I had no real broad-range image, it was just sort of blonde beehive and miniskirts, waving her arms around ... And when I came over, having always been fascinated with the States in general, and feeling that was the ultimate in life for a performer, it just got too big for me.' The enormity of Hollywood's history began to overwhelm her; she felt unconfident negotiating the intricate Los Angeles music and movie business, and settled for an American management that decided to play safe.

'The Americans were clamouring and saying, "We can guide you." Unfortunately it was the worst day's work that girl ever did,' says Pat Rhodes. 'They had no idea what she was capable of. None. They tried to push her into Las Vegas and New York cabaret rooms, which are not her scene.' Dusty went through a succession of managers, including the late Howard Portugais, Andy Williams's manager Alan Bernard and, later, the portly Barry Krost. 'A lot of work in America had been romanced by the American management,' Dusty said to me. 'After all, they had managed all the best people. I should have followed my intuition, though – my insides told me it was wrong. They were pushing me towards nightclubs, the equivalent of what I was trying to get away from in England. I did a few albums and there was no continuity to anything.'

'I don't think she had one good manager while she was out in the States,' observes Rhodes. 'They had no idea of her potential, and they never did anything with her. The worst thing you could do with an artist like Dusty was let her stagnate. Then she'd get frightened of going back to work. "Gosh, can I still do it? Will people want me? Have they forgotten me?" She was an extrovert onstage, but completely introvert off.'

Howard Portugais started his music industry career in 1966 as a roadie for psychedelic band the Electric Prunes, and soon became a successful TV agent and personal manager, working for International Famous Agency (now ICM). His clients included the comedian Groucho Marx, which Dusty majorly appreciated. Portugais told me that he and Bernard did well for Dusty, negotiating her out of an Atlantic deal she found restrictive, though he admits that he often disagreed with Bernard. 'I never saw her as a cabaret singer. Alan did. We would argue about this, as I felt music was going through a changing, transitional time and glitzy gowns were out of style.' Although she was determined to follow her inclinations, Dusty benefited from organized direction. 'She lost a mentor,' says Dave Shrimpton, former production manager at Philips. 'Johnny Franz gave her direction. Together they had a magic formula. But then she went four thousand miles away with Johnny still sitting in Marble Arch. There was a curious cut-off point at the end of the sixties, when her career was incredibly high. Then she went to America and suddenly there was nothing for the charts over here at all.'

Part of the problem for Dusty was her fear that American audiences would criticize her as not being 'the real thing', and she developed a phobia about going out on the road. 'She was terrified about touring,' said Portugais. 'We had put together a tour for her, opening at the Plaza in New York, and Alan was saying, "I don't know what to do, she won't even play a break-in date." So I told her, "C'mon, Dusty, you gotta play somewhere else beside US Customs." She laughed at that and finally said okay.'

In June 1972 Dusty did her first national tour in two years, opening with a short season at the lavish Century Plaza Hotel in Los Angeles. Critic Nat Freedland's review in *Billboard* was reserved. 'Miss Springfield was quite relaxed and mellow-voiced … Her voice did not cut through the walls of sound the way she used to on her records. Afterwards, at her reception, she was heard to complain about the room's sound set-up.' He added, however, that 'she tells flaky stories in great style'.

Dusty's self-deprecating air covered uncertainty about where she was going career-wise. She was unable to concentrate or commit herself to a sustained project, a situation exacerbated by protracted record-company wrangling. Although she still had one more album to record for Atlantic, she extricated herself from the contract, dissatisfied with their choice of material and direction. 'They were trying to turn her into what *Variety* would call a "chantoozie",' says her friend and one-time press officer, Norman Divall. 'To get her career off the ground in the States they wanted her to go to Vegas, be second on the bill to Dean Martin, get her face around.' In other words, to be the typical 'rich man's entertainer'.

Part of the last unfinished session she recorded for Atlantic is included on the *Memphis Plus* album, an amalgamation of *Dusty in Memphis* and later tracks. Two of these, 'Haunted' and 'I Believe in You', were released as singles in 1971. Although these bluesy ballads gained a *Billboard* Special Merit spotlight, they were too soulful for a white audience, and not black enough for the black radio stations. Neither made the charts. 'Dusty was ahead of her time, and in one sense avant-garde,' said soul connoisseur Dave Godin. 'American DJs and record people, to put it brutally, just couldn't understand why a nice white girl should want to sing like a black woman.'

Despondent, Dusty retired to her home on Laurel Canyon and fed the raccoons. Thinking she should put down roots, she had bought a house with a panoramic view, a large pool and a host of seventies 'gadgets'. 'It was sort of *nouveau riche*,' she said. 'The trouble was that I was not very *nouvelle* and not very *riche*. I staggered around that house for a while trying to convince myself that I really belonged, but every time I looked at the burnt-up hillside, I felt terribly alien.'

She tried to become 'Californian', lunching with ladies in Beverly Hills, shopping, socializing, eating elaborate meals and drinking the wine that went with it. 'That breeds extreme laziness in me,' she said. 'I handle idleness very badly. So I really had to kick myself in the butt and get out of there.' LA can be a lonely place. The city grew from a series of isolated communities to become a huge network of districts, without much in common and with no centre. And because distances between the different areas are so great, LA is dominated by car. 'People don't walk in LA, it's so spread out there's nothing to walk *to*,' remarks Wendy Fonarow. 'That means you drive everywhere. The car radio becomes important because that's the only thing that connects you to other people. You can be driving the freeways, bumper to bumper for hours, but never speak to anybody. It's terribly, terribly lonely.'

Consequently the phone has become a key instrument of social interaction. People drive cars and speak on the phone, make busy arrangements but rarely meet up. Parties take on the status of events. Driving is a problem for those who are drinking or doing drugs, so the answer is to take the car to someone's house and party there for several days. LA parties in the seventies were famous: people went on three-day binges, sampling swimming pools, saunas, hot tubs and outdoor waterbeds, as well as ingesting copious amounts of alcohol and cocaine. With plenty of space between you and nosy neighbours there was a sense of unlimited freedom. The idea of a moral spectator was something that belonged to Europe, or the old world, which everyone had left behind. As in Mark Robson's cult 1967 film *The Valley of the Dolls*, where Sharon Tate, Patty Duke and Susan Hayward play actresses going through drink, drugs, sex, disillusionment and more drink, excess was the order of the day.

'The drug scene, that's when it took off, man, in the seventies. The devil's dandruff was everywhere. It was *rulin'*,' soul diva P. P. Arnold told me. She had moved back to LA for a while after living in Britain in the sixties. 'If you weren't at the right party, you weren't happenin'. We all walked that road.' Lindsay Buckingham, guitarist with Fleetwood Mac, remembered when talking to me for the *Independent on Sunday* 'a seventies subculture of drugs that was the norm – it's become more of an aberration now. The way people were conducting their lives, it was difficult to get serious work done. But not much was known about the long-term effects of drugs, there hadn't been a long enough proving ground and not enough examples of people's lives going down the tubes. In the early seventies there was a hugely naive idea about it.'

Dusty embraced the LA life of excess. 'I wanted more of life, whatever it brought. That's all I've ever wanted,' she said. Party-going started off as a good way to network and became an end in itself, an antidote to the career insecurities that were beginning to dog her. 'LA is beautiful, but hard,' says Fonarow. 'If people are coming to you and you're not going to them, it's awesome.' But in a society where cultural values revolve around a hierarchy of fame, celebrity and money, LA can be cruel if your star is not in the ascendant. 'Everybody and their grandmother was in LA. It's a weird place, so competitive and so phoney. There's the hot-lick syndrome. Everybody's got the hot licks, they all love you. But you have to be connected when you get there. You can't just go and get a deal. Dusty went through a lot of stuff at that time. She was huge when she went there. Then she lost herself,' says Arnold.

Dusty's friend Pat Rhodes looks pained when she recalls how Dusty changed. 'She tried all this going to the wild parties bit thinking, Gosh, this is what you do out here. This is what we *do* in California. She was so quiet normally, she couldn't handle drink, and got drunk. She never drank, never smoked when we were on tour in the sixties. She was absolutely squeaky clean, I can promise you. People used to send bottles of champagne backstage and we quietly used to give them away. It seemed a shame to waste them.'

Rhodes remembers one Christmas Day on tour in Liverpool when she and Dusty were holed up in a hotel room with the band. 'It was horrendous weather, there was nothing to do, and they were smoking grass, killing themselves laughing and rolling round the floor. We thought, Oooh, drugs, ooh, but we were so desperate we decided to try some. We nervously puffed and blew straight out again. Of course, it didn't have any effect. Nobody told us you had to take it down and swallow it. To us, we thought we were *bad*.'

Later Dusty swore that she had never touched alcohol until she was twenty-five. 'I was just quiet, shy little Mary O'Brien who went straight out of convent school and into singing. After shows I was always the one that went home.' Then, one of the aptly named Temptations gave her a glass of vodka to ease her sore throat. 'It was 88 per cent proof, because that's what those boys liked,' she told the *Telegraph Magazine*. 'It never occurred to me to sip it. I drank it down, gagged a few times, and five minutes later I went, *Yes* – this is the answer to life. I was no longer afraid. Fuck the Brooklyn Fox – I can deal with it all.'

After a few years in California, Dusty wasn't so naive. She drank heavily in an attempt to combat feelings of isolation. Alcohol bolstered her ego at celebrity parties and jolted her out of the inhibiting shyness. She performed well for a while on the intoxicated high, partying for days with 'the wrong crowd'. 'I did the whole lazy self-destructive California bit, and thoroughly enjoyed most of it. But somewhere – you never know when – I crossed the line from heavy drinking into problem drinking,' she recalled. 'I was addicted to all sorts of things. So were many of us. I'm an addictive personality. A lot of us who went through the sixties went through a training period of being ravers. It was encouraged. The more you fell downstairs and indulged in lunatic behaviour, the more people said, "Oh, she's a right card, isn't she?" and actually it worked for a while.'

It also provided a distraction from her work, which seemed to be leading to a dead end. 'After two or three years on the American circuit, I was a *complete nutcase*. I didn't like that world *at all*. I couldn't deal with it. I had agents who would book me into clubs that were completely wrong for me and I'd get so frustrated I'd find myself in hotel rooms flinging crockery at the walls.' Operating through a haze of alcohol, Mandrax and, finally, cocaine ('[that] finished me off ... it just scrambled my life', she said), Dusty lost her focus and sense of self. 'I felt I was obsolete, with a feeling of uselessness and depression,' she confessed.

Getting back to music offered her a way out. Her move from Atlantic to the ABC Dunhill label to record her next album, *Cameo*, provided a brief respite and a chance to prove herself again. ABC was bought out by MCA Records in 1979, but in the early seventies it boasted an impressively varied roster of stars, ranging from Ray Charles to B. B. King. The Dunhill offshoot was a folk-oriented label that was successful when folk rock took off, handling such artists as Three Dog Night, Steppenwolf and the Mamas and Papas. It may have seemed an unusual choice for Dusty, but she was attracted to the ABC R&B element and, more importantly, to Dunhill songwriter-producers Dennis Lambert and Brian Potter.

'We were a hot company at the time,' recalls Steve Barri, then vice president of A&R at Dunhill and overall producer of the album. 'Dusty was aware of what was going on and she loved Lambert and Potter songs – ones like Barry McGuire's "Eve of Destruction" – which were all over the charts. I was behind Dusty's move to ABC, and really excited we got together for it.'

'She was an artist I personally loved. I'd grown up with some of her hits,' enthuses Dennis Lambert, who over the years has worked with the Four Tops, Natalie Cole and Smokey Robinson. Sessions were quickly arranged for the album.

'We had top players at the time and were hoping to come up with an equivalent to *Dusty in Memphis*. We cut the keys and tracks and, knowing that she was such a tremendous talent, we thought, My God, this'll be a breeze.'

When the time came for Dusty to do the vocals, the good feeling dissipated. 'She was her own worst enemy in the studio,' says Barri. 'She would take so much time. She'd do a reference vocal with a track to take home and learn – if we'd saved the reference vocals we'd have had a better performance. The disappointment was in the fact that we weren't able to *convince* her how good her reference vocals were, with more flow and feel. We wound up punching in so much, little details that destroyed the feel of the performance.'

'She could never accept that her vocal, cold, was fabulous,' adds Lambert. 'She had to satisfy a need to be hard on herself – she was in search of perfection.' Dusty was also strung out after a period away from the business. 'We could tell she was emotionally unstable,' says Barri, 'but it was hard to say why. She was having breakdowns in the studio, crying and carrying on, and having trouble keeping her pitch. That project was so draining, such a tough experience, that afterwards the feeling was one of "Thank God it's over." We were also recording the Four Tops at the time, which was so easy in comparison. It was a shame – she was one of the really exceptional singers, and she could've had hits.'

Cameo was released in April 1973 on Dunhill in the US and Philips in Britain. The cover design looked cheap and unprepossessing, and is ranked among Dusty's fans as her worst. A roughly hewn portrait of her is set in a circle amid shades of blue. The original intention was to print the cover in felt but, probably due to budget demands, it was issued on card, hence the clumsy, unflattering illustration.

Despite the studio traumas, the album was of a respectable standard. It was given a Special Merit Pick in *Billboard* and a favourable review: 'This album flows with each track,' it said. 'Her debut on this label showcases her sultry voice in a large orchestral setting.' *Cameo* opens with one of Lambert and Potter's finest, yet most underrated songs, 'Who Gets Your Love'. Leon Russell and Larry Knechtel play a classically inspired keyboard refrain, while Dusty pitches in with a poignant performance. She cut this record when the female singer-songwriter era was in the ascendant, and there are shades of a reflective Carly Simon in the tracks. She shows her funky edge on numbers like 'Easy Evil', and Ashford and Simpson's throaty 'I Just Wanna Be There'. 'Tupelo Honey', meanwhile, harks back to the *Dusty in Memphis* feel that Steve Barri was aiming for, with its horns and gospel intonation. In places Dusty sounds strained and overwrought, with the stress taking its toll on such overladen tracks as 'Learn to Say Goodbye', the song featured on the ABC Movie of the Week, *Say Goodbye, Maggie Cole*, a sentimental tearjerker starring Susan Hayward.

Cameo flopped on both sides of the Atlantic. The two singles released from the album, 'Who Gets Your Love' and 'Learn to Say Goodbye', barely tickled the charts. At the same time, though, Philips looked into their vaults and assembled a compilation of Dusty's former releases entitled *This Is Dusty Springfield Vol. 2: The Magic Garden*, a record following their 1971 collection *This Is Dusty Springfield*. Almost in protest at her gritty Atlantic outpourings, *Vol. 2* swayed with soft middle-of-the-road melodic Bacharach and Randy Newman standards like 'They Long to Be Close to You'. It was clearly a side of Dusty that made Philips feel more comfortable.

In a move to revive her flagging UK career, Dusty flew to London at the end of 1972 for a month-long engagement at the Talk of the Town. The opening concert was a disaster: as soon as she arrived in London, Dusty went down with bronchitis and spent several days in bed. Against doctor's orders, she decided to perform on the first night, with her friend Elton John waiting in the wings, ready to take over if she couldn't make it through her set. Dusty kept the audience waiting for forty-five minutes. It was packed with media celebrities, who became impatient, slow handclapping and hitting coffee cups with spoons. When she finally came on she was breathless and tearful, every inch the tragic heroine. She coughed heavily between numbers, her voice cracked and strained. 'There are many songs I'd like to sing, but I can't because they'd be an embarrassment to you and me,' she said, clearly distressed. For the rest of the set the audience were right behind her, *willing* her to finish. She struggled through it, then fled. Dusty was prepared to postpone the season, but the next morning she was shocked to discover that her four-week contract had been terminated.

'We had the manager Bernard Delfont yelling and screaming at us,' said Portugais. 'Even though we had a doctor's certificate they fired her.' After claiming £10,000 damages, Dusty played dates up north, in a converted Manchester cinema. 'These are the people who really count,' she said, trying to shore up her pride. 'They buy my records. They want to see me. They are my type of people.'

Afterwards she went straight back into the studio to record her second Dunhill album, provisionally titled *Elements*. Produced by Brooks Arthur, it was an attempt to continue the mellow pop feel of *Cameo*, with tracks by a young Barry Manilow, Carole Bayer Sager, Melissa Manchester and the duo Barry Mann and Cynthia Weil. Towards the end of its protracted recording the album title was changed to *Longing*, and adverts appeared in the trade press announcing its arrival.

If *Cameo* had been ill-fated, *Longing* was doomed. It was never released. One source close to the project says that had it been 'it would have been the end of Dusty's career'. In 1973 Dusty arrived at Brooks Arthur's studio in Nyack, upstate New York, considerably the worse for wear. Arthur told me: 'She wasn't handling her New York trip very well. Something had begun to tumble.' Usually impeccably reliable, Dusty had trouble getting to the sessions on time. The studio was booked for her between eleven and six during the day but she would often want to go on longer.

'Why don't you want to work late?' she would ask Arthur. 'Gotta go home to your wife and kids?'

'No, there's a guy booked in the studio at seven,' he'd answer.

'Who is this guy?'

'Bruce Springsteen.'

Then, Springsteen was virtually unknown.

'What kind of a name is that?' Dusty would retort. 'I'm sure you're making that up.'

Sometimes by six thirty at night Dusty's voice had warmed up and she sang well. Springsteen would arrive early and sit respectfully in a corner saying softly, 'Man, she's so fine.' These moments of sweetness were rare. Dusty's confidence was at an all-time low. Her lack of success convinced her that she had lost her musical ability, and she took further refuge in pills and drink. The problems began to escalate, reaching a desperate peak one night. 'She tried to damage herself, cutting her wrists,' Arthur recalled, still obviously saddened by the event. 'She tried to do herself in while she was in my care. I took her to Rockland State Hospital and checked her in as Mary O'Brien. I thought I'd keep it quiet. Goddamnit if there wasn't a British nurse there who said, "That's Dusty Springfield." The nurse contacted the press and I could no longer be discreet. The worst thing was it made me feel I wasn't taking good enough care of her. I gave her good meals, I rented her a wonderful home, I offered her the whole creative community of New York, but she wasn't in a condition to accept it. The tailspin lasted a long time.'

From then on Dusty tumbled fast. Jay Lasker and Howard Stark, president of ABC, told Arthur, 'We have to pull the plug on the record. Unless she straightens up we're not getting a thing for our money.' According to Arthur, 'It had all collapsed around her.' Dusty reached rock bottom. 'I was directionless and I was tired,' she told *Q* magazine, 'and record companies treated me as a tax write-off – and when record companies do that, there's nothing you can do. You can dance up and down and hang from a chandelier and set fire to yourself and they'll say, "Hey, that's *beautiful*," but they still won't promote you. So rather than crying about it, I just *stopped*.'

Throughout the seventies and into the early eighties Dusty lived on a knife-edge of emotion. She made several suicide attempts and swallowed her anguish in vodka and pills. 'She checked *herself* into a few hospitals,' said her former manager Portugais. 'That took an extreme amount of bravery. I remember once she was staying in a halfway house in LA after her release from hospital. She had no money, and a friend and I took her to lunch. She was living under the name Mary O'Brien, with people who were total failures. We cried all the way home.'

Portugais believed that Dusty never meant to succeed in ending it all. 'She always made sure somebody could find her. More than once she cried out for help. But unless you're sophisticated you don't see it. People thought she should just go back to work. She was unable to work, she was *afraid* to work. What kept her alive was her will to go on.' Dusty confirmed later that she never really wanted to die. 'I wanted to go to sleep for a very long time, like Rip van Winkle. I wanted peace and quiet but I never wanted to do myself in. I suppose all those Catholic whatevers come at you when your mind begins to enter those murky waters. You go to hell, you know, if you kill yourself.' What she discovered through this was her survival instinct, that she was a fighter at heart.

The climb back, however, was slow. She would be sober for a while, then relapse – 'Maybe it was a Tuesday, or somebody looked at me wrong.' She remembered painful moments, like the night she spent drinking in the Continental Hyatt Hotel on Sunset Boulevard and called down for another bottle of champagne. 'I thought it was fine,' she told *Telegraph* journalist Mick Brown, 'I was being a lady." And the room-service waiter said, "Haven't you had enough, lady?" And I thought, Christ, if he says that … Then you get really upset and think, Who the hell does he think he is? But it sticks.'

It took years of painful self-analysis, living in isolation with her cats, before Dusty was ready to face the world again. She said she never actually lost everything: 'There was no gutter involved, except in my head. I was fortunate in that I understood I had a major problem and knew where to get help.' She had a network of supportive friends who cared for her; some were ex-addicts 'who knew how to stay that way. It's very easy to *stop* drinking, *stop* doing drugs,' said Dusty, 'but it's not easy to *stay* stopped.'

There were bright spots in the dark years, like the time she met a girl in hospital who was poor and depressed. Dusty took her in a limousine to a Labelle concert at the Santa Monica Civic Auditorium and afterwards to a party hosted by Elton John.

She also struggled through some recording work, doing backing vocals with Canadian country pop artist Anne Murray on her 1975 album *Together*. These sporadic sessions kept her sane. She even tried love, and embarked on an insecure year-long relationship with a man called Howard. 'It wasn't a happy time,' she said later. 'He wasn't doing very well and I was unsettled so it was two worried, moody, very edgy people. It was a rubber-band situation. He kept bouncing in and out of my life.' Musician Tom Saviano remembered working with Howard in 1976 and told me: 'I was on the road with him. He was a really short guy who managed Phil Cody, an artist who writes for Neil Sedaka. He would always talk about Dusty and how he was madly in love with her.'

The relationship didn't last, but Dusty hated to think that it had failed. 'I'm a bad loser ... My trouble is I get lost in people. I've always thought that they should make up the part of me that I thought was missing. I gave people tremendous powers – the power to make me a whole person. Of course they couldn't and didn't want to anyway. I wouldn't know how to handle serenity if somebody handed it to me on a plate.' According to Portugais, her self-confessed 'Jewish mother' as well as her manager, 'When she was drinking she did tend to get mean and difficult, but that was the alcohol and the drugs speaking. Dusty was compassionate towards people and she had a big heart with room for everybody. She also had a sense of humour, which helped her survive.'

Unable to settle emotionally, Dusty moved around LA, going from Laurel Canyon to a cavernous house in Beverly Hills, then to a small place called Tarzana in the San Fernando Valley. After the strenuous, heady days of the sixties she lapsed into a numbing and troubled obscurity, wondering if she would ever really sing again.

After the humiliation of *Longing* she went through what she would later term 'The Long Silence'. It was four years of 'grey areas' before she found her voice again.

With her return to the pop world in the late seventies Dusty found that her most loyal fans were among the gay community. To them she was a showbiz heroine, a living legend in the mould of a Garland or a Piaf. In 1964 Dusty had said, with prophetic irony, 'I'm not the legendary type. You have to be a tragic figure to become a legend – like Garland and Edith Piaf. I don't have that quality. I don't particularly want it – not if you've got to slash your wrists to get it.' However, with her husky vulnerability and dramatic private life she embodied the camp pop sensibility. Her career had become like an operatic plot, scaling extreme highs and lows, and the pain of misfit isolation which many of her gay fans identified with.

In 1977 the news spread like wildfire that Dusty was ready to sing again. Emerging from years of seclusion and self-doubt, she attacked her next project with a determination and vigour. Dusty Springfield had called a truce with shy Mary O'Brien.

She was bored with sitting at home, and periods of sobriety meant that she was stronger. And she missed singing.

Having sat out her Dunhill contract Dusty's first move was to sign with the US label United Artists, whose company in Britain was Phonogram. Her choice of Roy Thomas Baker as producer marked a change of direction from her usual mellow ballad style. Geared towards rock, he had produced the loud, operatic melodrama of Queen, mainstream new-wavers the Cars, and ex-Mott the Hoople rock 'n' roller Ian Hunter. He had also worked with mega-rock groups such as Journey and Foreigner, and his outing with Dusty seemed an aberration.

Ever vigilant about musical changes, Dusty was well aware by the late seventies that the cabaret style, which had formerly been so successful for older acts, was now well out of date. Unlike Tom Jones and Shirley Bassey who slotted into the top Las Vegas bracket, Dusty was anxious to attract a new, younger audience. Punk was having a seismic effect on the business, shaking up notions of established stardom with a raw DIY approach. To compete Dusty had to toughen up.

She was aware, too, that women artists were becoming more outwardly politicized about the music business. In Britain, Joan Armatrading had revolutionized the image of the female singer-songwriter, projecting a powerful presence with her direct lyrics and complex, cross-rhythmic guitar. Kate Bush was exploring realms of free association and televisual pop art, while all-girl punk bands like the Slits and the Raincoats challenged notions of harmony and acceptability with their defiantly ragged chords and unruly style.

Coinciding with punk came the rise of disco and the proliferation of dance music. When Dusty returned she took a considered approach to the material, tentatively exploring new musical styles. In an interview with BBC Radio One, Roy Thomas Baker recalls how he coaxed her back into the limelight: 'She's very talented as a vocalist – phenomenal. We would work together right down to every last dot, each phrase and note ... I'd ask her to bend the end of a word up, and she'd write it down on her list, put a little dot at the top ... There were no ego problems and working with her was really good, but the record did go well over budget for one reason and another, and with both of us being perfectionists in our different ways, it cost something in the region of $420,000, which is quite a high budget, especially when you think of people putting albums together for $16,000. I think we ... allowed the other's indulgences, and the end product didn't warrant the money that was spent on it.'

Even though it wasn't a huge commercial success at the time, *It Begins Again* is an extraordinary example of seventies white soul – fluid, fragile, contemporary, poised and stuffed with session players at the top of their game. Crusaders' pianist Joe Sample, Steely Dan guitarist Jeff Baxter and drummer Ed Greene, for instance, while backing singers included Patti Brooks, Dianne Brooks and Brenda Russell. Dusty always hand-picked her singers, and here their swooping gospel notes are the perfect counterpoint to her husky contralto. It was definitely worth the money.

The album was recorded leisurely at the Cherokee Recording Studios in West Hollywood, and the orchestral arranger Sid Sharpe told me that Dusty was a model of decorum in the studio, a far cry from the wild, tattered scenes of her *Cameo* days. 'I thought she was a very nice person, full of life and ready to go. I didn't notice any signs of her being nervous,' he said.

Although the popularity of disco meant that synthesizers were beginning to supplant live arrangements, Dusty was keen to sing over a live backing and interact with musicians. 'She had a good feeling with the guys, she was able to give us cues musically,' says Ed Greene, who started his career with the Donald Byrd Group, and has played with everyone from Barry White to Dizzy Gillespie. 'We found it easy to be with her, especially with someone who's talking your language. She would explain to me what she wanted and sing the drumbeats to me. She kept saying, "I want the Ed Greene drum sound, the one that goes boom dakka boom." I'd actually patterned that feel after the Motown drummer Benny Benjamin, and we had heavy conversations about that man. Dusty and I were both R&B at heart.' She also exuded a certain fragility, and Greene remembers Baker being easy-going with her, 'not exerting too much pressure. It was an important album for her.'

Dusty wanted to give her album a feminist approach. She was conscious of the move away from romantic love songs towards a more self-defined attitude for women in pop. Nona Hendryx's song 'Checkmate' shows this confrontational strength, with a lyric that uses checkerboard imagery to describe a frustrating love affair. Dusty sings loud, with hints of gospel rock over a swirling piano rhythm. A long-term friend and confidante, Nona Hendryx was the raunchiest member of Labelle. After the break-up of the group she spent years struggling to establish the brand of surrealistic funk rock later popularized by Prince. Like Dusty, she was a woman experimenting ahead of her time.

There were tragic shades of Dusty's own past on the track 'Sandra', a narrative song written by Barry Manilow about a depressed, isolated housewife who swears she loves her husband

and kids, yet secretly drinks. Dusty sings, in the character of Sandra, that if she hadn't married so young, she could have had more time for herself. Sandra ends up 'accidentally' cutting her wrists while doing the washing-up. The kitchen-sink drama is set beside other standout tracks like the Lesley Gore ballad 'I'd Rather Leave While I'm in Love', the deeply vampy 'Love Me by Name' (her nod to the gay rights movement) and the gentle satire of LA life, 'Hollywood Movie Girls'. 'She sure was versatile,' says Sid Sharpe. 'Ballads, upbeat numbers ... she could have gone any way.'

News had begun to filter through to the UK that Dusty was releasing a comeback album. United Artists had put out 'Let Me Love You Once' as an appetizer, her first single in five years. Her Phonogram press officer Norman Divall, an actor and PR who went on to work for London's Capital Radio, remembers the excitement in the music business: 'Our marketing manager Lisa Denton went to LA to meet Dusty and came back with the tapes of the LP and some super photographs. They showed a Dusty we'd never *seen* before! She had shoulder-length straight hair, and everyone noticed immediately that the panda eyes had gone.'

By early 1978 the album was finished, and Dusty made plans for a major British promotion. She tried to keep her arrival date secret, wanting to come in four days before the official day so that she could meet old friends and become acclimatized to London once more. 'Of course the press caught her at the airport, of course there was a front page of the *Evening Standard*, of course there was a row with the photographers, the whole number,' says Divall. 'She wasn't prepared for them, she wasn't dressed or made-up, and she had travelled under her own name, Mary O'Brien.'

The press interest in Dusty's comeback was huge. Throughout the seventies her fans in the UK had been starved of releases: once Dusty had thrown in her lot with the American record company, their British counterparts had been less eager to promote her. Most Philips album releases in the seventies, like *This Is Dusty Springfield* and *Dusty Springfield Sings Burt Bacharach & Carole King*, were basic repackages of old material. Dusty was furious, saying: 'I had no control over that. There was nothing I could do. It bothered me when I had nothing else, and I tried to get a lawyer to make them stop.' She moved decisively, though, when she signed to United Artists/Phonogram, stipulating in her contract that her back catalogue was to be deleted as far as they were concerned. The reissuing of old material was a distraction, drawing attention away from the brand-new Dusty. She voiced this complaint many times over as she was anxious to shake off her sixties pop persona. She adopted the natural, sunny-Californian look to promote *It Begins Again*. The album sleeve depicted a mature Dusty, with soft, wavy hair, casual clothes and toned-down make-up.

Divall says, 'I'd been warned beforehand that she was unreliable, would change her mind at the last minute and refuse to see people, that she didn't like being photographed or interviewed, she was bad news. However, she sounded absolutely charming on the telephone and I thought if she seriously wanted to revitalize her career after a long period of being quiet, then I was going to approach it as positively as she was. I wouldn't listen to her critics. I had a meeting with her, we started talking at six p.m. and when I next looked at my watch it was ten past eleven. We got on like a house on fire. From then on she was co-operative, on time and didn't mind being interviewed – a publicist's dream.'

The press conference she held at the Savoy Hotel a few days later was a tough one. The British media turned out in force, and not all of them were kind. 'How much do you earn?' quipped one humorous fellow from a tabloid.

'Why? D'you want to borrow some?' was Dusty's quick reply.

She was fresh and on form, refusing to be fazed. A woman from the feminist magazine *Spare Rib* asked her about her sixties obsession with black artists, and there were questions from others about panda eye make-up, whether she regretted never having married and whether she was staging a comeback for the money.

Dusty fielded all the questions adroitly, with openness and humour. To the man from *Titbits* who asked about her marital aspirations she said, 'I don't think it would have helped me out of any emotional problems – perhaps it would even have increased them!' And when she was asked if she was returning because she was hard up for cash, Dusty answered, 'No, if I had to do it for that alone, I'd breed cats.' She had got through a lot of money, she said, and though she wasn't rich she wasn't destitute. At the end of the conference the journalists burst into spontaneous applause. She was back.

'A Love Like Yours' was the first single from the album but did not make the Top 20. The album release followed two weeks later. *It Begins Again* was Phonogram's biggest marketing campaign of 1978, with over five hundred in-store displays and countless radio plugs. The record entered the charts on 4 March, but only reached no. 41 and dropped out two weeks later.

Although Dusty had taken account of recent changes in musical taste, *It Begins Again* fell between two stools: it was neither MOR for the older crowd, nor distinctive enough for a generation used to rock and punk sounds. 'It probably won't disappoint ardent fans, but it's unlikely to win her any fresh converts either,' wrote Patrick Humphries in *NME*. 'Every track is impeccably chosen, the production meticulous ... cotton wool round a precious Ming vase. The voice is fine, but the material is not.'

The next single, a compelling disco throwdown called 'That's the Kind of Love I've Got for You' also missed the charts. Undeterred, the record company released 'I'm Coming Home Again' and Dusty returned to Britain the following year, 1979, to play a full nationwide tour. 'A lot of things I'm getting the advantage of on this tour – the sound systems, the lighting, the staging – those are things I was fighting for many years ago,' she said. 'It is ironic now to come home and see they are part of the accepted norm ... I fought for those things so hard, and it didn't really do my reputation any good.'

The tour was due to run throughout the UK finishing with three days at London's Drury Lane Theatre Royal from 19 to 21 April. It was rumoured that all the regional dates were cancelled because of poor ticket sales. Various reasons were suggested for this stroke of bad luck: a local newspaper strike was in progress; the promoter pulled out too early; on the posters she looked too much like her arch-rival Petula Clark. In reality, though, Dusty had become an anachronism. She was bitterly disappointed: she was popular only with her hardcore fans, people who loved her from the sixties along with a dedicated gay audience. The gay fans were out in force for the Drury Lane concerts, as many women as men. 'At gay events there are usually many more men than women, but not this one,' recalled John McElroy, an organizer of *The Dusty Springfield Bulletin*, the newsletter of the unofficial Dusty fan club. 'We were outnumbered. At the beginning of the concert Dusty said, "Give a butch roar or a girlish shriek, I don't mind who does what, sort it out for yourselves."' The concerts were a sold-out success, with scenes of sheer adulation in which fans threw themselves on the bonnet of Dusty's car. 'It was so emotional it was difficult to sing,' recalls her friend and backing vocalist Simon Bell. 'On the first night she was singing "I'm Coming Home Again". She got to the chorus, the crowd went mad and she started sobbing. She could hardly finish the song. I was trying not to cry – thank God I wasn't doing backing vocals on that.'

The shows were energetic, and the high spot each night came when Dusty performed 'Rollarena' on skates, in recognition of the seventies roller-disco craze. 'We worked out some choreography, where she was pushed from one side of the stage to the other, ending up in the middle of three singers in front of the mike,' says Bell. 'It was a miracle she got there. Every night she fell over. She couldn't see four inches in front of her face [she wears glasses offstage] and had never skated before. It was hilarious.'

The success of her Drury Lane dates made up for the disappointment of tour cancellations. Dusty's fans remained loyal, and from then on her records logged consistent sales, which, though never earth-shattering, certainly kept her around no. 60 in the charts. 'Baby Blue', for instance, a catchy disco stomper and her first twelve-inch single, reached no. 61 and stayed in the charts for five weeks. Philips were able to capitalize on her renewed popularity by releasing a *Greatest Hits* collection of twenty tracks. The sleeve was in dramatic silvery monochrome, depicting Dusty as a sixties icon, complete with mascara, blonde beehive and gown, and clutching a microphone. It sold well and drew the attention of a younger audience who had never heard of her before. Dusty might have preferred to move away from the sixties, but it seemed to work for her fans.

Dusty's next live date in England directly followed the Drury Lane triumph. In November she was featured on the BBC *Shirley Bassey Spectacular*, singing 'I'm Coming Home', and that December she starred in a charity performance attended by HRH Princess Margaret for the Invalid Children's Aid Association, which was filmed by independent producer Mike Mansfield. Although it was never screened, the film remains an emotional memoir of that night. The event took place at the Royal Albert Hall and, as before, was packed out with her gay fans. Dusty managed to offend Princess Margaret at the beginning of the show when she mischievously announced, 'It's nice to see that the royalty isn't confined to the box.' The Princess received £8,000 on behalf of the Invalid Children's Aid Association and was expected to chat to Dusty at the after-show party. Instead she shook hands with all the artists except Dusty and marched out. Evidently HRH wasn't amused by Dusty's veiled reference to the 'queens' in the audience.

'Princess Margaret actually sent a letter to Dusty afterwards, a typewritten apology for insulting the Queen, which she had to sign and send back,' says Simon Bell. 'It was annoying, because there's no way Princess Margaret would have done that to, say, Larry Grayson [a camp TV celebrity].' Perhaps Princess Margaret's annoyance at the incident was exacerbated by a remark Dusty had made playfully in a *Gay News* interview the previous year: 'I'm having a three-way with Princess Anne and one of her horses.' With jokes like this, Dusty consolidated her risqué reputation, and unlike other grandes dames of the pop scene, such as Cilla Black and Petula Clark, she was unable to stay out of trouble. Her irreverence was often a source of irritation to the show-business establishment.

Despite Princess Margaret's disapproval, though, the Royal Albert Hall concert was a major success. After being introduced by TV chat-show host Russell Harty, Dusty bounded onstage to the overture 'The Bitch Is Back', looking tanned, healthy and youthful. Giggling, cheeky and in good voice, she teased the crowd, singing key hits like 'I Close My Eyes' and 'Some of Your Lovin'' before a moving rendition of 'Quiet Please, There's a Lady Onstage', dedicated to Judy Garland. 'This is a song for all women who've been legends in their time,' said Dusty, summoning up memories of old demons. 'Sometimes the ladies involved give too much of themselves, sometimes not enough. This song is for all those women, no matter where they are.' The audience roared, and at the end of the concert a woman from the crowd clambered onstage and threw herself into Dusty's arms.

Dusty came back for several encores, overwhelmed with emotion. She had proved to herself that she wasn't washed up as a talent, and the audience's adoration convinced her that she was still a star.

However, while the concert represented the peak of Dusty's rousing British comeback, it was also a time of tension and grief. Some years earlier her mother, Kay, had developed lung cancer, and Dusty came over from the States to see her in a Hove nursing home shortly before her death. 'She looked like one of those horror masks all sunken. Her eyes were glassy from the drugs, but suddenly they focused and she just reached up this claw and tweaked my nose. I don't remember her ever doing that to me before,' Dusty said later. The following day she had to return to the States, but as soon as she got home she rang the nursing home. She was told that Mrs O'Brien had died. At that point 'the tweak' became very important to her. 'And it was horrific, too. I did come unglued then. I handled it very badly.'

Grief was mixed up with feelings of guilt that she hadn't been a model child, that she hadn't been in England when her parents were ill. Her father, OB, developed a heart condition, and although she had tried to establish a closer relationship with him when he was in his seventies, spending more time with him, taking him on trips to the States, there was still the memory of his 'snap Irish temper' between them. A few days before her Royal Albert Hall triumph, he died of a heart attack, alone in Rottingdean. He was found only because milk bottles were piling up outside his home. 'That has haunted me,' Dusty said. 'I feel very badly, not because I wasn't there but because no one was there. No one. I wonder if he was in pain. Was he incapable of reaching the phone? Did it happen fast? I will never know.'

Bereft of parents, and seeing less and less of her brother Tom, Dusty's old feelings of vulnerability and insecurity began to resurface. She had been fighting her drink problem and conquered it temporarily in time for *It Begins Again*. For her next United Artists album, though, she was less stable. 'I was afraid because I knew people who'd worked with her when she was in the dumps and I'd heard she had incredible drink and drug problems,' says David Wolfert, who produced *Living Without Your Love*, the follow-up to *It Begins Again*. Though Wolfert later worked with Dolly Parton and Stephanie Mills and became a Grammy- and Emmy-nominated composer, in 1979 he was not yet established as a 'name' producer. 'I'd heard Dusty on the radio the night before and thought I'd love to produce her,' Wolfert told me. 'I remember having to sell myself to her. I was a former studio musician, and I was young and nervous, working with one of the greats. She gave me a trial period, which luckily I passed!'

Wolfert was aware that he had taken on a major challenge. 'We didn't have Dusty's drink problems, but I did see a woman who was struggling with something, fighting hard. It was my impression that she had *already* come out of the chemical part of it, but she was fragile. Whenever she was needy, she'd ring up, and all these wonderful ladies would show up and just sit. Sometimes they were there from eight at night to eight in the morning. She needed them plenty to make sure she didn't drink, and I don't think the record could've been done without it.'

These incidents testify to the unwavering protectiveness and loyalty of Dusty's friends. Musicians on the session remember her clearly. 'Dusty was very vocal and a real live wire. She was different from, say, Michael Jackson, who is very quiet in the studio and hardly speaks,' recalls percussion player Gary Coleman. 'Dusty was intensely involved in what was going on, with almost an excess of energy. A lot of us in those days were wired for sound and half crazed. Most people, including me, were doing drugs to keep them going, and ninety per cent of artists of the time have or had been busted. We burned ourselves up and bottomed out. I'm now out of that scene.'

The sax player and arranger Tom Saviano remembers Dusty as being almost *too* vivacious. 'I'm intuitive with people when I first meet them,' he says, 'and can pick up emotions they're projecting. With Dusty I thought, Wait, what's wrong with this picture? Her being so outgoing with everybody showed me she was trying to hide something.' At the same time, she was careful to establish a rapport with the musicians, as if to disprove her 'difficult' reputation. 'All she had was compliments for what I was doing,' says Saviano. 'That made it easy in the studio. Who wouldn't like that? She was very sweet and warm. After I did the work for her she gave me a big kiss. A lot of artists you work with aren't that open and warm.'

After the eclectic mix of *It Begins Again*, the focus of *Living Without Your Love* was on orchestral ballads. The record company wanted to slot her back into mainstream Streisand-style easy-listening mode. 'They wanted to turn her from an R&B singer into something else,' says Wolfert, 'and on some songs she doesn't sound completely comfortable. She wasn't happy and she sounded to me like she faked it a bit. However, five or six songs on the album became hits for other people later ... "I Just Fall in Love Again" was a huge hit for Anne Murray.'

There was a heated debate about disco. Although he wasn't happy with some of the string arrangements, Wolfert felt that the live ballad-style format was more suited to a 'classic' singer of Dusty's calibre. But she was forever trying to escape that bag, opting instead for what was current. 'Dusty and I had many battles. I thought disco music was beneath her, and in that year it was the worst, it was pandering,' says Wolfert. 'Dusty felt that a lot of loyal followers were into disco and she would provide that. I thought disco was the lowest common denominator. At that time it had no real attributes of black dance music, it was just the same beat, the same mix and it could've had any vocals on top. What a shame to do that to Dusty Springfield!'

Ironically, 1979 was a year of challenging underground disco at clubs like Heaven in London and Paradise Garage in

New York, a tradition later seized upon by Dusty's eighties collaborators, the Pet Shop Boys. Dusty and her producer reached an uneasy compromise on tracks like 'Living Without Your Love', 'You Can Do It' and 'Save Me Save Me', all mixed with laid-back strings and beats into a kind of 'tasteful' disco. On 'Closet Man', Dusty explored more jazz-oriented tones. 'She had a great feel for the jazz–R&B crossover,' says Saviano, who enjoyed arranging the album's instrumental fusion. Chronicling the life of a gay man afraid to come out, 'Closet Man' is a David Foster song specifically for her gay fans. In the song, Dusty assures her friend that it is important to live life the way he wants to, that he can trust her to be discreet. It is the most experimental track, with complex plangent keyboards and jazz scat. In view of her usual reluctance to take a politicized stand on gay issues, this song was a surprisingly bold and open move.

Dusty also wades through lush balladry and songs that are almost self-confessional. Through swathes of emotive piano and guitar on 'Get Yourself to Love', for instance, she sings that if you don't trust yourself you can't feel sure of anyone else; while in her refrain and tour de force, written by Carole Bayer Sager, 'I'm Coming Home Again', Dusty confirms that she is only just beginning to accept she has a right to be herself. She was beginning to convey a sense of mature, lived experience in a way she had never done before. It was just a shame that the material she was singing didn't give her a chance to soar.

The release of *Living Without Your Love* in 1979 was greeted with indifference – later Dusty labelled it 'un-stunning' – and promotion was hampered by the collapse of the record company. 'It was barely released in America,' says Wolfert.

'United Artists got bought the week it came out and it was not promoted a whit. We were furious.' *NME*'s Graham Lock echoed the thoughts of many fans in his review, 'Why, oh why, didn't she stay with soul?' he signed. 'Why does she seem so lost? ... These new songs are just pretty, drippy and dull.' He goes on to stress the difficulty of her position. 'She's working in the dark – no other woman singer has followed a similar career, so there's no example to follow.'

The takeover of United Artists and her lack of success left Dusty floundering. In 1980 she signed a deal with 20th Century Records, which was later taken over by Phonogram, and released two singles for Phonogram in Britain as part of contractual obligations – 'Your Love Still Brings Me to My Knees' and 'It Goes Like It Goes'. Both fell flat, and she spent the next few years in record company wrangling, waiting for someone to take an interest in her again. Amid the confusion of numerous record-company takeovers, she had been left behind. Meanwhile, in Britain, the Philips *Greatest Hits* albums trundled on, compounding the assumption that Dusty was a sixties 'has-been'.

In the early eighties Dusty had another burst of energy and defiance. She recorded and co-produced *White Heat*, a critical success and one of her strongest albums for over ten years. At the tail end of the *Saturday Night Fever* enthusiasm in 1979, the mainstream opinion in the industry was that 'disco sucks'. But in the underground dance scene led by creative gay male DJs, disco was being reinvented; which led to the emergence of Chicago House and garage music. Dusty refused to accept the simplistic prejudice that disco was worthless pap, and began to explore the potential of music from which she had been steered away for so long. Inevitably this rejuvenated her iconic status within the gay community, a loyal following who recognized in her someone who had always been an 'outsider'; a woman who had never quite belonged.

8

Mine's a Gin and
Tonic, Smithey

'I HAVE AN IMMENSE number of gay friends. I always have
had. I'm in a business where at least fifty per cent of the
business is gay,' Dusty once said. She came out in a few press
interviews as bisexual. But, despite the greater visibility of
lesbians in showbiz, sport and the media, in the mid-nineties,
Dusty was protective of her private life and wary of discussing
her relationships with women. 'I know attitudes have changed,
but in general I don't know they've changed that much. It's a
veneer of change, a cosmetic change. Please, we're talking
Middle England here ...'

In moving to LA Dusty escaped 'Middle England' – the
swathes of suburbia from the home counties to the Midlands
and beyond, and the traditional values they represent. After all,
when Dusty began her career in the late fifties, anything other
than heterosexuality was seen as an aberration. Homosexual
acts between men were illegal until 1967; lesbianism, according
to Queen Victoria, didn't exist. 'Being a lesbian was not seen
as a nice thing. We'd been fed all this dreadful misinformation
about what lesbians were, and how we always lurked around

lavatories or railway stations to pick up poor little defenceless women,' recalled the late Jackie Forster, a gay activist and former actress and TV presenter. 'People were terrified of being found out at work, especially nurses, teachers, youth workers, midwives – anyone who had any contact with the body. There was tremendous self-oppression, because if you did say something you were on your own. There were no backup groups. That kind of picketing and support came later.' In the restrictive social world of fifties Britain, it was difficult to form lesbian partnerships. 'There wasn't a gay scene as such in the fifties and sixties. There were a few male gay clubs, which didn't welcome women,' Forster told me. 'It was almost impossible to find out where lesbians were. You couldn't ring Lesbian Line or *Gay News*. It was a subterranean ghetto world with not very pleasant places to go to. They always seemed to be in basements, with no kind of acknowledgement on the outside. It was just Dullsville, really. And nobody *dreamed* of changing it, because of being found out.'

The main meeting point for lesbians then was Gateways, a basement club behind green wooden gates off the King's Road, in Chelsea. 'It was tacky, a terrible place,' recalled Forster. 'There was nothing to tell you it existed on the outside, so you had to press a buzzer on the door and descend the stairs to a dark pit.' Inside there was marked 'butch' and 'femme' role-playing: some women wore cufflinks, natty gents' suits and short-back-and-sides haircuts, while their girlfriends dressed ultra-feminine with bouffant hair. To Frankie Culling, a singer in the fifties who was married and needed to keep her sexuality 'very hush-hush', Gateways was a liberation. 'It was loaded to me, the atmosphere was loaded,' she says. 'Very dark, very welcome and very sexy. I remember one night a beautiful-looking girl sat at a table with a hugely fat woman in heavy horn-rimmed spectacles. The latter came over to me and said, "My friend likes you, will you come home with us? There's only me, her and the dog." I thought, Oh, my God!'

The only other major network for lesbians was Kenric, a mixed gay social group that started in the mid-sixties. Kenric became a kind of code word. 'They'd book a pub for a meeting and call themselves "businesswomen" or "professional women",' recalled Forster, 'or they'd announce a get-together in somebody's house as a "library meeting". My lover and I went to one of these meetings in Notting Hill Gate – it just seemed to be an excuse for snogging on sofas. We said, in our naive way, "Well, where are the books?" They had to pull the sofa out and there was a handful of rather tatty paperbacks behind, nothing much else.'

Kenric reflected the cautionary times. It was a low-key, word-of-mouth affair, and for a while married women had to have their husband's signature to be 'approved'. Forster remembered Dusty and her then lover going to both Gateways and Kenric in the sixties. 'Dusty and she knew Gina and Smithey [the pair who ran Gateways], and they stayed within that circle. They sometimes wandered into Kenric meetings, but Dusty was never really on "the scene". Even at Gateways she'd keep herself very much to herself,' Forster remembered.

'The scene', however, embraced Dusty from the beginning. 'At Gateways they'd play her records all the time, along with Doris Day and Julie Andrews. We adored Dusty. Everybody bought her records. Especially "You Don't Have to Say You Love Me", that was a sell-out. When we started discos, that was always requested,' said Forster. 'Dusty was attractive just because to us she was a glamorous singer and a lesbian. I think if she'd sung crap we'd have still loved her, because even though she never imposed it, or mentioned it, she was our role model.'

There were few visible gay women on the pop scene at that time, apart from singer Polly Perkins, who was famed for speaking palare (gay argot), wearing Carnaby Street pinstripe suits and singing songs like 'Superdyke'. She had more novelty value, though, than staying power. 'Looking back, I think I was a bit camp for some of them, dear,' she later told the girl group fanzine *That Will Never Happen Again*.

By the late sixties an identifiable lesbian culture was beginning to grow, and the film *The Killing of Sister George*, in which Beryl Reid plays an ageing butch actress whose life falls apart after she loses her job and her young lover, brought it right out into the open. 'My lover and I went to see the film dressed like Conservative MPs' wives – skirts, nylons and masses of make-up and handbags. We thought we were the only ones,' said Forster. 'Part of the film was shot in Gateways, and there was a wonderful moment when Smithey had her line. "Gin and tonic coming up," she said to Beryl Reid, and the cinema went mad. We realized everybody there were dykes, all dressed up like MPs' wives. The roar she got! After that, women began to *pour* into Gateways.'

The gay scene opened up considerably with the emergence of Campaign for Homosexual Equality (CHE) and the Gay Liberation Front (GLF), Britain's first activist gay movements. 'It was mostly men, but then women joined in all these carry-ons. It was *joyous*,' said Forster. While CHE campaigned within the system against job discrimination and legal inequalities, the GLF 'zapped' events like the Festival of Light gathering at Central Hall in Westminster in May 1971. The Festival of Light was a Christian evangelical alliance with celebrity figureheads such as Cliff Richard, Mary Whitehouse and Malcolm Muggeridge, who were actively opposed to the 'amoral' permissive society. The GLF seized the headlines by storming the event dressed as nuns, releasing white mice and covering the venue with leaflets. The same year, all the gay groups assembled for London's first Gay Pride march. 'This was when gay politics really developed,' said Forster. 'Until then it had been terribly underground.'

Dusty began to draw attention to the issue. In 1978, when she was living in Los Angeles, she gave an in-depth interview to *Gay News*, criticizing the hypocrisy in American show business: 'There is a very strong anti-gay feeling in Hollywood, which is extraordinary in an industry which is seventy-five per cent gay ... Because industry heads are very anti-gay it's *very* tough for most gay people and difficult to speak out. There *are* a few brave people and there's a growing number of *enraged* people, straight and gay, who are not going to put up with it any more.' But she was still wary of publicly nailing her colours to the mast. 'I respect gay people. That doesn't make me one and that doesn't *not* make me one. I'm *me*. I have a gay following. I'm grateful for it. I want to keep it,' she said to *Gay News*. Throughout her career Dusty had attracted the attention of the tabloid press. Her peroxide bouffant, black make-up and convent school education spelled trouble. The combination of vulnerability and rebel glamour ensured that she was at the mercy of the headlines rather than controlling them.

Ironically, the shy Mary O'Brien side of Dusty always longed for a quiet life and couldn't fathom why the press was so interested in her. She went out of her way to avoid the press, but this only inspired journalists to try to uncover scandal. And Dusty provided a good story: mystery, drug abuse, indeterminate sexuality – it was a ready-made pop singer soap opera.

'I don't know why they were such bastards,' says Pat Rhodes. 'They'll rake up anything, whether it's "lesbian", "nympho" or "drunkard". People don't know how vulnerable and easily hurt she is. I've seen her sit and cry over something in the press that's totally uncalled-for, saying, "Why? Why do I get this?"' Those who are outspoken or oddballs in the pop world are considered fair game. Elton John, for instance, was reported to have had sex sessions with rent boys, and although he won a million pounds in libel damages from the *Sun*, it ruined two years of his life. 'The whole world fell in on me,' he said. 'It took a hell of a long time to prove my innocence. I went through a year and a half with that shadow hanging over me ... I could sit at home but the people who work for me had to listen to all the gossip and the lies. People tend to believe what they read – halfway through there was even a danger of me believing it! ... I was on the edge of a nervous breakdown.'

Dusty and Elton John were close friends with a lot in common – they both had a goonish sense of humour, and both flirted with the camp expression of gay culture. On the one hand they courted flamboyant Hollywood-style stardom and, on the other, presented a private, almost asexual image to the world. In terms of tabloid pop, this was a teasing combination.

For years Dusty was deliberately vague about boyfriends in her press interviews, focusing conversation on her pop career. But her work required the illusion of sexual availability. 'Because that's the way success goes, it's not enough to be a singer. You have to be a clothes peg, wearing nice things which make nice photographs. You have to make amusing conversation, which makes pleasant reading in the morning papers,' she said. She had grown up in a Catholic family where sex education came through the post, wrapped in brown-paper-covered Catholic manuals, and 'sexuality was never discussed ... it didn't exist'. She had been taught that men were mysterious and dangerous, and it wouldn't do to 'lead them on'. With the invention of Dusty Springfield she dealt with this question by creating a look modelled on drag queens, a larger-than-life parody of stereotypical femininity. According to critic Charles Shaar Murray, 'She was as close to being a drag queen as you can get if you're a biological woman.'

For Dusty, it was important to be as unsexy as possible: 'Neat, yes, perhaps a bit exciting, but I have to be the kind of girl another girl would leave her boyfriend with,' she said in 1963. She claimed later that at the height of her sixties fame she was 'living the life of a nun'. When Mick Jagger asked her out, she was too terrified to go. Singer Tony Orlando asked her to send him a telegram when she'd lost her virginity. Inevitably, as the sixties drew on and Dusty didn't get married or find a boyfriend, there was speculation about her sexuality. At first she was dubbed 'the bachelor girl', seen to be dating one or two men here and there. For instance, her picture was taken in an after-show clinch with singer Eden Kane in 1964. 'I've taken him home to meet my parents,' she said coyly, 'but we have no definite plans.' Later, she added, 'Men are afraid of me because I'm famous.'

Tabloid coverage of her private life gradually became less dignified. By the end of the sixties she had had many affairs, but never named names and never said whether she was involved with boys or girls. The hints were there, though. A Marcelle Bernstein article in the *Observer* in 1968, for instance, detailed her living arrangements with songwriter/artist Norma Tanega. '"All the orange things and all the toys in the flat are Dusty's," remarks Norma. It was she who decorated the £20,000 house Dusty is moving into near Campden Hill Square, Kensington. Norma spent over £6,000 on the conversion and every fitting is properly star-like: the vast sunken bath is reflected in amber glass, [and] the double bed looks quadruple at least.' The article goes on to discuss their phone bill and their eating habits.

It was while she was living with Tanega that Dusty had a passionate six-month affair with folk singer and activist, Julie Felix. A beautiful woman of mixed Mexican and Native American heritage, Felix travelled around Europe before moving to London in the early 1960s and gaining fame as the resident singer on *The Frost Report*. She hosted her own BBC2 show, and released best-selling singles like 'I Can't Touch The Sun' and 'If I Could (El Condor Pasa)'. She met Dusty on the set of *Ready Steady Go!*, and the two forged an instant connection.

'Dusty was living in Kensington and I was on the King's Road, not far away, so we would go back and forth. We were both with other women, so our time together was double-secret,' recalls Felix. 'We were naughty and we liked the intrigue. Because it was so hidden neither of us thought about changing the dynamic. I was infatuated with Dusty, but she was living with Norma, and I was devoted to my partner Val.' Although their partners didn't find out, Val suspected. The latter worked as a dress designer and once made a dress for Dusty to wear for a performance on Felix's TV show. The dress had a big, bouffant skirt with feathers, but at the last minute Val said she had run out of feathers. 'Dusty looked like a pregnant chicken!' says Felix. 'So we had to run around and get a different dress. I don't know if Val did that on purpose ...'

The secrecy of their affair sometimes caused unbearable tension. On one occasion, Felix was getting ready to leave to go back home to Val, and Dusty tried to stop her. 'She hit me,' says Felix. 'It was just the once. Violence is terrible, but in a strange way it proved she really cared about me. We'd been drinking some wine and she was taking Mandrax, and I think the combination was bad. I left, and I don't think she remembered it later.' Dusty sometimes found it difficult to control her emotions. 'She could be jealous. Her moods would go up and down – but sometimes she was lovely and considerate and the sweetest person on earth. She had a lot of charisma. She was like a magnet – people would want to be near her and around her.'

Dusty's explosive outbursts at this time were obviously affected by the pressure cooker of fame, and the need to hide her sexuality. 'She was active on the gay scene,' says Felix. 'One time I went to Gateways with her, but I was terrified of being found out. My mother would say the word "lesbian" as if it was worse than being a serial killer.' Felix remembers that as high-profile performers they had to be constantly on their guard. 'We had to lie. I still feel the scars. I could never really be authentic. As a young girl on TV the first thing I'd be asked was, "Do you have a boyfriend?" I had to skirt around the subject all the time. I'd be doing three or four interviews a day with people asking personal questions. It was such a harsh pressure, like being in a vice. You want to talk about your life, but you can't admit to who you love.'

The result of this was a feverish sub-world of clandestine meetings and songs that had secret, nuanced meaning. 'When she recorded "I Close My Eyes And Count To Ten", Dusty said it reminded her of me. That made me feel very special,' recalls Felix. She also remembers Dusty secretly ringing her once from Germany and racking up 'an unbelievable phone bill'. Felix found it slightly easier to hide her lesbian sexuality because she had been known to have a relationship with David Frost, and she had a child. 'But for Dusty it was really hard because she was so high profile. She was pestered year after year. I remember one night going to an event with Dusty and hanging out with our hairdresser friend John Adams. At one point she came up to me and hissed, "Don't be so close to John. I want people to think he's with me!"' Felix says that Dusty hated lying – 'she had very strong moral concepts and believed in human rights' – but she had to throw journalists off the scent.

When Dusty made a brave statement in 1970 to the *Evening Standard* that her affections were as easily swayed by a woman as a man, the desire by the press to prove that she was a lesbian became obsessive. She was dubbed 'the woman who was rumoured to be gay before Navratilova even learned to play'. Eventually the rumours seeped into her working life. While most musicians who played with her had nothing but admiration for her singing, some had reservations about her sexual reputation. 'It was a kinda icky situation,' recalls Bobby Woods, the pianist on *Dusty in Memphis*. 'I didn't want to get too close to it. At that time people didn't dare come out of the closet. In the country where I came from, if someone found out someone was homosexual you either got hung or run out of town. It was that strong. I was a naive Southern Baptist boy. I'm not judging her, that's between her and the Almighty.'

Of Dusty's relationship with a smart, witty black American soul singer, who had sung backing vocals on Dusty's records and who was a constant source of support, a friend in the sixties rock business says, 'They were very revolutionary. They were just being themselves, doing what they wanted. We all were. We were pioneers in that respect. We paved the way for it becoming acceptable to today's generation.' Jackie Forster added, 'There was great excitement when a press article said, "Dusty's gone to America with joy." Joy was her new lover, which of course we all knew.'

Julie Felix and Dusty briefly rekindled their relationship out in LA. 'I went to her house in the Hollywood Hills, and remember her cats sleeping all over the bed with us,' says Felix. 'She took me out to dinner. She had to borrow a credit card from her record company. And I remember going to some parties that were full of gay women. I was partly scared and fascinated. Dusty said to me, "You ought to get to know some of these women. They'll pounce on your bones!"'

While Dusty was very confident and at ease in these social situations, Felix felt more intimidated. 'Vicki (Wickham) said I was really soft and easily emotional. It's my Latin blood,' she laughs. 'Dusty liked women who dominated her and who were strong. I was too sensitive. It was a good thing I didn't get more involved, because it could get so crazy.' Dusty had many partners, including a leading women tennis player. At parties she also celebrated her 'fag-hag' image, playing the bantering, theatrical diva and surrounding herself with gay male friends.

'She could be so funny. In the darkest moments she could have a laugh,' says Felix.

Gay men responded to Dusty's warmth, her vulnerability, and to her stage show, which pulsated with melodrama. John McElroy, of the *Dusty Springfield Bulletin* and the unofficial Dusty fan club, said that many of his members were gay. 'The attraction is in her voice, the wonderful vulnerability she projects. If you listen to some singers live, after a few seconds you relax, because you expect them to get it out. Somehow Dusty's voice sounds so fragile, as if any minute it may crack. No matter how many times you see her, even miming to a record on TV, you're on the edge of your seat, willing her to get through.'

Unlike her sixties female competitors, Dusty quickly became a recognizable icon: male TV comedians mimicked her act, dressing up in wigs, gowns and massive false eyelashes, and calling themselves Rusty Springboard.

'Dusty always stood out. She had terrible taste in clothes, she didn't fit in with the glam things sixties girls were supposed to, and she modelled her looks on drag queens,' said the late writer Kris Kirk. 'She was open about the fact she liked gay men, and she was seen in gay clubs long before other women performers were identified with the scene. Also you can get high on her, she has a painfully sad voice that expressed for gay men feelings they felt themselves.' Drag queens also loved Dusty. Her dress designer Fred Perry told me about a night in LA when he went round to see Dusty and her house was 'full of queens. They raided her wardrobe, and one of them, a particularly big bloke, was wearing her dresses!'

Dusty gained gay fans early in her career because of her musical style and her love of Motown. Gay men have always been at the forefront of dance music, whether as soul consumers or as performers, and Dusty was seen as a bridging point in terms of her musical choices. The rumours about her sexuality and lesbian lovers enhanced, as well as damaged, her reputation. 'It was like she was within this secret showbiz clique,' says Kirk. 'She did things like speeding in sunglasses and behaving like a prima donna. She's had a very operatic life.'

In 1982 Dusty appealed directly to her gay constituency with the recording of *White Heat*. She had always aspired to be a disco diva, and loved the impact of Hi Energy, a speedy-disco style driven by over 120 beats per minute. It featured female vocalists like Donna Summer, Gloria Gaynor, Barbara Pennington, Evelyn Thomas and US gospel-disco singer Loleatta Holloway diving through peaks, crescendos and never-ending soprano notes over a fast backing track. An intense, frenetic sound, it gripped metropolitan clubland first, then laid the basis for pop hits in the eighties and nineties.

To the gay community these women were heroines. 'Their vocals were meaningful, they related to gay people's experiences and dreams,' says Andy Doyle, a seasoned eighties clubber. 'Just look at the titles – "Coming Out of Hiding", "Stranger in Disguise", "Cold Shoulder" – they said so much.' These, together with the warm irreverence of songs like 'He's a Saint, He's a Sinner' and 'So Many Men, So Little Time', evoked gay men's experience more accurately than the 'straight' romance of the regular charts. The connection between gay man and disco diva has always been a special one.

On *White Heat*, Dusty explored her disco potential. Accustomed to singing with plenty of string arrangements and a live band behind her, the album was a departure towards a more synthesized sound. 'I felt she was looking for a new image,' says bass player Nathan East. 'She was developing a fresh situation for herself – coming back into pop down another street. She felt that uptempo dance music was the move to make.'

In keeping with her fresh outlook Dusty went to live in Toronto for a year, the centre of the Canadian gay scene and a city with a soul tradition that had spawned cult outfits like the Nanette Workman Band. Toronto was alive with gay bars like the Music Room, the Fly by Night and Chez Moi. It was also a highly politicized scene with feminist Take Back the Night marches, and the anti-censorship 'Men Loving Boys Loving Men' case that dragged on between 1976 and 1979 and involved the gay newspaper *Body Politic* in the most famous non-criminal case in Canadian history. Violent police raids on gay Toronto bathhouses in the early eighties also sent thousands of people on to the streets in protest. 'It was an exciting time to be there,' recalls Judy Thornton, a Canadian Dusty fan and gay activist. 'It felt like a small sexual revolution was happening.'

Against this backdrop, Dusty worked hard on her new record. She collaborated jointly with the producer and soul aficionado Howard Steele, gaining a prominent co-production credit. 'She was right in there, suggesting alternatives,' says Nathan East. 'She liked to work with musicians, she had a hands-on attitude. We had to be chameleons. I didn't find that painful, though. I respect an artist who takes an active interest.' He was also struck by Dusty's sense of purpose. 'I got a feeling of strength from her, a strength that came from dealing with the ups and downs in the business. She was a pioneer at the time, surviving all those eras. She also had a great sense of humour; she was one of the cats. You didn't have to watch what you said and worry because there was a girl in the room.'

The result of the *White Heat* session for Casablanca Records is a focused form of dance pop, with the tingling hedonism of tracks like 'Donnez-Moi' and 'Gotta Get Used to You'. They are intense Hi Energy performances: 'Donnez-Moi' showcases a synthesized Eurodisc chic, written and arranged by Jean Alain Roussel. Dusty also interprets material from a younger generation of songwriters. She sings Elvis Costello's 'Losing You', formerly titled 'Just a Memory', in a way that's as clipped and complex as its writer's own delivery. 'I Don't Think We Could Ever Be Friends' is a gutsy dance track with lyrics written by Sting. Raunchy Canadian vocalist Carole Pope from the band Rough Trade also contributed two songs. 'I Am Curious' features Dusty's voice mixed way back, sharp and nasty like Prince, while the closing track 'Soft Core' sets her tart vocals against a delicate acoustic piano. She sings like Liza Minnelli, intoning with a vaudeville cabaret tinge that a sadistic lover has brought out a hidden spitefulness in her.

The savage humour of 'Soft Core' hints at Dusty's darker, self-destructive side. Although she had overcome the worst of her drink and drug problems, Dusty sometimes slipped back into self-doubt, suffering major crises of confidence and quelling her insecurity with alcohol. In the early eighties she met up with Tom Jones in Vancouver for a TV special. 'She didn't really know what she wanted to do,' he told me. 'She was losing not only the chance, but the desire to do it. Part of the problem was Los Angeles. There are a lot of promises made there, but without a good solid record contract it doesn't help you very much. You have to be very self-contained.'

It was also at this time that Dusty was in an abusive relationship. She talked about it later when she was working with Karen Townshend, wife of the Who guitarist Pete, on a project to help battered women. 'They were circumstances I should never have been in but that women get themselves into. I've been in that trap that I've seen other women in, you get so frightened that you are ashamed to tell anyone what's going on, you retreat. I did get myself out in the end – it had been a very destructive relationship.'

Dusty's spirits dropped further when the release of *White Heat* in the US was delayed until 1983. She said later that she was amazed it came out at all: 'Every time I made an album, the company I'd made it for would be swallowed up. They'd fire everyone you'd been working with and the enthusiasm would disappear with them. 20th Century Fox Records was the original company which got swallowed up by a reactivated Casablanca which then got eaten up by Phonogram. Then I had to fire the original producer because he had put half the budget up his nose ... there was a point where I began to feel that I was just some company's tax loss.'

Yet despite the complications *White Heat* emerged as a critical, if not commercial, success. The cover is a strange bleached-out shot of Dusty's face in close-up, with the dark eyes staring out and lips and cheekbones scribbled in. On the back she appears in a motorcycle helmet – it was rumoured that it covered bruises on her face, inflicted by her then partner.

The reviews for *White Heat* were mixed. 'Without any potential classic songs, *White Heat* needs time to grow on the listener,' wrote Bob Grossweiner in *Goldmine*. Graham Lock of *NME*, though, was ecstatic: '*White Heat* is essentially modern music: the force of those great sixties melodramas has been reignited in an eighties context of synths, voice treatments and upfront sexuality. It's possibly a personal risk – a huge leap away from the relative security of the cabaret circuit into the dangerous currents of pop commercialism – and perhaps that's why *White Heat* also feeds on a tension that grips from start to finish.'

Unfortunately Phonogram UK did not share his enthusiasm. According to publicist Norman Divall: 'Phonogram lost enthusiasm for her. When I left Phonogram, copies of *White Heat* were ready, but they were saying, "We're not sure about it. Everything we've released of Dusty's recently hasn't taken off."' They offered to release the album if Divall would take on Dusty's press as a freelance. He readily agreed. 'We both thought it would be wonderful, but then Phonogram didn't release it. By then she had become a cult following in Britain and she needed that elusive hit single to broaden her appeal.'

Dusty spent the years following *White Heat* trying to regain her status. In 1984 she recorded the old William Bell and Judy Clay song 'Private Number' as a duet with Spencer Davis, for the small Allegiance record label. In the studio he 'had fun working with her, but I also found her to be a very nervous, neurotic lady'. The result was a soporific dance track with Davis sounding languid and Dusty trying to sound like Tina Turner. By then the forty-five-year-old Turner was having a surprise revival success with 'Let's Stay Together', and Dusty didn't see why she, too, shouldn't succeed as an older woman in pop. But the *Evening Standard* remarked of 'Private Number', 'Two sixties dinosaurs team up for a duet ... ah, nostalgia.'

The charts were geared to youth, and a woman's image had to be fresh, her sexual availability evident. In her next British single project, Dusty was not just slightly off-key but also overweight. When anxious or under stress, she had always been prone to overeat. Years of zero promotion and wrangling with record companies had taken their toll.

Canadian fan Judy Thornton remembers seeing Dusty perform a short set in the early eighties at a late-night dance club in Toronto. 'Dusty was with Nona Hendryx and Carol Pope. Nona was wearing silver and she was fab. Carol Pope had just left her band Rough Trade and was singing solo. She was incredibly sexy, even overtly sexual onstage. It seemed Dusty was there as the added bonus. She was wearing this weird brown satin jumpsuit thing that wasn't very nice. She wasn't on form, her voice was tired and she seemed rundown. My sister who'd come with me said, "Poor Dusty, she's having a bad day."'

Dusty's faltering confidence was most apparent during the London Hippodrome fiasco in 1985, when flamboyant club entrepreneur Peter Stringfellow invited her to record for his new company Hippodrome Records. On paper, the £100,000 deal looked like harmless fun and a novel way to bring Dusty back into clubland and mainstream popularity. She was to record a single, linking its release with personal appearances at some of Stringfellow's clubs, the main performance being at the Hippodrome itself, a glittering emporium in London's Leicester Square with an equally large gay clientele. Dusty camped up her appearance for the occasion, wearing silk and sequins, her outrageously permed hair dyed candy-floss white and pink. Broadcaster and journalist John Peel remarked after her Hippodrome press reception that her silver-sequinned suit made her look like 'a minicab driver in Bacofoil'. It was difficult to strike the right image.

'She is the epitome of glamour,' Stringfellow enthused at first. 'She's so charismatic and outrageous. Stars today have to be like that. And she's popular among young people. Kids today are into legends. They have a great respect for Dusty because she lived through a pop period they missed.'

For the Hippodrome recording Vicki Wickham was tied up with her management company in the States, so Dusty's former manager Vic Billings handled the arrangements. Of the project, he said, 'There's only one word for it – horrendous. It was not so much her fault as Peter's. The whole thing was a disaster.'

Billings was keen for Dusty to start with a catchy uptempo track called 'My Love Life Is a Disaster'. 'Sounds funny, I know, but it was a very good song,' he said. 'I was pleading with Peter to go with this disco stuff, because I'd been working with Hazell Dean and it was very successful for her. But no, he wanted "Sometimes Like Butterflies", a great second or third record, but not something to start with.' It was hastily recorded, and Dusty's vocals sounded rough and off-pitch. Billings blames the poor quality on disorganization in the studio. 'Peter was going to get all these top-flight producers who never materialized. He wanted Pip Williams, the leader of Jimmy Ruffin's backing group, as producer, but Pip wasn't the producer for Dusty. In the end she half produced it herself, and Peter was going in and doing mixes and someone else was doing mixes and she was fighting with Peter. We'd get into a meeting at eight and still be there at midnight arguing, and I'd be in the middle saying, "Shut up, the pair of you." It was dreadful.'

Simon Bell, one of Dusty's backing singers from the session, remembers it as hard, traumatic work. 'She was surrounded by total amateurs, people who were playing at making a record.

There was no one in charge, Peter was so overawed that he'd managed to get her. Dusty also had reservations about the single, feeling it wasn't commercial enough. The engineer wasn't experienced enough – really Dusty produced it because all he did was say "yes" to everything. She was capable of doing better and the people in the studio were accepting stuff that wasn't good enough. They wouldn't push for another take.' It seems surprising that Dusty the perfectionist didn't push for further vocal takes. 'She was going through a period of doubting her own ability,' says Bell. 'When she was worried, her voice was not so strong, and she felt inhibited because she was surrounded by a bunch of wankers, basically.'

Despite the record's flaws, Dusty received generous press attention, with interviews in the music papers and national dailies. Journalist Alan Jackson remembers going to interview her in a small London mews house when TV personality Magenta Devine was doing her publicity. 'It was a sunny day, but the curtains were closed because the light was too harsh. Magenta also had sunglasses on. I thought, What's going on with everyone here?' he remembers. 'I heard this pacing upstairs. Dusty kept me waiting for an hour, then she walked down like Linda Evans in *Dynasty*, all dressed in lilac silk with her white blonde hair fluffed up like a halo round her head. She was very shoulder-padded, and her eye make-up, lips, fingernails and satin shoes were all purple. She carried two tiny kittens in her arms, saying, "Look at my darlings," as if she wanted to distract your attention from her. Then when the photographer started shooting she said, "Pray, sir, be gentle with me, the lady has had a sleepless night." She came across as mad as a hatter, but so sweet. Really kind.'

Favourable press pushed up the record's high advance sales, which, had distribution gone according to plan, should have landed it at no. 40. 'Unfortunately they hadn't got the records in the shops,' said Billings, 'and at five p.m. on a Friday afternoon someone from the Hippodrome had to go to EMI's factory and pick up two thousand records to take down to EMI's shop in Oxford Street – can you believe? She'd had a lot of plugs, but that was it.'

The record peaked at no. 82. When Billings suggested an Albert Hammond song as a follow-up, Stringfellow said he didn't have enough money and folded the record company. 'He should have bought the expertise to run it,' said Billings. 'Instead he was making all these records with Frizzby, a right old carry-on, real crappo stuff. And he was opening a club in America at the same time. Having said that, I adored Peter. He's a great guy.'

The incident blew up out of all proportion, with gossipy media reports of the Dusty/Stringfellow slanging match. 'Peter knew fuck-all about the record industry,' Dusty later said in a frank report in the *Sun*. 'And to make it worse he wouldn't listen to my advice ... My relationship with him was one of the incidents that made me so fed up with the business, I nearly gave up for good.'

Stringfellow lashed back, reported in the same article as saying, 'She is absolutely right about the fact that I knew fuck-all about the record business. But, then, I wasn't the one who refused to go on TV chat shows to plug my new record ... She wouldn't go out to promote it at all. She refused to sing in public, claiming it was too difficult. How can you possibly get a hit with a record when the artist won't perform the thing so people can listen to it?' He rued the fact that his naivety cost him a great deal of money. 'Although I had another couple of artists on my label, Dusty was the main big name. I reckon in the three years I kept the label going I got through more than a million dollars.'

At the same time as the Stringfellow debacle, speculation resurfaced about her sexuality. Dusty became deft at fielding the inevitable question. 'You're going to ask me if I'm gay, aren't you?' she said squarely in 1985 to the hard-nosed Fleet Street journalist Jean Rook. Rook was taken aback. She had been intending to pop the question at the end of the interview, but Dusty had beaten her to it. 'Then tell me you're not,' she challenged.

'God, you've got me into a corner, haven't you, coming straight out with it like that instead of "Why aren't you married?"' Dusty said. 'Let's just say I have a strong gay following.' When pressed further, she admitted, 'Look, let's say I've experimented with most things in life. And in sex. I suppose you can sum it up that I remain right down the middle.' Rook found she liked the woman 'who can "nuke" you with her eyes'; she admired Dusty's sense of drama and comedy, and said, 'I could still go home, unscathed, to my husband and son.'

In April 1988, after much negotiation, Dusty agreed to allay some of the rumours by talking frankly to the sleaze-gossip king of British Sunday papers, the *News of the World*. She decided to exercise some control over the story that they would one day print by talking to them personally – and getting paid handsomely for it.

The scene was set in a Bedfordshire health farm, with pictures of Dusty working out in the gym, lifting weights and pumping the exercise bike. Under the unflattering headline, 'LUSTY DUSTY'S BATTLE OF THE BULGES', she discussed her problems with alcohol and drugs, then brought up the subject of her sex life. 'I'm sick of being asked about it, so perhaps by talking I'll shut people up ... I have tried sex with both men and women. I found I liked it.' She went on to say that the criticism she had had to take about her sexuality had hurt deeply. 'I think my life and career might have been easier without these constant gay rumours. My sexuality has never been a problem to me but I think it has been for other people. They seem to want me to be either gay or straight, they can't handle it if someone's both. How many other women entertainers can you name who've admitted they're bisexual? Believe me, some are.' And they all feel restricted by a business that demands women flaunt heterosexuality as part of the package. For Dusty, forced to compete for chart places with younger, evidently heterosexual women like Mariah Carey, the strictures were clearly defined. It's a received truth in the business that male record buyers need to feel that the singer to whom they're listening is available for seduction. If they know she is a lesbian the spell is broken. A lesbian then becomes an affront and a threat. As one top gay female singer once said to me, 'If you came out, they'd call you an old dyke and that'd be the end of your career. Commercial suicide.'

It has been easier for gay men to achieve mainstream success. In the eighties, chart-topping artists such as Boy George, the Communards and Frankie Goes to Hollywood made open, politicized statements about their sexuality. There is a vein of camp gay male dance music, dating back from the Village People's 'YMCA', that has consistently sold. There was even commercial success for Tom Robinson in the late seventies when he rode punk's new wave with the anthem 'Glad to Be Gay'. It wasn't until the nineties, though, that women in the mainstream arena tested the water, and most were cynical about what would happen if they tried. In Britain the introduction of Clause 28 in 1988, a Conservative local government Bill banning the 'promotion' of homosexuality, created uncertainty in the gay community about how open they could be and encouraged some of tabloid pop's worst 'queer-bashing' excesses, with headlines that cemented, even celebrated, old prejudice.

However, the entertainment world has always been at the forefront of image manipulation, overturning many entrenched values. Pop's 'gender-bending' experimentation of the seventies, with David Bowie and Mark Bolan, and the eighties, exemplified in Boy George, allowed for an ambiguity of image. A few early eighties female stars like Grace Jones and Annie Lennox began to play with image, subverting male dress codes to project a sense of androgyny. But much of it remained at the level of teasing – Grace Jones had a much-publicized relationship with he-man Dolph Lundgren and Annie Lennox took many cues from her partner Dave Stewart. As the decade wore on women artists found they could be more open and honest in the way they presented their sexuality. Singer/ songwriters like Michelle Shocked and Tracy Chapman, for instance, patently rejected conventional notions about image. To some extent, they were excused because of the genre in which they worked, a kind of intellectual folk-roots protest singing that from Joan Baez and Joni Mitchell onwards has a tradition of bohemian 'eccentric' females.

Then, in the nineties, more mainstream artists, like k.d. lang and US stadium rocker Melissa Etheridge, challenged the status quo by coming out as gay. Within hardcore alternative rock, punk-inspired movements like Riot Grrrl and Queercore triggered the rise of lesbian and gay-identified acts like Tribe 8, Random Violet, Malibu Barbie and Sister George. 'The queer scene and the punk scene have always been linked for me,' said Random Violet's singer Allison Hennessey. 'Both are about being as loud about it as you can, so that everyone will see and hear it.' Skin, the beautiful, bald singer of rockers Skunk Anansie, spoke openly of her bisexuality. And in the commercial arena, Madonna flirted with 'lipstick lesbianism' and a new kind of androgynous image for the video 'Justify My Love', cross-dressing and kissing women as well as men. Rumours abounded over her 'intimate friendship' with comedienne Sandra Bernhard, and it became hip for girls to turn each other on.

Dusty had been born at the wrong time. During her sixties heyday, any suggestion of lesbianism would have ended her career. 'Without question the lesbian issue was the icing on the cake of her "difficult reputation",' says her friend, songwriter Allee Willis. 'It would have been fabulously scandalous if she'd been having hits, but it came at a time when she was tumbling down. You'd never just hear about drugs, you'd hear about the tough females that came along with it. It made her less of a controllable cutie doll, unlike Sheena Easton, who has an image that can be manipulated. It didn't allow Dusty to fall easily into the category of pop songstress, and she was dependent on music producers, arrangers and A&R to assemble material for her. Her "reputation" complicated matters. She had a bum rap.'

Willis sees Dusty as a 'path-carver', a trailblazer weighed down by the burden of being the first woman in pop associated with lesbianism. She was also one of the first performers to speak out and put gay sexuality on pop's agenda. 'It's not such a big deal to be gay now,' says Willis, 'but then it definitely wasn't hip.' Dusty made herself vulnerable by talking about bisexuality, and got ridiculed by the tabloid press. Until other female pop performers spoke out, she was isolated.

Though younger artists in the nineties found it easier to be open about their sexuality and were mystified as to why anyone should hide it, Dusty came from a different generation. 'There's this dichotomy between who I really am and who people think I am, which is wildly inaccurate. I've fought categories all my life. The agenda doesn't fit – it's not my agenda,' she said in 1995. Dusty felt that Middle England, the Catholic Church and a conservative pop industry all disapproved of her, while at the same time her inner conflicts were unresolved. When under attack from both the outside and from within, it is hard to speak out. Tennis player Billie Jean King was a friend of Dusty's and a star from the same generation. She, too, had been raised by strict parents in the forties and fifties. She, too, found herself unable to speak out, even when her 1981 palimony dispute with former lesbian lover Marilyn Barnett was splashed worldwide through the media. King called their seven-year relationship a 'mistake', and it wasn't until a 1997 Virginia Slims press conference in Chicago that she felt able to sum up her feelings. 'I've struggled with my sexuality for years,' she said. 'But times have certainly changed ... In fact, if you want to talk about your sexual orientation, the acceptance level is way up. I can tell you that in the seventies there was this huge fear about coming out. The whole environment has changed. But it takes individuals coming out to help personalize it ... I think it is really important to come out because the truth does set you free, there's no question.'

Although the general climate has become more tolerant, the

pop industry is still uncertain about how to market a lesbian artist. As funky gay singer-songwriter Adele Bertei says, 'Popular music has always maintained a silence on gay love, and the truth of the oppression we live with has to be spoken, too ... that we're human beings who have a right to be respected for who we are. That shouldn't be a problem for the record industry. If someone is upfront about their sexuality, then people are going to be attracted to them whether they're straight or gay.'

Dusty might have had a rough time with the press, but most of her friends remained loyal. Some found her emotionally exhausting, the victim of her own sensitivity. 'She was a fool to herself, that girl,' Petula Clark once remarked, while dusting her nose with a pre-show powder-puff. When Dusty was on form, however, she commanded respect. 'She was like Marlene Dietrich. She'd be the loyalest friend in the world, but you do something stupid professionally and she'd bollock you for it. She was professional herself and expected other people to be the same, especially those working for her,' says her friend Norman Divall.

When he spoke to me in 1988, Vic Billings likened her to an old-style movie star. 'She would have been someone like Greta Garbo, wanting to be alone and languishing in her bedroom all day, maybe reaching over for the occasional chocolate. Dusty's a very kind, genuine person. She's temperamental as hell, but that's to do with the talent. You could willingly throttle her one minute and then you want to hug, cuddle and protect her the next. She has a few people she trusts, she homes towards people she's known a long time. Sometimes she plays up and you think, Ooh, God, you're such a cow. She's like a little girl in many respects. She'll push and push, asking you to do things, all to prove that you really care for her. It's all bound up in this insecurity. She's a person who needs a lot of love and kindness.'

Pat Rhodes saw Dusty's 'difficult reputation' partly as the problem of being a woman in a man's world. 'Women are seen as difficult. A man is seen as standing up for his rights. She was not supposed to know best but half the time she knew better than the people themselves. She was easily led, though. She let herself be swayed by people who weren't right for her and she hadn't learned how to suss them out. It broke my heart sometimes.'

In the early eighties, Dusty was ridiculed for her age, weight and sexuality but by the end of the decade her fortunes began to change. As the pop market opened up to alternative lifestyles and role models, older sixties artists began to reinvent themselves, and Dusty was greeted with a new respect. The story wasn't over yet.

9

Britgirl

'NOW THE MUSIC industry is two thousand times better, with female singers like Annie Lennox and Alison Moyet. In the sixties there was no one like Sinead O'Connor. She's fabulous, young and Irish. Where was she in the sixties?' Dusty said to me in 1988, talking with renewed optimism. In a changing music industry, which was becoming more open to strong, self-defined women, Dusty's talent found another outlet.

That year she quit LA for good. 'Parts of this city are really naff, parts are glamorous,' she told me. 'I like the convenient aspects to it, things like twenty-four-hour cleaners, but I don't like the heat. And musically Americans get frightened if you fling a lot of stuff at them, playing several different styles makes them nervous. Besides, I'm tired of LA. I've been homesick for a long time. I've been waiting for the groundswell of movement in Britain, and now seems the right time to come back.'

It was with her move, first to Amsterdam (while her cats were in quarantine), and then back to the UK, that Dusty's career took off once more, giving her a new high, and her first major hit since 1968. She re-entered a scene where women like Sinead O'Connor, Suzanne Vega and Tracy Chapman were successful on their own forthright terms. Back in the early sixties, though, top-selling solo female singers were few and far between. When girls *did* make it, they were expected to conform to a certain pattern. 'Whereas guys in the sixties could be mad, bad, dangerous to know and do politics, a female singer was inevitably shoved into being nicey, nicey for Mum, Dad and all the family on entertainment variety shows,' remarks music writer Charles Shaar Murray. 'Compromise was built into the set-up.'

The best new material generally went to the boys, while up-and-coming female vocalists had to fight for their cast-offs. With a limited range of images available, most sixties women in pop went for the bright, fun-loving style. After all, it sold records. Before the creative individualism of the seventies and eighties, the careers of Britain's top pop girls were guided along similar channels, meaning there was room for only a few to break through. In the battle for chart places, Dusty fought all the way, keeping her sense of quality tuned, and her professionalism uppermost.

By 1964, it was becoming fashionable in the British record industry to copy the American girl-group sound, with a slightly cleaner home version. Each of the four major companies had their token female star, groomed for acceptable family pop entertainment. Lulu, the Glaswegian singer from Dennistoun Palace in Glasgow's East End was signed to Decca; Cilla Black, the wise-cracking cloakroom girl at the Liverpool Cavern Club that made the Beatles famous, was on EMI; Sandie Shaw and the effervescent Petula Clark were on Pye; and Dusty, of course, was with Philips.

The tradition of the British female singer with the reassuring 'girl-next-door' image had been set during the Second World

War when bright blonde Vera Lynn sang for soldiers overseas on a lively request programme, *Sincerely Yours*. Known as the Forces' Sweetheart, she seemed like the kind of girl who'd listen to your problems and make you a cup of tea. Her optimistic, lush orchestrations were followed by the crooning style of the fifties. Ruby Murray, Alma Cogan, Anne Shelton and the young Petula Clark popularized this ballad format, carrying on the trend for British girl singers to sing light and sweet, with material that veered towards show tunes and standards.

When Dusty came on the scene with the Lana Sisters in 1958, female vocalists were expected to perform without undignified raunchiness. The Lana Sisters' harmony pop packed a punch – '... a lively rocker that moves along at a fair old pace with guitars twanging all around' is how *NME* described their single 'Someone Loves You, Joe' in May 1960 – but it was heavily circumscribed by the middle-of-the-road variety sound beloved of their competitors, the Kaye Sisters and the Beverley Sisters.

As the Lana Sisters, Dusty, Riss and Lynne could easily have sung complicated jazz harmonies. However, they adhered to a strict pop formula, with simplistic songs like 'Seven Little Girls Sitting on the Back Seat', all delivered with impeccable timing and perfect diction. The weightier hits they wanted just weren't on offer. 'We found we were competing against all those boys,' said Riss Chantelle, 'Tommy Steeles, Cliff Richards, Adam Faiths – the 2i's coffee bar in Denmark Street was brimming over with them.' Despite their limited material, the Lana Sisters – who later became the Chantelles – were an attractive, lively act, managing to secure in their brief career a wide range of slots on TV and radio. 'We were raring to go. We didn't want anyone standing in our way. We had to fight. We had enough with all those boys!'

Despite their gutsiness, though, Dusty and the girls never managed to break through. 'We would've got a lot further but in 1959 we had an onslaught of American girl groups like Brenda Lee, and the Ponytails. There was all that as well as Larry Parnes and Marty and the rock 'n' roll boys. We'd have done better if we weren't a girl group,' said Chantelle. 'It became easier when I formed the Chantelles and toured with acts like the Beatles and Cliff Richard.' It was really the Vernons Girls, by the sheer force of their numbers and talent, who began to open up alternative avenues for British female singers. The group originally worked as clerical staff at Vernons Football Pools Company in Liverpool. For employees' recreation, the company encouraged the organization of a seventy-strong choral society, from which sixteen girl members emerged in 1957 as a group in their own right. The Vernons Girls became resident performers on Jack Good's ITV rock 'n' roll show *Oh Boy!*, backing such artists as Cliff Richard, Marty Wilde and Dickie Pride.

With their tight sweaters and short skirts, the Vernons Girls created a stunning visual impact. They continued as a trio in the early sixties, recording strong and sometimes eccentric pop numbers like 'Dat's Love' for Decca. The Vernons were considered slightly ahead of their time, but by the early sixties, the success of girl groups like the Ronettes and the Crystals in America showed British record companies that upbeat female pop artists were viable. They were still reluctant, though, to invest money in this genre. 'In the sixties it was very difficult to launch the career of a female singer,' says former Philips employee Dave Shrimpton. 'Girl singers were tried and promoted, but we had a bigger success rate with male acts, like Cliff Richard, Tommy Steele, Adam Faith and Marty Wilde. It seemed women were less likely to be played on the radio, they were less accepted.'

According to sixties *NME* journalist Keith Altham on UK Channel 4 documentary *Britgirls*, 'The feeling was still prevalent that a woman's place was in the home, and if she was on the stage then she'd better behave herself. The girl singers basically were considered to be a short-term proposition. Their potential was limited.' It would have helped if their material had been better. This was long before the tradition of solo performers writing their own songs, so they had to rely on songwriters or US cover versions. Many women weren't given access to the hits or the hitmakers of the day, and no matter how well the artist was promoted, if her songs weren't strong enough she would never achieve the high-chart profile she desired.

Sandie Shaw once remarked to me that 'women weren't considered the big meat'. Most of the working acts that came out of Britain in the sixties were male beat groups, riding on the crest of the wave created by the Beatles and the Rolling Stones. Amid the 'serious' talent, women singers were seen as ineffectual. Aspiring female pop singers were viewed as dolly birds whose job it was to sing what was put in front of them. 'There was pressure to be a girlie,' singer Beryl Marsden said on *Britgirls*. 'I did it once and I was very unhappy about it. I did a TV appearance wearing a tiara, this horrible great pink chiffon dress and high heels, and I got very upset so I never allowed it to happen again.' She says that stars like Sandie Shaw and Dusty were noticeable for 'standing up for themselves and not going for the pretty-pretty image'.

Although the Big Four – Dusty, Cilla, Sandie and Lulu – were vigorously promoted with major record-company backing, they were the token female artists. On a broad scale little commitment was shown to women by the majors, so consequently there was a vigorous 'underground' female pop scene. Many women occupied a kind of 'second division' pop status, releasing inspired one-offs or occasional cult classics, while an even larger number threw in their lot with session singing. Former Vernons Girls, the Breakaways were an example of a highly respected backing trio who released songs of their own.

Several girl groups appeared brandishing instruments, but they were always treated as novelties – and sometimes a girl would pop up in an otherwise all-male band, like Megan Brady, female bassist in the Applejacks, the band that scored a Top 10 hit in 1964 with 'Tell Me When', and Honey Lantree, the drummer in the Honeycombs for their hit 'Have I the Right'. There was a cluster of beat-girl belters like Billie Davis and Beryl Marsden, who opted for a straight raw R&B style. 'There weren't a lot of female singers around because they couldn't associate themselves with the songs. The majority of female singers who had made the charts were Susan Maughan types – pretty songs and party clothes. But in Liverpool you had to be one of the boys,' says Marsden. Briefly signed to Decca, Marsden sang warm bouncy numbers like the Shirelles' 'Everybody Loves a Lover', but didn't make a big impact on the charts. Meanwhile, Woking-born mod Billie Davis achieved a little more success with her raucous 1963 hit cover version of the Exciters' 'Tell Him'.

But the unofficial queen of the beat girls, the Glasgow blues shouter Lulu, enjoyed a much higher profile: her 1964 hit version of the Isley Brothers' 'Shout' propelled her into the major female pop league. 'I loved black American music, especially Motown. It was hot,' she says. Lulu's energy kept her in the public eye for years afterwards, but 'Shout' was probably her pop pinnacle.

There were plenty of novelty acts, too. Girls in specs, girls in tartan, girls singing with dancing men in bowler hats. There was thirteen-year-old Lorraine Silver whose soulful 'Lost Summer Love' later became a Northern soul smash; the teenage Orchids from Coventry, who 'hated schoolgirls' and considered themselves fully fledged mods; and Polly Perkins, the lesbian singer in a pinstripe suit.

Only a handful of vocalists had consistent success in Britain, and still fewer dented the international market. Cilla Black, for instance, recorded successful UK versions of US hits like Dionne Warwick's 'Anyone Who Had a Heart', had over a dozen Top 20 hits and was skilfully managed by Brian Epstein to the top of the pop industry. She had a bawling Mersey magic, a mod bob and the right team behind her. She also had a charm that kept her at the top in Britain, but which never really translated overseas. After cabaret stints and a regular BBC series in the seventies, she came to the fore as a wisecracking TV celebrity in the eighties, hosting prime-time shows *Blind Date* and *Surprise Surprise*.

Sandie Shaw was also a consistent hitmaker, given a strong selection of songs. '(There's) Always Something There to Remind Me' was the first of fifteen Top 40 hits, most of them produced by Chris Andrews. After her chart-topping entry into the Eurovision Song Contest, 'Puppet on a String', her career faltered, and she didn't emerge again until the eighties, with a completely different, punk-inspired sound. She, too, never cracked America. Although Sandie had her wild side, her sixties image, along with Cilla, embodied the Best of British. It was a humorous, quirky, girl-next-door image that was as restrictive as it was successful.

By contrast, ex-convent girl Marianne Faithfull began singing mournfully sweet folk-pop ballads like 'As Tears Go By', but was never really acceptable for a family audience, with her reference to 'dope' while appearing on *Juke Box Jury*, and her much publicized (if in part alleged) sex 'n' drugs 'n' Mars Bar affair with Mick Jagger. She was identified more with the sixties hippie counterculture, whereas UK pop preferred its heroines straightforward and squeaky clean. Ironically, Dusty felt she had more in common with Faithfull than with all the other Britgirls put together. 'I think I'm a maverick,' she said, three decades later. 'I don't even know why. I probably identify most with Marianne Faithfull. There's a lot of pain there too.'

Early on, Dusty battled to break free of the limits of British pop, expressing her revulsion at the process of packaging pop girls for a few years before hiving them off into pantomime and summer shows. She wanted longevity and international stardom, but with musical authenticity and an honest expression of self. She made full use of talented soul singers such as Madeline Bell and Doris Troy for backing vocals. Their powerful voices plumped up her sound and gave her the edge over competitors. She learned a lot from them and repaid the compliment by recording backing vocals for them, under the pseudonym Gladys Thong.

Another UK vocalist anxious to break free of the expectations placed on girl singers was Kiki Dee, who became Dusty's backing singer and close friend. Signed to Philips and later to Motown in the States, Dee released some striking soulful covers of US hits like 'Running Out of Fools' and 'I Dig You Baby'. Despite thorough promotion on Philips's part, she didn't become a star until after the sixties. The large mod following who were then the major consumers of soul in Britain took their music seriously, and were wary of a white British girl releasing singles that were covers of the US soul classics they loved.

Dusty neatly circumvented this problem by releasing only original material as singles. It meant that she created more work for herself. 'It was hard in the early stages. We had floods of material and a load of crap, but it was easier later on, especially when we had a good relationship with songwriters like Burt Bacharach and Carole King,' said her manager Vic Billings. This ensured a quality that Dusty sustained throughout the sixties, never releasing anything that might be even faintly embarrassing. She stamped each single with her presence, making it difficult for classics like 'You Don't Have to Say You Love Me' to be identified with anyone but herself.

'You can hear the quality in the records she made,' says Bob Stanley, nineties songwriter/producer and sixties enthusiast. 'She worked with very gifted writers and arrangers, even the backing singers were top quality. Obviously she had a lot more control than her contemporaries. Her records don't sound like they were thrown together in five minutes, like Lulu or some of Sandie Shaw's later stuff sound to me.'

According to Billings, 'We had some lovely songs that we lost, or nearly lost. Valerie Simpson once played us "Ain't No Mountain High Enough" on the piano and we said, "We gotta have it." She said, "I can't, really, I've just signed with Motown." And Carole King played us "Goin' Back". At the time she was breaking up with Gerry [Goffin] and he'd written it for a boy, and wouldn't allow the lyric to be changed. Luckily for us there was a group in London called Goldie and the Gingerbreads who had a record released on Decca called "I Think I'm Goin' Back". Within two days it was stopped, with Gerry threatening to sue. He was furious. He then rewrote the song and sent me a cable saying, "Good luck with Dusty. Here's the lyric."' It turned out to be one of her best recordings.

As a performer Dusty was more authoritative than the rest of the UK beat girls. There was a single-minded focus that came out onstage and in her studio recordings. When she lost her direction in the seventies, the music floundered with her. For two decades she had spent so much time trying to escape the strictures of the sixties British music industry that little did she suspect, by the late eighties, pop from the sixties would again be big business. A trend for sixties revivalism swept through music, fashion, advertising and the media, with Levi's 501 jeans commercials leading the way in the selling of glossy retro imagery. Knowledge of the sixties was cool, something to aspire to, and yesterday's stars were treated with fresh respect. No longer old dinosaurs, they were seen as experienced elder pop spokespeople.

As the eighties recycled pop culture from former decades, sixties music came to the fore, with the sounds of ska, Motown, protest folk and Stax hitting the airwaves. Both mod and hippie fashions reappeared, along with moptop hairstyles and psychedelic design. Dusty was swept up and carried along in a nostalgia boom created by a younger generation curious about sixties idols. The success that she'd been chasing for such a frustrating length of time finally tapped her on the shoulder. 'It just sort of plopped into my life and changed it,' she said. 'I'd gone through a very down time. Nothing was happening ... I was sitting in someone's garden in California under one of the few trees that were there and a feeling came over me that it was going to be all right, everything was going to be all right.'

In 1988 there were several successful and unlikely duets in the British charts. Tom Jones teamed up with electronic provocateurs Art of Noise for his swarthy hit version of Prince's 'Kiss'. Camp underground punk star Marc Almond linked his fortunes with the sixties hero Gene Pitney in a rousing remake of 'Something's Gotten Hold of My Heart', while Euro-house music aficionados Yello created a one-off unholy alliance with Shirley Bassey for 'A Rhythm Divine', featuring her vocals, soaring, glitzy and melodramatic, over a disco backbeat. Queen's Freddie Mercury linked his love of overwrought rock opera with the authentic operatics of Montserrat Caballé in 'The Golden Boy'; Lulu had another smash hit with her rerelease of 'Shout'; and Petula Clark brought out a bestselling house mix of her old hit 'Downtown'.

A couple of years earlier the idea behind such unlikely collaborations began to take hold when Morrissey from the Smiths managed to get his favourite sixties female star Sandie Shaw to sing his song 'Hand in Glove'. Released on former punk independent label Rough Trade, this was a new and welcome departure for her. 'Female singers then seemed to be giving everything away and hiding nothing. That's what made them more dramatic, more interesting to me,' Morrissey later explained. The record he did with Shaw triggered a rush of pop duets, with older, more established stars exposed to a new generation of teen consumers. It was a new dynamic that worked.

Younger acts always want to commune with their heroes, while the latter are flattered. It keeps their profile challenging and up to date, and, most importantly, creates hits.

The Pet Shop Boys – Neil Tennant and Chris Lowe – were among the first of pop's young style brigade to approach a sixties idol. In 1989 they worked with Liza Minnelli, but Dusty Springfield was their primary target. Five years earlier they had been a small group in search of songs and some artwork for their records. They were attracted to a strange motorized art piece designed for the song 'Neutron Dance', a huge hit for the Pointer Sisters in the US. Artist and Grammy award-winning songwriter Allee Willis, who had written hits for Earth, Wind & Fire such as 'September' and 'Boogie Wonderland', co-wrote 'Neutron Dance' with Danny Sembello and created the art piece.

A bright, effervescent socialite who lives in the Los Angeles' Valley, Willis recalls how she was approached by the Pet Shop Boys' manager Tom Watkins. 'He came to my house and was really impressed with my collection of fifties artefacts, because he collects them too.' Willis and Watkins struck up a 'fast and furious' friendship, which resulted in Willis doing some graphic portraits for the Pet Shop Boys. When Neil Tennant realized that she was also the songwriter behind 'Boogie Wonderland', he became ecstatic. A great fan of black music, he managed to persuade her to write them a song.

'I wrote "What Have I Done to Deserve This?" when I was having a pathetic time in England, hence the song,' says Willis. 'We cut the demo as a duet. My style is to assemble parts that don't go together, so there was a seemingly sing-song-y melodic chorus with a sixties swing, coming out of rap. The boys immediately thought of Dusty Springfield for the chorus.'

As luck would have it, Willis had got together with her a few years before that, because she had heard that Dusty liked her material. 'At that time it was definitely not a happening period for her,' recalls Willis. 'She was looking for stuff to sing. She came over to my house and ten minutes after she arrived there was a power failure that plunged the whole house into darkness. We didn't get many songs done, but we got wildly drunk in the kitchen.'

When Willis came up with Dusty's song some time later, at first Dusty refused. 'Who are the Pet Shop Boys?' she asked blankly. The Pet Shop Boys held off from finishing their first album, waiting for Dusty to record the track with them. Eventually they had to release it without her, but held out hope. In the meantime they rose to fame in the UK, having a massive no. 1 success with 'West End Girls'. Later Dusty recalled hearing the song while driving along the freeway. She was so impressed she almost had an accident. 'There's a symphonic quality to it, a larger than life quality, [plus] that kind of offhandedness,' she said. 'There was a pulse to it ... no one had done that sound. So, I suppose, it struck me the first time I heard Phil Spector ... "Funny how potent cheap music can be." I never in a million years thought about working with them.'

Despite their high profile, it was two and a half years before Dusty agreed to work with them and finally flew over to the studio in London. Vicki Wickham had become her manager and was impatient with Dusty 'vegetating in LA for so long'. She firmly believed that this was the kick-start that Dusty so vitally needed. And Dusty behaved herself accordingly. 'We'd heard she was difficult to work with,' admitted Neil Tennant, 'but actually she was just very professional. We had quite a laugh with her because it was the first time she had made a video and she seemed to think everything was pretty crazy. Also she asked if we thought the duet would get to no. 1 and told us she'd only had one so far. She laughed when we said, "Ha ha, we've already got two." She slapped Chris for saying it.'

Dusty was nervous about being back in the studio after the Hippodrome fiasco. 'It was eerie. Vicki and I were giggling away because the Pet Shop Boys are so different. Thank God I'm so versatile,' she said. 'I couldn't work out what they wanted until we'd finished the session in London. Then I realized, it was the sound of my voice. It was that simple!' Whenever she got nervous or irritable the Pet Shop Boys would say reassuringly, 'It's just a pop record!'

'She's very husky and breathy with an intensity and desperation to her voice that's fantastically sensual,' enthused Tennant. 'She sort of floats off on another plane.' *That* voice rises supreme over the Pet Shop Boys' muted synth-rap backbeat on 'What Have I Done to Deserve This?' A moving, light-hearted song, it is the epitome of the sixties-meets-the-eighties pop collision, with shades of sophisticated boystown disco and shimmeringly bright melody. On the record sleeve, Tennant and Lowe sit with snarlingly camp moodiness astride a sixties motorbike, while Dusty's face looms behind them, iconic and majestic.

The record gave her back her dignity and a fresh, hip image. Dusty's face pops up in the video singing cheekily while dancing girls, red carpets and feather boas float past. She looks relaxed and sunny in a way that is reminiscent of her *Ready, Steady, Go!* days. Released in August 1987, the single shot to no. 2 in the British charts. It was also a massive hit in America, reaching no. 1.

'Gratitude is a new feeling to me,' said Dusty later, in a BBC Radio One interview, 'I was always accused of being a very ungrateful child. "It will show on your face one day, my child," my mum used to say. It was there in the scowl … I'm really grateful to the Pet Shop Boys, and I feel embarrassed to say that. It sticks in my craw to be grateful. I am, because they had the faith in me that I didn't have. They saw something in me that I was about to lose.'

Willis was delighted. 'It's always a pleasure and a relief to have a hit,' she says. 'Everyone was really glad for her. It was a great feeling as a writer to be part of her resurgence. She had got to a point where she didn't want to have anything more to do with the music business, it brought up all that insecurity complex. She couldn't get a record deal because of her reputation, basically. Now she's able to make peace with the fact she's so great.' Also cheered by Dusty's success, singer Tom Jones saw parallels with his own experience. 'I'm glad that, like me, she found her way, found her niche again,' he says. 'Dusty is a good comparison to me. We both came out around the same time, we can cover the same musical areas, we both got a bit lost in America, and we've both come forward again.'

The following February, Dusty appeared onstage with Neil Tennant, singing 'What Have I Done to Deserve This?' at the BRIT Awards, a testimony to the fact that she was back on top. Soon after the success of 'What Have I Done to Deserve This?', Dusty kept up her US profile by recording a duet with Richard Carpenter entitled 'Something in Your Eyes'. Self-doubt hit her again before she walked into the studio: she was in awe of the legacy left by Karen Carpenter. She still managed to turn out a skilled performance on this ballad, even though she is not shown on the record's picture sleeve and there is a tiny credit under Richard Carpenter's name saying, 'Lead vocals by Dusty Springfield'. She took that as a snub.

'Something in Your Eyes' reached no. 12 in the American Adult Contemporary Chart in November, and got to no. 84 in the UK. The single didn't go higher partly because of Dusty's reluctance to come over to Britain for promotion and face the inevitable questions about 'comebacks'. 'The word "comeback" always alarms me,' she says. 'It implies you're trying to be what you were. Press-promoted comebacks have always surrounded me with drama and animation. It's embarrassing.'

For a long time she felt hampered by the old sixties image. 'The fans won't let me let that go,' she said to me in 1988. 'That's quite a fight. It was twenty years ago – they don't want you to change because your image is part of their growing up. I've changed my hair, I've got older and an element has got resentful. I don't want to be exactly what I was, I'm a different person now and my life is taking directions I least expect.'

The Dusty revival continued apace with the rerelease in December of 'I Only Want to Be with You' on the Old Gold label. That song has proved to be Dusty's most successful, having been covered five times since in various guises. It became a hit for the Bay City Rollers in the early seventies and went to no. 4 in 1979 for Annie Lennox and the Tourists (the band that later transmuted into the Eurythmics). Ten years on, it entered the chart again, lamely sung by page-three model and showbiz personality Samantha Fox. When asked what she thought of Fox's version, Dusty said, 'She's got bigger titties than me!' She also remarked, 'I think it's really rather good … It's not very different from my version, they've just put on that galloping bass. I wish I'd written the song.'

Dusty's hit singles were then respectfully packaged in *The Silver Collection*, a Phonogram compilation released in early 1988. It was her first CD LP, and a monumental success, catching precisely the right pop moment. The album has a gatefold sleeve featuring a flattering sixties shot of Dusty the mod, complete with a fringe, chin-length hair and heavy mascara. The picture was given the Warhol treatment inside, with Dusty's face repeated in rows, her image bleached out and then touched up in Day-Glo colours. The sleeve notes pay tribute to her achievements. This time round Dusty felt that Philips, now Phonogram, had released an acceptable greatest-hits album. 'They're making a real effort for once, and doing it right,' she said.

The album went gold, proving to be a phenomenal seller. Buoyed up by the public reaction ('The public are very forgiving,' says Pat Rhodes. 'If you say, "Sorry, this is what happened," they'll welcome you back.') Dusty packed her belongings and moved back to the UK. 'She had been stagnating in LA doing nothing but was petrified about making the change,' recalls Rhodes. 'I think it helped enormously working with the Pet Shop Boys and realizing how much they admired her. That boosted her confidence enough to come back.'

For the first three months Dusty stayed at Rhodes's house in Palmers Green, north London, living as part of the family. 'She was no bother at all,' says Rhodes. 'She said to me, "All I need is a bed, a telephone and a TV." She didn't have to be anybody special. She didn't bother with make-up and sometimes spent the day in pyjamas. She'd get up at night and pinch chocolate biscuits from the fridge, then leave a note in the morning – "I owe you a packet of digestives."' Living with Rhodes's family enabled Dusty to settle back gently into UK life and feel secure. 'She was like the girl next door. I knew her as Mary O'Brien, that was the real Dusty. Onstage she was a frightened woman who never thought she was any good. At home she was relaxed. All she wanted was my spagetti bolognese and roast dinners, particularly roast parsnips.'

Dusty's return consolidated her position as queen of the sixties. This was emphasized in the orange juice manufacturer Britvic 55's TV commercial. In tune with hip revivalism, the advert is a highly stylized pastiche of the sixties shot in black and white, featuring stars such as Eric Burdon, Sandie Shaw, Brian Poole and the Tremeloes and Georgie Fame. Dusty is revealed at the very end as the ultimate star, a mystery woman who gets out of a Sunbeam Alpine sports car to greet a throng of waiting fans. Until she turns round with a Britvic orange juice in her hand, her identity throughout the commercial has been concealed. As she takes a drink and smiles, the male voiceover says, 'Britvic is for real!'

This stylish commercial was a far cry from the one she did in the sixties for Mother's Pride sliced bread. Media resurrection of the past enabled Dusty to reinvent and celebrate her former self, to reclaim that period as a source of strength rather than embarrassment. By 1989, with the release of the film *Scandal* and her recording of the theme song 'Nothing Has Been Proved', a cycle was nearly complete. The film was set in 1963 – the year Dusty began her solo career – when the British government was being rocked to its foundations by the Profumo scandal, involving call girl Christine Keeler and Mandy Rice-Davies. Tory war minister John Profumo had to resign because of his affair with Keeler, who was reputedly connected with suspected Russian agent Eugene Ivanov. Her mentor, osteopath Stephen

Ward, committed suicide and Keeler herself was convicted and imprisoned for prostitution.

It was a tragic situation that, twenty years later, remained unresolved, with accusations of cover-up and trial by media. Hence the densely written song 'Nothing Has Been Proved'. An uptempo ballad produced by the Pet Shop Boys, it became another hit for Dusty, peaking at no. 16 in the UK charts. The video showed her dressed in purple, singing softly against a background of black and white sixties news footage about the Profumo affair. 'That was such an incredible song, it really was a gem,' she said fondly. 'There's a lyric that, to half its audience, nobody understood a word of, but it didn't matter because it had a sound.'

To promote the single Dusty appeared on several chat shows, speaking about the issues the film had raised. Many drew parallels with her sixties experience. She professed to have been unaware of the enormity of the scandal at the time as she was concentrating on her career. 'We were busy making our own little scandals, blundering through the sixties,' she said. 'I spent the first five years of my career not really knowing what naughty words meant – like "love nest". Someone was always caught in a love nest sipping champagne. The sleaze factor of it didn't hit me till a few years later when I became aware of all sorts of things!'

In resurrecting the strong – and saleable – elements of her past, Dusty was able to move forward after years of hiding from and being denied the limelight she deserved. It was a relief for her to be upfront and on TV – a media personality once more. In talking about *Scandal*, though, Dusty drew parallels with the darker side of press manipulation. 'The film gives clarity to the situation and approaches it from an angle people wouldn't expect. It deals with Christine Keeler's actual feelings for Stephen Ward, whereas most people think she didn't have any feelings. They thought she and Mandy were just good-time girls – but she wasn't. She never got over it; to this day she could never come to terms with his death and the way she got treated by the tabloids.' The Profumo affair was a peculiarly symbolic moment in British history. Apart from political intrigue, it introduced two long-standing British traditions that frame the image of Dusty Springfield: the swinging sixties and the rise of chequebook journalism. Dusty, too, has suffered from the underbelly of tabloid journalism.

By the time Dusty celebrated her fiftieth birthday on 16 April 1989, she was feeling a new confidence and fresh hope for the future. The two hit singles with the Pet Shop Boys meant she was able to quell the self-doubt that had plagued her, particularly during the low period of the seventies. 'There was an innate feeling I had first time round – maybe it was stupidity – that everything would be all right. Certainly I don't know how – the first time I had no contacts, knowledge or experience. I just knew it was going to be all right. And there's been a return of that feeling. It seems to be the right time,' she said.

She signed an album deal with Parlophone, EMI, the major company that just a few years before had given her a wide berth. After the success of 'What Have I Done to Deserve This?', more and more people in the record company saw her potential. With its upfront, straightforward title, *Reputation*, Dusty's first new album in eight years, played lightly on the themes of scandal and notoriety that have coloured her career.

It was a characteristically long time coming. Soon after the release of 'Nothing Has Been Proved', Dusty was talking about doing a whole album, but *Reputation* didn't emerge until the following year. Delighted to be working with the Pet Shop Boys, Dusty initially wanted to showcase on her album what she saw as the best of British production talent. There were rumours that Phil Collins would be involved, and Dusty enthused about his ability to 'do wonders with an old song. Look at "Groovy Kind of Love".' She was also enthusiastic about the UK funk/soul band Level 42. 'The bass sound on that! That was what I wanted from musicians in the sixties. I was the first person to ask someone to play an electric bass and they didn't know how to do it. It was a slog.'

Various names, including Climie Fisher's, were bandied about in Dusty's choice of collaborators. Apart from the Pet Shop Boys, the end result didn't feature any of these names, but American industry pro Dan Hartman took up the challenge for side one. 'When Dusty recorded "Send It to Me", Dan Hartman was in ecstasy, behaving like a sixteen-year-old fan,' says Simon Bell, who sang some backing vocals on the album. 'Because he had been a singer himself, he had the ability to coax the best out of her.'

Speaking to me from his home in Connecticut in 1990, Hartman described how at first he thought that Dusty Springfield didn't exist. 'I called her management many times about the album, but the lady never returned my calls. Then a few days before we were due to start recording, she finally got back to me.' A sought-after producer of black dance music, Hartman became famous as a singer in the mid-eighties with a smooth white soul sound that was similar to Hall and Oates. An enthusiastic 'hands-on' producer, he recorded with Dusty at his Connecticut studio as well as in London, drawing out of her the ebullient pop/soul that he is happiest with. For the London sessions, Hartman sensed that she was preoccupied and uncomfortable. 'Then when I had the pleasure of her coming to my Connecticut studio, she got over the nervousness and we clicked. All she had to do every day was get up, have breakfast and sing. It's her soulful interpretation that stands out, and I felt it was important to let that flourish, to let her feel free. She's best when at her free-est point.'

Hartman is proud of 'Send It to Me', seeing it as 'optimum Dusty Springfield "radio" pop', and his admiration also goes out to the Pet Shop Boys-produced rap 'Daydreaming'. 'Dusty's so incredibly hip – she always gravitates towards the unusual. When they've been in the business as long as she has, a lot of people tend to lose touch with what's on the edge, but she's right there.' The *Independent* was slightly more sceptical about Dusty's taste on *Reputation*. 'If it were 1987, this would sound bang up to date,' their critic remarked. Some of the Hartman tracks do sound a little derivative, but 'Send It to Me' is pleasant arch-pop that has Dusty's vocal sliding with the melody, while 'Born This Way' goes back to the slinky survivalist shout of her funky sixties days. Black music heavyweights Geoffrey Williams, Tawatha Agee and Vaneese Thomas, daughter of infamous 'Funky Chicken' Rufus Thomas, provide the backing vocals, showing that Dusty could still summon up the best.

Hartman brought out Dusty's light-hearted side – off-duty as well as in the studio. He recalls one evening when he was going through his singles collection. 'I found an old B-side that Dusty had written herself, and I put it on really loud. She came screaming out of the shower, hair dripping over her face and shouted, "What is that? What're you playing that for?" She then admitted that she liked it a lot.' Hartman remembered Dusty as 'a bit manic, very private, sentimental and a real prankster'. It's that warm enthusiasm that permeates most of the album's first side.

The reverse side is completely different, with the Pet Shop Boys adding swathes of cool irony and a transcendent techno edge. Dusty would have preferred the duo to oversee the whole thing. 'I wanted them to produce the whole LP, but I think they wanted it to be just half them. I don't want to fall out with them, [but] it's ended up sounding like two different albums,' she said.

The Pet Shop Boys tracks proved to be most popular, especially the hit 'In Private', which, when it first came out as a single in November 1989, the Motown-inspired pop beat just sounded throwaway. The melodramatic hookline, however, refused to sit down, and the record was played everywhere, peaking at no. 14 in the British charts and entering the Top 10 in charts all over Europe and Japan. In 1990 it was one of Germany's bestselling singles, and also became a favourite on the New York club scene. In the burst of publicity surrounding its release, Dusty made an appearance on *The Dame Edna Experience*, the TV chat show with the scathingly witty Barry Humphries in drag as its host. Considering Dusty's appreciation of camp, it was a suitably celebratory pairing.

The single struck a chord with the late eighties pop audience. Singing about the possible conflict between private life and public image, Dusty pointed out with pop simplicity the dilemma of fame and stardom. The video did little to enhance the song, however, parading a succession of vacuous models on the telephone. Its image was strictly cheap and cheerful, without doing justice to the clever twists of the song.

As well as the *Scandal* theme 'Nothing Has Been Proved', the Pet Shop Boys side of the album includes a long bewitching house mix called 'Occupy Your Mind', where Dusty went acid existential. Always willing to 'have a go', on 'Daydreaming' she came out with a delicious transatlantic rap that echoes Neil Tennant's deadpan style, yet also contains a shivery quality of regret.

After a year of discussion and careful planning, *Reputation* finally came out in June 1990. Although the recording was completed some time before, protracted negotiations about the sleeve shots delayed its release. According to a friend, EMI were anxious to market Dusty one way while she wanted another approach. *Reputation* was eventually issued with a grainy, studiously enigmatic shot of Dusty on the cover. The monochrome images emphasized her heavily smudged eyes, high cheekbones and soft perm, while the graphics blazed a classic Dusty pink.

Within three weeks of release, the album sold over 60,000 copies and went silver, only to drop out of the UK charts shortly afterwards. 'She was really pleased that it entered the chart so quickly,' recalls Simon Bell. 'Then she called me up the week it went down, really disappointed. I told her, "But, Dusty, three years ago you wouldn't have even had an album in the chart!" It's funny how soon you get used to being back.'

Being back meant that Dusty had to get used to a chart turnover that was far more rapid than in her peak sixties days. Whereas in the past a single could take weeks, even months to climb up the charts, by 1990 a record was judged a success or failure within two weeks of release. However, *Reputation* was her most successful album since the sixties, recorded in an atmosphere of support and co-operation, and yielding three hit singles. 'It makes everybody happy that she's belting it out again,' said Bell. 'She was very relaxed for *Reputation*. Usually she's nervous, very critical of herself, but I don't think she was as destructively nervous as before. On, say, "Sometimes Like Butterflies", she knew she wasn't good, but on this one she was surrounded by people who knew what they were doing and really cared.'

Press verdicts on the album were generally kind: *The Times* mentioned its 'polished, surefooted air', *NME* that it had 'the sound of two decades colliding and nobody getting hurt', and the *Daily Telegraph* remarked that it showed 'an impressive return to form by a true original'. In the light of her success, Phonogram issued her entire back catalogue on CD, in batches of two or three at a time. In 1990 only a few artists such as the Beatles and the Rolling Stones had been granted this industry accolade, so Dusty was up there with the CD gods.

It is ironic that the teenage generation who had rejected her ten years before welcomed her back as sixties pop queen. Yet again it was the gay subculture, along with the popularity of melodramatic pop in the late eighties, that rescued her career. By then pop had become a pastiche of itself, borrowing madly from different eras, styles and genres. A top sixties star like Dusty was highly sought after because she had rarity value. She was the Original. 'It was a time in history when things lined up right for us. I don't think that will ever happen again. You can't repeat that,' Dusty said in 1995, three decades after her success as the leading British beat girl.

The respect of younger bands for their idols is sometimes touching. Jon Marsh of the nineties acid pop band the Beloved recalls the day he nearly hit Dusty with a pool ball. 'We were at the studio one day. I was playing pool, accidentally jerked the pool cue, and the ball shot into the air. Dusty was sitting with her back to us, and it whistled past her ear.' Marsh was mortified. 'She was very cool about it,' he says with admiration. 'She just turned round and smiled.'

Where many sixties stars had faded, opting for a life out of the limelight, Dusty still felt the urge to compete. A born Irish fighter, she functioned best with a sense of defiance. When Simon Napier-Bell suggested to her at one point that she was past it, Dusty reared up. 'I could say that to myself but God help anyone else who does,' she told *Girl About Town* in 1990. 'It gave me the kick in the arse I wanted. Sometimes I need someone to say something disgusting to me, to energize me. So I'm quite grateful to Simon. He doesn't know how helpful he was.'

After the success of *Reputation*, many expected Dusty to return quickly to the studio. But it was three years before she began work on her next album. And it was during those sessions that she learned something that would test her resources and her will to fight in a way she had never fought before.

10

Goin' Back

'YEAH, SO MUCH is going to happen – all or nothing,' Dusty said in 1993, just before she flew out to the States to record the follow-up to *Reputation*. Although the record had put her back on top, she retreated, and didn't go out on tour, so after *Reputation*'s momentum died away her career once again went through a lull.

At times Dusty was unable or unwilling to capitalize on her success. To coincide with the release of *Reputation*, an entire edition of *Arena*, the prestigious BBC Two arts documentary slot, was planned to focus on Dusty's career. However, as filming neared completion, Dusty could not find the two extra days needed to finish the programme so the project was shelved. It wasn't until 1994 that a documentary, *Dusty: Full Circle*, was finally aired. Mock-interviewed by comedians Dawn French and Jennifer Saunders, Dusty comes across as relaxed, but also bemused and self-deprecating. The attention that stardom brings still made her feel uncomfortable.

Her next musical project was a safe, one-off showbiz duet with Cilla Black called 'Heart and Soul'. 'Cilla was the heart and Dusty was the soul, basically,' says TV promoter Nick Fiveash, who worked on the video for the song. Released in 1993, the single was the standout track on Cilla's *Through the Years* album, a record commemorating her thirtieth anniversary in the business. Fiveash remembers bringing Dusty into the studio to film a performance of 'Heart and Soul' for Cilla's ninety-minute TV showcase special. 'The pair of them were in great spirits,' he recalls. 'It was so interesting to see two sixties legends, women who were so opposite to each other. The song "Heart and Soul" had been written especially for them. There was no choreography, they just got down there to this empty studio and off they went. They spent a lot of time laughing and making up sixties dance steps. After the third take, Dusty was parodying sixties moves – waving two fingers across her face, things like that – and Cilla was roaring with laughter in the background.'

Fiveash then assembled a promo video for the song with Vicki Wickham. They unearthed old footage of Dusty guesting on Cilla's sixties BBC shows, including their rendition of a comedy song 'If You're Ever in a Jam'. That was intercut with up-to-date material and duly dispatched to the media. Although it had been a lark, the record wasn't a hit. 'The single got to no. 74 in the charts,' says Fiveash, 'and as for the video, ITV's *The Chart Show* voted it the worst promo video of the year. Cilla said to me, "Well, at least we got top of something."'

The non-impact of the single was soon forgotten as in the summer of that year Dusty embarked on a new phase in her career. 'On 19 July 1993, I started my job as MD of Columbia in London. I called Vicki Wickham before lunch on that first day, introduced myself and said, "I wanna do a record with Dusty,"' remembers Kip Krones, a Nashville-based artist/manager who had worked with the Moody Blues and a range of singers and producers. During his time at Sony UK he signed acts as varied as Kula Shaker and Michael Ball, but his pet project was Dusty. 'At my age, growing up in the music business, she was the best female pop singer of my generation,' claims Krones. Vicki Wickham couldn't believe her luck, that there was no catch, that a record label MD, who was not wearing polished shoes, Armani suits and 'talking bullshit', purely and simply wanted Dusty.

Mindful of how *Dusty in Memphis* had become a legend in the business, Krones wanted to make a *Memphis* for the nineties, only this time in Nashville. 'I thought *Reputation* had been an interesting album, but it was more about production than her voice. It was not a singer's record. We wanted to make a classic singer's record. I knew she was singing well and wanted to stay active, so this record would be a sorta companion piece to her *Dusty in Memphis*,' explains Krones. 'Also I had in mind a 1994 release date. It would have been twenty-five years since the release of *Memphis*, and had all that pageantry attached to it. It was an obvious record company dream.'

Wickham was overjoyed. 'Vicki said, "That's so nice. Thank God the head of the label signing you wants the kind of record you want to make,"' remembers Krones. He claims that part of the rapport between him and Dusty was down to the fact that they had the same birthdate, 16 April. 'I've read Jerry Wexler said she was difficult to work with, but I felt that was incorrect. Dusty and I have the same temperament, I understand her. It's just that she's always been suspicious of record companies.'

Plans were quickly underway. Krones hired Nashville songwriter Tom Shapiro to produce the record. A BMI Songwriter of the Year, the easy-going, ebullient Shapiro crossed several genres. 'He wasn't a hillbilly songwriter,' says Krones, 'he had gone to the Berklee College of Music and he'd had soul as well as country hits. He wrote George Benson's "Never Give Up on a Good Thing", which was my favourite song in high school.'

For the next few months Shapiro gathered material for Krones, either playing it over the phone to him or sending packages of tapes. 'I was committed from the beginning. It became a labour of love, picking material from four thousand miles away,' says Krones. Word got around. The idea was to concentrate on Nashville writers, reflecting the fact that a sophisticated songwriting community had grown up there, one that spanned rock and pop as well as country. By the mid-nineties, Nashville rivalled New York and LA as a music centre for rock as well as country. As more and more writers submitted songs, the cream of the international crop began to approach Shapiro. Diane Warren, for instance, the one-woman LA hit machine who has penned such mainstream smashes as 'If I Could Turn Back Time' by Cher and Starship's 'Nothing's Gonna Stop Us Now', assiduously courted Krones, Shapiro and Dusty. The self-confessed 'infamous Valley Girl' who'd been brought up on Brill Building hits finally ended up with two songs on the album, including 'Wherever Would I Be', the duet with Daryl Hall.

'I flew to London to meet with Dusty and we were in agreement on most things. Song selection went easy,' Shapiro told me from his studio in Nashville. 'Originally the album was going to be a following to *Dusty in Memphis*, but as we got into it, we realized it would be more of a pop album with country touches.'

It became apparent that what people wanted was to contribute to a slice of history. Dusty's reputation as a vocalist and soulful interpreter of other people's songs was now towering. While flattering, this widespread reverence ironically acted against her. In many people's eyes she belonged to the 'old school', and this maybe stopped her from taking risks or reinventing herself as utterly contemporary. Some mainstream sixties artists like Shirley Bassey and Cliff Richard are quite happy to stay within the category that made them, whereas Dusty had always been pulled in several directions, both to stay 'classic' and to explore completely new sounds. It was this creative tension that fuelled her new album.

Provisionally titled *Dusty in Nashville*, recording began at the end of 1993. A short flight from Memphis, situated amid the rolling hills and fertile farmlands of central Tennessee, the city has been the capital of country music since the 1920s. Thousands of Irish and British rural migrants settled there, fusing their folk song with the more urban sounds of Tin Pan Alley, religious hymns and ex-slave songs. Their music found a focus in Nashville's main radio station WSM ('We Shield Millions' is the slogan of its insurance company sponsor), which in the late twenties began broadcasting the Grand Ole Opry show, a 'hillbilly' jam session that became country music's elite live showcase, featuring acts like Uncle Dave Macon, influential guitarist Sam McGhee and star band singer Roy Acuff.

By the end of the Second World War, Nashville was packed with recording studios and artists' agencies, selling the commercial down-home-easy-listening Nashville sound pioneered by stars such as Patsy Cline, Jim Reeves and later Barbara Mandrell. Although in the seventies and early eighties Nashville was seen as a bland, conservative force and a centre of Bible-thumping religion, there was a real network of talented working musicians and songwriters behind the preachy slogans, flowery frocks, bootlace ties and rhinestone glitter of 'Nash-Vegas'. By the late sixties Nashville made half the records in the USA, and many of the best session players in the country lived there. Top artists like Bob Dylan, Johnny Cash and 'outlaw' country star Willie Nelson recorded there. And in the late eighties it saw the development of emancipated female 'new country' acts like Nanci Griffith, Mary Chapin Carpenter and the young Mindy McCready.

'It's a very creative environment for artists, it's not a high-stress place, unlike New York or LA, where the cost of living and traffic weighs you down. Dylan loves to come here. Even though he's famous, nobody bothers him. In this town, Dylan's just another writer,' says Daryl Sanders, journalist and MD of Treason Records, a Nashville-based independent rock label. There is still the glitzy country side to Nashville – the Opryland theme park, for instance, complete with a 4,424-seater theatre, and the Country Music Hall of Fame, preserving Boxcar Willie's hobo hat and Elvis Presley's gold Cadillac, painted with crushed diamonds and Oriental fish scales – but rock music and back-to-basics songwriting are winning out. 'Country executives are flippin' out on Music Row because they see the day when rock and pop will be bigger,' says Sanders. 'It's a battle between the old guard and the young turks.'

Once again, Dusty showed the knack of being in the right place at the right time. 'You keep tripping over people from LA and New York [in Nashville]. It's attracted a mass of outside songwriting and production talent and it's diffused musically from its early core self while keeping that,' she said at the time. 'I had a very strong feeling that life goes in circles and this was a very large circle. And it was right that I went back there.'

As Dusty flew into Nashville she was revisiting her past: she had gone there more than thirty years earlier with the Springfields. Then her career was just beginning, and she had been brimming with exciting, ambitious plans; now she arrived older, wiser and more reflective. Gone were the ballads balanced on a knife edge, the R&B tracks infused with the white-hot urgency of the day. Instead, this collection (eventually christened *A Very Fine Love*) was wry, gentle, gracious; an uptempo exploration of love and leaving, fighting and commiseration. 'I am a woman of a certain age,' she said. 'I'm very comfortable with that and want to reflect it in my music.'

For the Nashville session she worked with top players like guitarist Biff Watson, pianist John Jarvis and Glenn Worf on bass. Each song was painstakingly recorded, capturing some of that open lazy Southern soul feel that infused *Dusty in Memphis*. There's the devotional opener, 'Roll Away', showing off Dusty's distinctive, warm vibrato; then the catchy title track, complete with lazy rhythm and Stax-style horns. Most moving is the ballad 'Go Easy on Me', a song that echoes with the emotional pull of lived experience, along with 'You Are the Storm', a ballad revolving around the idea of not being able to give a lover some shelter when they are the raging storm.

There are a few star turns on the album. Daryl Hall duets with Dusty on the Diane Warren song 'Wherever Would I Be'. One half of Hall and Oates, the biggest selling duo in US pop history, Philadelphia-born Hall came from the same tradition as Dusty. Dubbed a 'blue-eyed soul singer', he had immersed himself in black music from an early age, and with Oates developed a style that combined R&B with adventurous pop. Their strongest point musically was the album *Abandoned*

Luncheonette in 1973, but they really hit pay dirt in the late seventies and early eighties with glossy pop-soul singles like 'Rich Girl' and 'I Can't Go for That (No Can Do)'.

Hall and Dusty worked well together on the song. 'He was a charm, and she was a great fan of his,' recalls Shapiro. 'He was a real pro. He took his time with her and said, "I want to stay here till it's right." She was delighted.' A rousing, full-blown mainstream radio ballad, 'Wherever Would I Be' ended up on the soundtrack of the no. 1 box-office hit movie *While You Were Sleeping*, a romantic comedy starring Sandra Bullock. 'No one anticipated that it would be such a huge film,' says Kip Krones, 'so it was great advertising for the album.'

It was a good year for Dusty in terms of film soundtracks. Just as she was doing her album in Nashville, another neat reference was made to *Dusty in Memphis* with the Quentin Tarantino movie *Pulp Fiction*. The standout track on this hip, tongue-in-cheek gangster film was Dusty's version of 'Son of a Preacher Man', a song that introduced her to a whole new generation in the UK and the States. In the film Dusty's dusky voice rings out as John Travolta's character Vincent Vega slinks into his boss's house (a swanky seventies blaxploitation mirage of white and cream), stoned on heroin, while Uma Thurman's gang wife Mia, crisply dressed and perfectly made up, cuts up coke on a mirror upstairs. It is a decadent yet seductive sequence, made all the more powerful by Dusty's sensual tones. No doubt the song helped to make the *Pulp Fiction* soundtrack one of the biggest sellers of 1994.

Another key track on Dusty's Nashville album was 'Where Is a Woman to Go', a tour de force of woman-identified new country pop featuring the First Lady of Country Mary Chapin

Carpenter and feisty Texan singer K. T. Oslin on backing vocals. In this song, written by Oslin and Jerry Gillespie, a broken-hearted woman goes to drown her sorrows in a bar on the wrong side of town, and asks the bartender to give her a stack of quarters so she can play every song on the jukebox that makes her cry. A powerful, ironic tearjerker, the robust harmonies show that a strong sense of kinship existed between the female performers. Dusty warmly commented on Oslin being her kind of person. 'Both of us are fiercely irreverent about our work and about record companies, and she's very funny about it,' she said in the *Dusty Springfield Bulletin*. 'She says all sorts of things I wish I'd said and has the nerve to say them ... [also] she said, "Girl, don't ya ever sing a country song, it'll drive us all outa town." No one could pay me a higher compliment.'

There are also parallels between Dusty and Carpenter. A multi-Grammy winner, Carpenter rejuvenated country music in the late eighties and nineties in the same way that Dusty dominated British girl pop in the sixties. Both women have fought inner turmoil, drawing on that to bring a striking sense of honesty and directness to their work. In 1989, for instance, Carpenter ruminated on the strange loneliness of the thirty-something career woman with the song 'Middle Ground'; and in 1992 her multiplatinum album *C'mon, C'mon* featured the famous song 'He Thinks He'll Keep Her', a cold dissection of a dead-end relationship. 'It's [about] the realization that this woman is somewhere that she shouldn't be and it's up to her to empower herself to do something about it. I've met people who have not lived "the examined life", in other words they haven't looked inside themselves,' she once remarked, saying that the process of looking inward can be powerful – 'that sense of isolation gives you a feeling of strength'. It was a sentiment Dusty could identify with, and it's not surprising that she, Carpenter and Oslin had a rapport in the studio. 'They were like three little girls on a spree,' recalls Shapiro. 'It brought the best out in Dusty. That song is one of the highlights on the album.'

But while she had some transformative moments, there were other songs that didn't work so well. 'Lovin' Proof', for instance, a chugging sixties-influenced song, just sounds formulaic, while 'Old Habits Die Hard' is similarly lacklustre. 'On first listen I loved "Old Habits Die Hard", then it was "No, no, no!"' says Shapiro. 'But Dusty loved it, she wouldn't let go of it. She was adamant. She thought it was a hit, I thought it was bubblegum.'

Dusty spent over thirteen weeks in Nashville, and in the middle of recording an ice storm took down electricity supplies, so she spent three weeks with Pat Rhodes and an American friend Elaine, touring in the Smokey Mountains. 'She was very interested in American history and visited Civil War graves,' says Rhodes. 'One day we went to a Native American reservation and she was very upset, thinking about the way the people had been driven off their land. We went to an Indian village and bought a lot of silver jewellery to help them out a bit.'

Towards the end of her stay, Dusty's mood was growing fragile. The album was taking a long time to record, as Dusty's voice lacked its former power. Unbeknown to her then, she was very ill. 'Dusty had this problem and nobody knew. It made it difficult to get vocals down because she was having a lot of trouble, she would tire easily. She was weak, so each night we could only do a little vocal – a line or two here, maybe a verse there,' remembers Shapiro. 'The sessions weren't easy. She has *great* ears, and she knew she wasn't up to par. It was painful for her. We had to work real hard to get it right.'

Dusty admitted later to *You* magazine that she was having difficulties. 'I had eaten like a hog. I wasn't concentrating on my body. I was concentrating on getting through it all. I kept getting terrible infections ... I couldn't get well. I stumbled through the record.' Rhodes remembers taking her to see a doctor in Nashville. 'He examined her and said, "I don't think the problem is with her throat." I think the man knew she had cancer in her body. Dusty wasn't vigilant. She wasn't deliberately self-destructive, but somewhere in her mind she didn't think she was worth anything, so why bother? Also she didn't like her own body, didn't like to touch it. She was so shy, always hiding herself. She wasn't the type to cuddle and got panicky if you hugged her. I think that's why she never really settled down with anyone, and why she didn't look after herself.' When Dusty got back to England she started dieting and noticed a large indentation in her breast. Hell! she thought. What's that?

After seeing her GP she was sent straight to the Royal Marsden, one of London's key hospitals for cancer treatment. Rhodes went with her and waited outside the breast cancer clinic. A diagnostic doctor chatted merrily about cats while she examined the abnormality. When the results came up on screen there was a pursing of the lips. Eventually she said, 'I'm afraid it's a tumour and it's the one we just don't want.' Dusty came out of the room and started walking quickly down the corridor. 'Can you phone Vicki?' she said to Rhodes. 'Tell her it is.' Rhodes stopped dead in the corridor and threw her arms around Dusty.

For Dusty, the shock was enormous. At first she was enraged 'that this was happening to Miss Springfield and it was highly inconvenient because she had this record, for God's sake'. She called her brother Tom and went with him and a few friends into town for lunch. The Irish fighting spirit kicked in, and she was even able to laugh. But it was later on at home that the news really hit her. 'I saw my cat lying there asleep [and thought], Who's going to look after you? It was like somebody had run a train through me. I wept and wept and wept.'

Over the next two weeks, doctors worked out a course of treatment for her. That was when she first realized that cancer wasn't necessarily a death sentence, that it can be fought. She began six months of arduous treatment, with chemotherapy to shrink the tumour, an operation to remove it, followed by radiotherapy. When Dusty first had chemotherapy, she felt nauseous, but then, she said, 'I think my body liked the chemicals. I've poisoned it over so many years in the past that it went, "Yes! Poison!"'

One of the hardest facts to face was that, because she felt continually exhausted, she would not be able to work during the treatment. This was a blow not just to Dusty, but to everyone involved in making the album. 'She got diagnosed the same day we started mixing the record in London,' remembers Kip Krones. 'She came into the studio, started to cry and told everybody what had happened. We kept going, kept mixing the record, but it was difficult because we lost about nine months.'

The release date of A Very Fine Love had to be put back a year. 'We had a real problem. It was tragic for the record,' Shapiro says frankly. 'Dusty was a pain, but I did become fond of her. You wanna kill her, then you want to kiss her. And selfishly, I thought, we have a special record here. It definitely would've been a big seller right after release, we had all kinds of plans. The whole promo was building and building, then … nothing. I felt bad about that.'

Although at first she was paralysed with fear about what the team at Sony would think – would they yell at her? Would they fire her? – Dusty made her health a priority. Luckily the record company were supportive, reiterating their commitment to the album, but as far as Dusty was concerned the most important thing was to get well. 'It's a long time since being a star was the most important thing to me, but it's even less so now,' she said at the time. 'I don't need to be adored, to hear that applause. If I never heard it again, I would still be fine.'

By May 1995 Dusty had been given a temporary all-clear and was well enough to do promotion for the album. While there was a lot of press interest, plus the obligatory round of chat shows, *A Very Fine Love* didn't get the radio play that Columbia hoped for. 'The general feeling was that it was wishy-washy in places, and didn't have a standout track,' says Jo Donnelly, who steered Dusty's press campaign for the album. Record company staff also felt railroaded by Krones, and this caused tension behind the scenes. 'He really championed Dusty, he was very bullish about it,' says Donnelly. 'He was so blinkered – if we had a marketing meeting there would be three hours on Dusty and five minutes on everything else. It was his absolute dream to sign Dusty, and he was such an enormous fan. When an MD is in that position, it can be hard to work with.'

Krones admits, 'I probably got more involved with it than I should have, but it was awfully difficult to bring the company to the same fever pitch for the release. All the internal promo we'd done before had to be put on the back-burner. Such a thing was unprecedented – from spring '94 to spring '95 the record sat there waiting for Dusty to get better. My enthusiasm had to keep going for two years. It was tough.' It was even harder to break the record in America, even though it featured heavyweight US artists like Daryl Hall, K. T. Oslin and Mary Chapin Carpenter. 'It didn't sell that well. It was signed to a UK company, and the US looks at UK releases as second-class citizens. Also Dusty wasn't young and incredibly interested in visiting every radio station in America. That would have helped.'

Even though *A Very Fine Love* wasn't a huge hit album, Dusty had some sympathetic press. According to Fred Dellar at *Vox* it was 'pedal steel meets soul at its most sophisticated ... a record that will vie with the best to emerge from [Nashville] this year'. And though it was rated as 'fairly boring' by *NME*, Dusty herself was said to 'still sing better than anyone else ... one of the greatest singers in pop history'.

She made some notable TV appearances, in particular a virtuoso performance on BBC music show *Later ... with Jools Holland*. The audience sat on the edge of their seats in reverence, not just for the way Dusty sang 'Where Is a Woman to Go', but also for her backing vocalists – Alison Moyet and Sinead O'Connor – two younger female stars influenced by her take on classic pop. Legendary bass player Mo Foster was in her band that day and he remembers Dusty was overawed that Sinead in particular wanted to sing with her. 'She was in the dressing room beforehand saying she was so excited to be singing a song with Sinead,' he recalls. Maybe Dusty felt a connection through her Irish heritage, and, like her, the younger artist was a rebel who struggled with her mental health and the challenges of the music industry.

Dusty seemed grounded in a way that she never had been before. Over the course of her illness she had developed a sanguine philosophy: 'I've grown up a bit. Now I can say, this is important to me but it's not *that* important. If it all went wrong, big deal. It's such a *release*. You can breathe.' Grappling with the shock of a life-threatening disease had given her an entirely new perspective. It made her see the excesses of the past as an ironic luxury. 'If I'd gone on doing drink and drugs it probably would have killed me at some point. Because even if it was indirect, I would've had a car crash. Too many people died from all that kind of stuff. The messes you get into, they're life-threatening situations. That was my own doing. Before it took over my life, I'd initially chosen to do that. But I didn't *choose* cancer,' she said, in an interview with writer Alan Jackson. 'With drink and drugs you think, Fuck it, I'm having a good time. And you don't *get it* for the longest time. While it works it's *great*,' she continued, with pleasure in her voice. 'You have the best times of your life, no doubt about it. I'm grateful for all those times. But I didn't choose this. I'm quite a controlling personality and I have no control over this bloody thing – except to show up and *fight* it. Just fight it.'

In the same way that Dusty had raised awareness thirty years earlier by speaking out against racism, she was honest and positive about a social issue that directly affected her. 'Having been in and out of the Royal Marsden on a daily basis, you see so many survivors. In a way it's a privilege for us to be able to talk about it, if asked. There are so many women who can't,' she said. She mentioned singer Olivia Newton-John who the same year had released *Gaia: One Woman's Journey*, a conceptual album that, via spirit guides, forests and universal love, dealt with her battle against breast cancer. Self-penned songs like 'Trust Yourself' and 'Not Gonna Give in to It' were a far cry from her vacuous seventies persona. 'I saw her a couple of times and thought, God, you look great. Then, God, I think I know how you felt,' said Dusty. 'What I liked was her turning her life into something new. I admire anyone who can take life and shake it up like that.'

Breast cancer affects one in eight women in the UK, and it is the most common cause of death in women aged 35–49. For many years it was an issue that was underfunded and under-discussed. 'When I was diagnosed with breast cancer in 1989 there wasn't that much support around – especially for women in their twenties like me. Now that's all changed, there's so much more awareness,' Caroline Rust, one of the volunteers for the Breast Cancer Care (BCC) helpline, told me. In the late nineties she was part of a network of trained volunteers offering women one-to-one support. The only national breast cancer support charity in the UK, BCC was set up by Betty Westgate, who had a mastectomy and wanted to relieve other women of the loneliness and distress she had experienced. By 1997 the helpline received over twenty thousand calls a year.

Dusty was very aware of the teamwork and dedication it took to tackle her disease. 'God, if ever it comes home to you, it's the people who get paid piss-all to help people like me. They do it every day. I thought I was hard done by going round the M25 from where I live for radiotherapy. One of the nurses treating me travelled about sixty miles a day to work. She'd work these long hours, then go home to two kids and a husband. She has the hard part. I just have to show up and go home again. Okay, I'm going to get tired, but what about her?

The nurses are so supportive. And you're part of a team that's about getting you well.'

They were such a source of support that when the treatment ended she missed them. 'I always knew the hardest part would be when that stopped. Because then you return to life, but you return slightly dented, literally. You're tired. They're on the phone if you need them, but they're so busy I'm not going to bother unless I'm about to slit my throat. It's about returning to life and life's demands. And the demands of the music business are extraordinary at the best of times.'

When *A Very Fine Love* came out, Dusty was in remission, optimistic about getting 'full clearance' within the next few years. 'I've had so much junk put in my body, wonderful junk, that it's beaten for now,' she said. Despite her new peace of mind, Dusty still found the question of image and promotion a difficult one to negotiate. 'She was absolutely lovely and quick to put me at my ease. But she was terribly insecure when it came to doing a photo shoot,' says her press officer Jo Donnelly. There was one occasion when Dusty became friendly with the art director on a magazine photo shoot and ended up spending a day at a lab ten miles away, fascinated at the way people's heads were turned back to front, eyes were put upside down, and spots determinedly retouched. 'I'd love to retouch my whole life,' she quipped.

Dusty was aware of her growing laughter lines. As an older, high-profile woman in pop, she had encountered more than her fair share of sexism. 'STAR NEIL DWARFED BY A GIANT OF POP' bellowed one *News of the World* headline after Dusty's appearance at the BPI awards with Neil Tennant in 1988. At that time Dusty was overweight and self-conscious about her age. The 'report' waded in with a series of insults: 'Dusty Springfield reckons she has to dress up like a dog's dinner for a quick howl with Pet Shop Boy Neil Tennant. They took the stage at the BPI awards for their own version of the Little and Large show ... the ballooning belter, just over eleven years from collecting her old-age pension, reckons she can still teach skinny Neil, thirty-three, a thing or two about heavy rock ...' The *Sun* went even further with 'investigative reporter' Rick Sky proclaiming with erudite wit: 'Dusty Springfield has earned herself a new nickname – Dumpty Springfield – after piling on a staggering THREE STONE.'

Being called 'roly-poly', 'Lusty Dusty' and a 'pop star fatty' brought up all the insecurities Dusty had had as a chubby girl at school. She was also furious that her weight problem should be so publicly used against her. 'I was angry at why it's necessary for women to be a certain shape – 'cos I've noticed certain male singers of late who're definitely not the shape they used to be, but who still get large hit records,' she said. 'Yet, apparently, it's necessary for me to be a cadaver, to actually look quite ill, in order to achieve the necessary ... I've taken to defensive dressing – which means covering up my faults, knowing how to hide what you need to hide.'

Dusty's anxiety about her looks was exacerbated by the tabloid coverage. After the media taunts about her weight, she spent many months working off the pounds, going to health clubs and fitness classes until, by the time of the promotion for her 1988 single 'Nothing Has Been Proved', she had lost forty pounds. She looked young and trim, but the jibes left their mark. After lengthy cosmetic preparations for one interview with the *Daily Mirror*, she kissed her publicist then dashed back into the walk-in wardrobe. 'I caught my nose on Murray's,' she wailed. 'Now I'll have to check my make-up all over again.'

Seven years later she was still worried about her appearance. Once during promotion for *A Very Fine Love* the film crew spent an hour meticulously setting up a room in London's Langham Hotel before Dusty did an interview. When they finished, she saw herself in the monitor and said, 'This is my bad side. Do you think you could rearrange the room?' Because she was so apologetic, the crew did just that. After another hour she was happy. 'She was so sweet we didn't mind doing it,' recalls one of the crew, 'but to us the difference was imperceptible. She just looked like Dusty Springfield.'

After the promotional hoopla around *A Very Fine Love* died down, Dusty retreated once more. Finding herself stretched by the release of the record, she was thankful to have some peace again. But by the summer of 1996 her new-found calm was broken by bad news. The cancer had come back. She discovered another lump in the same breast, and went back to the Royal Marsden to endure more bouts of chemo and radiotherapy.

Over the next eighteen months her health was up and down. Sometimes it looked as if she would be able to start work on her next single, sometimes it didn't. At the beginning of 1997 it seemed that she was responding well to treatment, but by the autumn, any work was out of the question. 'The cancer had gone to her bones. That put the kybosh on everything,' recalls Rhodes.

In February 1998 she had to decline an invitation to the BRIT Awards ceremony because she was worn out by extensive chemotherapy. That night the deputy prime minister John Prescott had a bucket of cold water thrown over him by anarchist pop band Chumbawamba – but far more memorable was the announcement that Dusty was unable to attend. The evening's host, comedian Ben Elton, said to the audience: 'We had hoped that Dusty Springfield, that icon of music, would be here tonight. I know everybody in the industry will send her our love and our very best wishes.' Her illness made headline news.

In the wave of concern that broke after the report, Vicki Wickham declared to *Scotland on Sunday*, 'Dusty is a real survivor but she has had to put everything on hold for now. She's very determined to fight this and hopes to start work on her next single as soon as she can.'

Dusty stayed as positive as possible, but the impact of secondary cancer was hard to bear. 'When it comes back it's shattering, shattering,' cancer sufferer Ray Owen told me in 1998. 'Immediately you first get cancer, death is what you think about. Then, over a period of time, you get blasé about it. Until you go in after four or five years and the breast nurse says, "You've got spots on your spine." Then it's harder to fight back.' A BCC counsellor, she provided valuable volunteer support for older women. She had a double mastectomy at fifty-four, and was 'clear' for several years before it returned, in her bones. 'I rarely used the word "cured",' she said. 'You might be clear for five years, but it can still come back. People think that once you have secondaries that's it. I'm proof that it's not.'

Cancer was no longer frightening to her because she dealt with it by talking to others. 'Everybody has fear. In the beginning your headaches are tumours, your stomach ache is another cancer, but I say to everybody, "Learn to pace yourself. Give yourself goals, things to look forward to. You have to fight for yourself here. You're living with cancer, but don't let it be your whole life."'

Dusty learned to pace herself. In the summer of 1998 she was pottering in her garden and enjoying the World Cup on television, but making another record was 'out of the question'. In May she sold her 275 song rights to Prudential Insurance for up to £6.25 million, the same company that had paid £35 million for David Bowie's songs the previous year. 'It's a one-off deal,' said Tim Biggs, spokesman from Prudential. 'She is a legendary pop figure so we are delighted to have bought them. Dusty felt the time was right. Future dealings will depend on her health.'

Shortly before Dusty signed her Prudential deal, Linda McCartney lost her long fight against breast cancer. This tragedy accentuated the need for Dusty to stay positive, so she socialized and kept active. According to a close friend, 'Her fierce wit was still very much intact.' Friendship had been the one constant in Dusty's life. She was most loyal to those who needed her and who accepted her for what she was. Her main backing singer Simon Bell started off as an ardent fan in 1964, chasing her taxi from the stage door after a show in Glasgow. 'There was a picture of me and her in the Scottish *Daily Express* with her signing my wrist in the hotel foyer,' he says, smiling. Fifteen years later he became her backing singer, getting a slot on her London Drury Lane dates through their mutual friend Madeline Bell. 'I was chosen because I knew Dusty's old songs better than she did.' He became a close confidant, often cat-sitting for her after she'd moved to Amsterdam. 'She proved to be a good friend, especially one night when I had a very traumatic experience in a relationship and was ready to do myself in. She was in the middle of bleaching her hair, but she just dived in a taxi and came over, all the purple stuff still on her head. When I saw her I went from hysterically crying to laughing. You just wanted to put your arms round her.'

Shortly after her first diagnosis Dusty said: 'I've got great neighbours, but I find the most solace in calling someone who's seen me through really rotten times and been there for me. Simon is a very good friend and a wonderful singer. He has been there for me, and I've been able to cry to him.'

Despite a coterie of close friends, Dusty often felt happy with her own company, and there hadn't been a significant lover for some years. In 1998, at the age of fifty-nine, Dusty was living alone, but had come to relish solitude. 'I'm happy being on my own. Genuinely. I don't want a close relationship,' she said. 'There have been times when I've been lonely, but *true* loneliness, it seems to me, is when you don't choose it.' Her main solace throughout her life had been her cats, who were constant companions.

Fanatical about her cats, Dusty owned nearly two hundred over the years, and at one time kept nine in the same house. Whenever she left LA, she would book her pets into the Blackford's Hotel for Cats, where they would be fed their favourite foods. 'They have a chef. They'll get fried chicken, melon, doughnuts, pizza – all the things they're not supposed to. They're hideously spoiled.'

Pat Rhodes believes that the secret of their long friendship was that they were both animal lovers. 'We were into hedgehogs. We would stand out in the garden waiting till it got dark and we didn't move, or speak, watching the hedgehogs come out. We'd kill ourselves laughing watching these little things laden with fleas. The neighbours must have thought we were stark-staring bonkers.' Cats were a calming influence on Dusty when she was at her most anxious and insecure – she could talk to them without being answered back and she found them more dependable than humans. She would spend a fortune on caring for adopted strays – one cost her five hundred dollars in vet's fees.

When she was living in LA she threw herself into campaigning work for the Wildlife Way Station, a 160-acre ranch off Tujunga Canyon Road in the San Fernando Valley, which looks after more than two hundred animals. Its founder and president, Martine Collette, set it up in the early eighties as a refuge for exotic animals that had been abandoned or abused. She and Dusty campaigned vociferously against the trend for unscrupulous pet-shop owners to sell wild animals such as lions, tigers and coyotes to people as pets.

Dusty spent much of her time at the Station, nursing animals back to health and clearing cages. 'It's tough being a singer but if a three-hundred-pound bear jumps on you, it's tougher. Also, shovelling shit proved to be a very levelling experience,' said Dusty.

But it was domestic cats that gave her the most pleasure. 'I think they're amazingly beautiful and sensuous,' she said. 'They get up in the morning and they look great. They're comic and affectionate, and they can see a phoney straight away.' Dusty's concern for cats determined her mobility. She decided to move back to the UK from California in the mid 1980s, but it wasn't until the summer of 1989 that she plucked up the courage to put her two cats, Nicholas Nicholiavich and Malaysia, through quarantine, in a graduated move back to London. She eventually arrived in her childhood territory of Buckinghamshire to live a 'dull, but clean life' in the countryside. After a lifetime spent travelling from place to place, she found that the quiet English life felt like home.

After declaring a truce between Mary O'Brien and Dusty Springfield, a process that began with her move from LA, Dusty gained fresh recognition. In the nineties she went from critically acclaimed cult status to the iconic. In January 1999 she was awarded the Order of the British Empire in the Queen's New Year Honours List. Two months later, she was to be inducted into the US Rock 'n' Roll Hall of Fame alongside luminaries Paul McCartney, Bruce Springsteen and soul man Curtis Mayfield. As a key figure in the development of British pop, she was finally given her due. 'She didn't actually sound black, but a white girl with a helluva lot of black friends. And that's not a criticism,' enthuses Charles Shaar Murray, biographer of John Lee Hooker and Jimi Hendrix. 'She wasn't indulging herself in sub-Al Jolson routines like other sixties wannabes. She understood that soul was more than putting on a rasp and sounding like LaVern Baker.'

In the sixties Murray was a counterculture writer for the underground newspaper *IT*. Then, as a rule, he listened to Jimi Hendrix, blues and psychedelic rock, not bland pop. 'We regarded the big Italianate ballad as the worst. I wouldn't have dreamed of buying it done by anyone else, but when Dusty did "I Just Don't Know What to Do with Myself", she made it cool. I adored it. There was a mischievous warmth in her voice, a richness and an understated power.' Novelist Michael Bracewell also saw something highly distinctive in Dusty. In his 1997 book *England Is Mine: Pop Life in Albion from Wilde to Goldie* he writes: 'England had not produced a Joni Mitchell, a Patti Smith or a Janis Joplin, and with the exception of Dusty Springfield's magnificent succession of soul-baring singles ("You Don't Have to Say You Love Me" or "I Close My Eyes and Count to Ten") it seemed that women would remain as either fans or girlfriends in the world of pop.'

Musicians, too, continue to take inspiration from her sound. Bob Stanley, songwriter/producer with the nineties British pop band St Etienne, says, 'Dusty's voice had an incredible delicate quality for someone with such a powerful voice.' He likens Dusty's influence to that of another sixties legend, Scott Walker. 'Like him there's a mystique around her, and in the nineties she became massively hip.'

Though she was often asked to write her memoirs, Dusty was reluctant. First, there were all those years she couldn't quite remember; then there was 'the backlog of pain that's easily tapped into. It's like striking oil. There's this gush of emotion.' The Mary O'Brien who went thousands of miles, like Dorothy in search of Oz, never quite found that sense of place. 'I'm a transient,' she said. For a while after she moved to her house in Buckinghamshire she sometimes found it too quiet, too secure. When she felt restless she would drive to the airport nearby, park her car and just watch the planes. She would 'eat crap' there late at night, relishing the impersonality of it all. She'd observe people saying goodbye, hello, crying, laughing, arguing. Nobody noticed her because they were too busy with their own dramas, too busy going somewhere. 'Dusty was really two people. I related to her more as Mary O'Brien,' recalls Rhodes. 'And her brother Tom wouldn't talk about her as Dusty Springfield. It didn't matter how many fans queued for her autograph, she never thought she was great. Not once. Not even later on.'

Dusty always felt a vacuum in her life, a deep, unquantifiable sensation. Once she talked about *Latecomers*, Anita Brookner's novel about a supposedly happily married man who feels a strange, distant melancholy. 'It's about a feeling of wanting to be somewhere else all the time. It's almost a homesickness – but you don't know where home is. It's an intangible ache that is there, and I recognize it,' she told writer Alan Jackson. 'I can't quite put a name to it, but I acknowledge it in that I can sit on my back step and watch a plane go over and burst into tears, but I can't associate with it. It's a free-floating loneliness, not attached to a person or place. I am smart enough to know that I can't put that right by doing a geographic oh-if-I-move-to-Virginia-I'll-be-happy because I've done that, and it doesn't work. It's an inside job.' Towards the end of her life she did experience that calm sense of belonging. 'You can only reach that feeling if you get very still. Sometimes I'd sit on the same back step and just … let it in.'

There was poetry in her words, in the way she told stories, in the way she perceived herself. 'I'm like a seagull over the marine bed, the way they swoop when you throw down food. Except I'm a very selective seagull,' she once said mischievously to the *Observer*'s Jon Savage. 'I don't just sweep down for crumbs: it's got to be a whole loaf of bread in the water.'

In selecting material Dusty used that voracious intuition. 'A good love song has to make me cry,' she told me. 'There's a connection between the pit of my stomach and my eyes. That's the Irish melancholy in me. A song has to be immediate, it cannot grow on me. Once it sends a message to my tear ducts, then it's right.' What will endure are the sharp, husky tones of her voice, rising high over the music. At her best, she stunned everyone into silence. Having once lost herself, the survivor and humorous iconoclast, pop's Great White Lady finally made it back.

11

What's It Gonna Be

AT THE END of 1997 Dusty's friend Simon Bell moved into her house near Henley-on-Thames to help care for her. 'I stayed for a while. We didn't expect her to survive fourteen months, we were told it would be quicker. It was a special time,' he recalls. Bell did the shopping, took Dusty to doctor's appointments, and kept her company. 'I'm quite happy sometimes to sit in silence, and I think Dusty appreciated that. It's good to have quiet moments. There were friends who would irritate her, who would fidget and talk and couldn't sit still, and she couldn't wait for them to be gone.' Bell and Dusty would watch old BBC shows, and once the director James Cameron sent her a copy of *Titanic* on two VHS tapes. 'That was a good night,' recalls Bell. 'We enjoyed watching those.'

What Dusty craved, more than anything, was information. Even when she was losing her battle against cancer, she would get Bell to research the latest treatments. 'She had a lot of anger that this was happening to her,' he says. After conquering many of her psychological demons through therapy, Dusty was ready to fight the cancer. 'I was aware of how often she had self-harmed. For somebody who'd spent a great deal of time being self-destructive she really wanted to live.' Despite anger over her illness, Bell felt that Dusty had come to terms with issues that had troubled her in the past. 'I thought she would be difficult to handle,' he admits, 'but she was more peaceful than I expected. She seemed to be happy and she looked back on her music with pride.'

Rhodes also visited Dusty in Henley. 'We'd look out on the garden and watch the rabbits playing,' she recalls. 'It was a nice house. It had a spiral staircase and two dressing rooms. Outside everywhere you looked it was beautifully green.' On the morning of 2 March 1999 Dusty lapsed into a coma. Rhodes went to the house and was worried by what she saw. 'She did not look peaceful,' she recalls, 'so I went to find a priest to give her a blessing. After he had gone she was completely relaxed. I held her hand and sat talking to her for a while, saying that she didn't need to worry about us. She wasn't selfish – she'd always worry about me and Simon, that we were okay. I said, "Dust, I feel you've had enough and you want to let go. Just let go and drift off." I knew I wouldn't see her again. I remember getting in the car at four p.m. I sat there in the driveway for half an hour because I couldn't drive. The tears flooded down my face. It's as clear as day in my mind – the nice turquoise colours she had in her room, the green lawn outside, her face after the blessing, completely relaxed. I drove home and her brother Tom went down in the evening. Then at eleven p.m. I got the phone call.'

Dusty died peacefully at home that night. She was fifty-nine, just six weeks short of her sixtieth birthday. Too ill to go to Buckingham Palace for her investiture, Dusty had received her OBE at her bedside in the final stages of her illness. Retaining her deadpan humour to the end, she remarked, 'It's a nice medal.

But couldn't they have got a better ribbon? It's a bit frayed!'
When news of her death broke, the reaction was phenomenal:
the Queen said she was saddened, and stars, including Cher,
Elton John and the Pet Shop Boys, paid tribute to Dusty as one
of the finest female vocalists of her generation. Neil Tennant
and Chris Lowe commented, 'She brought pleasure to millions
of music lovers around the world. She will be sadly missed.' It
was as if Britain had only just realized what a great singer they
had lost. Dusty was cremated following a ceremony at St Mary's
Church in Henley on 12 March. The town centre was completely
closed, as thousands came to attend from all over the country.
'The fans stayed up all night threading daisies through the
railings. There were daisies everywhere,' recalls Rhodes. 'Dusty
wanted people to sing and dance at her funeral, like an Irish
wake. She'd asked for a Mexican tent with Mexican food and
music and people having a good time. She didn't want people
to wear black. Unfortunately the executors didn't arrange this,
and the funeral was in an ordinary hall. I wore light grey, and
I remember people tutting.' There was a bright note, however,
with the coffin being transported in a camp, theatrical horse-
drawn hearse, along with a wreath that spelt out Dusty's name
in bright flowers. Even then, it seemed, she was having the last
laugh. 'Since that day Dusty's grave has *never* been without
flowers,' says Rhodes. 'She won't be forgotten.'

Dusty was inducted into the US Rock and Roll Hall of Fame
two weeks after her death and over the next two decades, rather
than fading from cultural memory, Dusty's legacy grew. 'She
is regarded more highly now than she was in her later years,'
Bell says. 'After her death there was nothing but her past, and
it was clear to see how good she was. Dusty had such power

and versatility, and they keep finding obscure tracks by her, like "Spooky", which ended up on a Carlsberg advert in 2007. She did so many different things, so there's always something that is current. Dusty is still my favourite singer, that's never changed. She is still the best singer I ever heard.' Every year they can, Bell and Rhodes organize 'Dusty Day', a fundraiser for the Royal Marsden Hospital, celebrating Dusty's life and music.

Dusty's story has been a source of fascination for many film and theatre directors. In 2000, for instance, singer Mari Wilson starred in *Dusty the Musical*, which toured the UK for five months. 'Dusty is iconic and I grew up listening to her, so I didn't want it to be a tribute act or impersonation, rather my interpretation of her songs,' Wilson told blogger Kate In Brockley. The show had a nostalgic feel, focusing on wife and mother Carol, who is reliving the freedom of her sixties youth. Produced by Paul Farrah, who went on to do the Buddy Holly musical *Heaven Can Wait*, it was endorsed by Dusty before her death. In the years that followed several film projects were announced – in 2007 it was *Brokeback Mountain* director Ang Lee, with Charlize Theron slated for the starring role; then in 2008 Nicole Kidman was producer and star of a proposed Dusty biopic through Fox's Blossom Films company, while Number 9 Films tried to produce a film with Bond girl Gemma Arterton, and even Madonna expressed interest in the leading role of a TV movie about the singer.

In the end *My Left Foot* director Jim Sheridan's *Dusty* will be the first feature film about Dusty's life. With support from Screen Ireland, it's inspired by the star's Irish heritage. 'This is a woman 50 years ahead of her time,' Sheridan said to Irish Central.com when the film was announced in September 2023.

'Her Irish and Catholic background gave no hint of the visionary and transformative crusades she led. I can't wait to get on set.'

What fascinates people is the extremity of Dusty's story. 'The more distance we have, the more we realize how ahead of her time she was. She was in control in the studio at a time when women didn't call the shots. We'd all kill to sound like she did. I thought, If I had that talent my life would be made,' says playwright and author Jonathan Harvey, who wrote the acclaimed 2018 theatre show *Dusty: The Dusty Springfield Musical*. 'But she had drug and alcohol problems, she was fucked up, and that is so present on her records. There is a break in her voice and you don't know if she will get through to the end. There's a generation now that know her records, but don't know about her life. You think she has it all, but she doesn't have peace of mind. We can see that she's like us, a bit messy.'

From his award-winning play *Babies* in 1994 to the stage musical *Closer to Heaven*, his collaboration with the Pet Shop Boys, Harvey has always taken a dramatic and darkly comic approach. 'When I started researching this I was shocked. Oh my God, she was homeless and in a psychiatric hospital. I didn't realize it had got that bad,' he says. 'I wanted to open in the psychiatric hospital, but Vicki [Wickham, the producer] said, "Can we leave it to the second act before she's sectioned? It might be a bit much for the audience to take upfront."' Despite the harrowing aspects of Dusty's story, Harvey also saw joy and transcendence. 'If you're telling any other showbiz story, people never come back from that. But she did come back and win success again.' One of the biggest challenges for Harvey was combining the original story and Dusty's songs. 'I didn't want to do a tacky jukebox musical,' he says. 'Dusty was really cool, she wasn't an idiot. I wanted to honour her, so worked hard on those transitions from talking to singing. It had to feel organic.' Set in the mid-sixties at the height of her career, the show vividly captured her perfectionism and complexity, with Katherine Kingsley in the lead role.

Dusty is reimagined and reframed time and time again because she touches a chord. Many have tried to pinpoint the nature of her appeal, talking abstractedly about 'a great voice'. One of the most perceptive comments came in an interview I did with Derek Wadsworth, the top arranger and trombonist who had worked with Dusty for many years. 'She didn't have a great natural voice like Tom Jones or Aretha Franklin. It was a light voice. She couldn't project very far, she was a microphone singer,' he says frankly, 'but she was extremely expressive. She knew how to bend a note until she had got it right. She was a hard grafter and a great musician.'

Wadsworth recalls her inviting him over to her Holland Park flat, early in her solo career. She put on several Motown records, saying: 'I want you to take this down.' Accustomed to jazz and swing, Wadsworth found the music simplistic.

'It's just a little riff,' he said dismissively.

'But listen to what the guitars are doing.'

Wadsworth then began to hear it differently, how the guitars bounced off each other, how the voices worked with the rhythm. 'Dusty had analysed the whole of the backing,' he says, 'she wasn't just a singer who went out in a pretty dress and sang a tune. All the different elements of the arrangements were in her head.' Through Dusty, he learned how to adapt to the changing pop world and became the first rock arranger in Britain. 'She didn't want to let go of what she'd learned and loved – the ballads and the Latin – and she was also into rock and soul. She was a great pioneer for the music that then swamped the country.'

Dusty expressed fragility, heartbreak and grace. Her songs show us an emotional reality, what it is like to struggle and despair, to live on a knife-edge of tension, but also what it's like to triumph and let go. That's why she appeals to everyone from young pop fans to soul aficionados. 'Dusty occupies a unique place in the memory of rare soul fans,' says Stuart Cosgrove, author of the soul trilogy *Detroit 67*, *Memphis 68* and *Harlem 69*. 'At Wigan Casino her song 'What's It Gonna Be' had all the archetypal brilliance of Motown, the sophisticated vocals, the bracing singers and the uptempo beat. It was a record so in demand but so difficult to find that it was even bootlegged – an unusual accolade for a British pop song. Her voice is pure soul – the indescribable something that soars above pop.'

Dusty's other major achievement was inventing that look – the impossible beehive, the smudged eyes, the glittering gowns. In true diva style, she had a succession of wigs that she named Cilla, Sandie and Lulu, and a host of gay fans who appreciated the fact that she had modelled herself on drag queens. Though friends said that Dusty could be 'as temperamental as hell', she also exuded the graciousness of a Southern belle. Only she could stand in a muddy cow field in Ireland in her white stilettos and sparkling gown before a concert at a tiny village hall, then go onstage and do a perfect set. And one of her favourite presents was a T-shirt from her stage director Fred Perry. She was so delighted with it, she wore it as a nightshirt. The slogan on the front read: 'THIS IS NO ORDINARY HOUSEWIFE YOU'RE DEALING WITH!'

She kept her gentle, deadpan humour to the end. Never one to let circumstances get in the way, when she was going back from the hospital one day in an ambulance she made the driver stop. She got out, went shopping, and climbed back in again. It was this insouciance that endeared Dusty to everyone who met her.

Although she has gone, Dusty's irresistible spirit and her voice, captured on record in all its vulnerability and passion, will endure for ever.

Dusty Springfield:
A Discography 1959–2024

This discography includes all Dusty's key UK releases. Cassette releases are not catalogued where they do not differ from the original vinyl records. Many thanks to John McElroy and Paul Howes of the *Dusty Springfield Bulletin* for help in compiling this discography. (All details were correct at time of going to press.)

The Lana Sisters

Singles

Chimes of Arcady / Ring-a-my-Phone (Fontana 267025 IF. 1959)

Buzzin'* / Cry, Cry Baby (Fontana H-176. 1959)

Mr Dee-Jay / Tell Him No (Fontana 267055 TF. 1959)

(Seven Little Girls) Sitting on the Back Seat / Sitting on the Sidewalk (Fontana 267081 TF. 1959)

My Mother's Eyes / You've Got What It Takes (Fontana 267092 TF. 1960)

Tintarella di Luna (Magic Colour of the Moonlight) / Someone Loves You, Joe (Fontana 267109 TF. 1960)

Down South / Two-some (Fontana 267130 TF. 1960)

---

* Buzzin' was also featured on an EP called 'Drumbeat' (TFE 17146), which featured six songs from the BBC TV show of the same name.

The Springfields

Singles

Dear John / I Done What They Told Me To (Philips 326469 BF. May 1961)

Breakaway / Good News (Philips 326481 BF. August 1961)

Bambino / Star of Hope (Philips 326486 BF. November 1961)

Goodnight Irene / Far Away Places (Philips 326509 BF. January 1962)

Silver Threads and Golden Needles / Aunt Rhody (Philips 326522 BF. April 1962)

Swahili Papa / Gotta Travel On (Philips 326536 BF. August 1962)

Island of Dreams / The Johnson Boys (Philips 326557 BF. November 1962)

Say I Won't Be There / Little Boat (Philips 326577 BF. March 1963)

Come on Home / Pit-A-Pat (Philips 326600 BF. July 1963).

If I Was Down and Out / Maracabamba (Philips 326627 BF. January 1964)

Silver Threads and Golden Needles / Island of Dreams (Philips 326975 BF. June 1969)

Island of Dreams / Silver Threads and Golden Needles (Old Gold OG 9240. 1982)

EPs

The Springfields: Dear John / I Done What They Told Me To / Good News / Breakaway (Philips 427 488 BE. 1961. SBBE 9068)

Kinda Folksy No. 1: Wimoweh Mambo / The Black Hills of Dakota / Row, Row, Row / The Green Leaves of Summer (Philips 433 622 BE. 1962)

Kinda Folksy No. 2: Silver Dollar / Allentown Jail / Lonesome Traveller / Dear Hearts and Gentle People (Philips 433 623 BE. 1962)

Kinda Folksy No. 3: They Took John Away / Eso Es El Amor / Two Brothers / Tzena, Tzena, Tzena (Philips 433 624 BE. 1962)

Songs from the Hills: Das Kostet Keinen Pfennig (Settle Down) / Ich Geh' Ohne Ruh' Durch Die Strassen Und Gassen (Island of Dreams) / Alles Gold Und Alles Silber (Silver Threads and Golden Needles) / Sag Mir, Wo Die Blumen Sind? (Where Have All the Flowers Gone?) (Philips 433 643 BE, released in Germany)

Christmas with the Springfields: The Twelve Days of Christmas / Mary's Boy Child / Away in a Manger / We Wish You a Merry Christmas (P125E, Free with *Woman's Own* 1962)

Hit Sounds: Silver Threads and Golden Needles / Island of Dreams / Little Boat / Say I Won't Be There (Philips 12538 BE. 1963)

Vinyl albums

Kinda Folksy (1961)

Wimoweh Mambo / The Black Hills of Dakota / Row Row Row / The Green Leaves of Summer / Silver Dollar / Allentown Jail / Lonesome Traveller / Dear Hearts and Gentle People / They Took John Away / Eso Es El Amor / Two Brothers / Tzena, Tzena, Tzena (Philips mono BBL 7551, and stereo SBBL 674)

Folk Songs from the Hills (1963)

Settle Down / There's a Big Wheel / Greenback Dollar / Midnight Special / Wabash Cannonball / Alone with You / Cottonfields / Foggy Mountain Top / Little by Little / Maggie / Darling Allalee / Mountain Boy (Philips mono 632 304 BL)

The Springfields Story (1964, double album)

Dear John / Breakaway / Bambino / Far Away Places / Silver Threads and Golden Needles / Two Brothers / Aunt Rhody / The Green Leaves of Summer / Allentown Jail / Gotta Travel On / Pit-a-Pat / Island of Dreams / The Johnson Boys / Little Boat / Cottonfields / Foggy Mountain Top / Maggie / Alone with You / Settle Down / Say I Won't Be There / Come on Home / Maracabamba / If I Was Down and Out / No Sad Songs for Me (Philips mono BET 606 A-B)

The Springfields Sing Again (1965 and 1969)

Repackage of *Kinda Folksy* LP (Wing mono WL1078 and stereo Fontana SFL 13098)

Songs from the Hills (1966 and 1969)

Repackage of 1963 album *Folk Songs from the Hills* (Wing mono WL1132 and Fontana mock stereo SFL 13081).

Island of Dreams (1971) (Contour mock stereo 6870 530)

CD album

Over the Hills and Far Away (July 1997)

47-track compilation covering almost entire output (2-CD set; Philips 534 930–2)

Dusty Springfield (Solo)

Singles 7"

I Only Want to Be With You / Once upon a Time (Philips BF1292. November 1963)

Stay Awhile / Something Special (Philips BF1313. February 1964)

I Just Don't Know What to Do with Myself / My Colouring Book (Philips BF1348. June 1964)

Losing You / Summer Is Over (Philips BF1369. October 1964)

O Holy Child / Jingle Bells (Philips BF1381. B-side with Springfields. November 1964)

Your Hurtin' Kinda Love / Don't Say It Baby (Philips BF1396. February 1965)

In the Middle of Nowhere / Baby Don't You Know (Philips BF1418. June 1965)

Some of Your Lovin' / I'll Love You for a While (Philips BF1430. September 1965)

Little by Little / If It Hadn't Been for You (Philips BF1466. January 1966)

You Don't Have to Say You Love Me / Every Ounce of Strength (Philips BF1482. March 1966)

Goin' Back / I'm Gonna Leave You (Philips BF1502. July 1966)

All I See Is You / Go Ahead On (Philips BF1510. September 1966)

I'll Try Anything / The Corrupt Ones (Philips BF1553. February 1967)

Give Me Time / The Look of Love (Philips BF1577. May 1967)

What's It Gonna Be / Small Town Girl (Philips BF1608. September 1967)

I Close My Eyes and Count to Ten / No Stranger Am I (Philips BF1682. June 1968)

I Will Come to You / The Colour of Your Eyes (Philips BF1706. September 1968)

Son of a Preacher Man / Just a Little Lovin' (Early in the Morning) (Philips BF1730. November 1968)

Am I the Same Girl / Earthbound Gypsy (Philips BF1811. September 1969)

Brand New Me / Bad Case of the Blues (Philips BF1826. November 1969)

Morning Please Don't Come (duet with Tom Springfield) / Charley by Tom Springfield (Philips BF1835. February 1970)

How Can I Be Sure / Spooky (Philips 6006 045. September 1970)

Some of Your Lovin'/ Son of a Preacher Man / You Don't Have to Say You Love Me (Philips 6006 151. Maxi single. August 1971)

Yesterday When I Was Young / I Start Counting (Philips 6006 214. May 1972)

Who Gets Your Love / Of All the Things (Philips 6006 295. April 1973)

Learn to Say Goodbye / Easy Evil (Philips 6006 325. August 1973)

What's It Gonna Be / Bring Him Back (Philips 6006 350. March 1974)

Yesterday When I Was Young / The Look of Love (Philips 6006 446. March 1975)

A Love Like Yours (Don't Come Knocking Every Day) / Hollywood Movie Girls (Mercury DUSTY 1. February 1978)

That's the Kind of Love I've Got for You / Sandra (Mercury DUSTY 002. June 1978)

I'm Coming Home Again / Save Me Save Me (Mercury DUSTY 003. April 1979)

Baby Blue / Get Yourself to Love (Mercury DUSTY 4. September 1979)

Your Love Still Brings Me to My Knees / I'm Your Child (Mercury DUSTY 5. January 1980)

I Only Want to Be with You / You Don't Have to Say You Love Me (Old Gold OG9242. 1982)

Private Number (duet with Spencer Davis) / Don't Want You No More by Spencer Davis (Allegiance ALES 3. March 1984)

Sometimes Like Butterflies / I Wanna Control You (Hippodrome HIPPO 103. August 1985)

What Have I Done to Deserve This? (duet with the Pet Shop Boys) / A New Life by the Pet Shop Boys (Parlophone R 6163. August 1987)

Something in Your Eyes (duet with Richard Carpenter) / Time by Richard Carpenter (A&M AM406. September 1987)

I Only Want to Be with You / Breakfast in Bed (Philips BRITV 5. December 1987)

I Just Don't Know What to Do with Myself / I Close My Eyes and Count to Ten (Old Gold OG9763. 1988)

Nothing Has Been Proved / Nothing Has Been Proved (Instrumental) (Parlophone R 6207 single sleeve, RG 6207 gatefold. February 1989)

In Private / In Private (Instrumental) (Parlophone R 6234. November 1989)

Reputation / Rep U Dub 1 (Parlophone R 6253. May 1990)

Arrested by You / Arrested by You (Instrumental) (Parlophone R 6266. November 1990)

Heart and Soul (duet with Cilla Black) / A Dream Come True (Cilla Black solo) (Columbia 659856 7. October 1993)

Goin' Back / Son of a Preacher Man (Philips SPRNG. April 1994)

Singles 12"

Baby Blue (Disco version) / Baby Blue (Mercury DUSTY 412. September 1979)

Sometimes Like Butterflies (Extended Mix) / Sometimes Like Butterflies / I Wanna Control You (Hippodrome 12 HIPPO 103. August 1985)

What Have I Done to Deserve This? (Extended Mix) / A New Life / What Have I Done ... (Disco Mix) (Parlophone 12R 6163. CD CDR6163. August 1987)

I Only Want to Be with You / Breakfast in Bed / The Look of Love (Philips BRITV 55. December 1987)

Nothing Has Been Proved (Dance Mix) / Nothing Has Been Proved (Extended and Instrumental) (Parlophone 12R 6207 single sleeve, 12RG 6207 gatefold and CD CDR 6207. February 1989)

In Private (12" version) / In Private (7" version) / In Private (Instrumental version) (Parlophone CD CDR 7234. November 1989)

In Private (12" version) / In Private (7" version) / In Private (Instrumental version) (Parlophone 12R 6234. November 1989)

In Private (Remix) / In Private (Dub) / In Private (Bonus Beats) (Parlophone 12RX 6234. November 1989)

Reputation (Lots of Fun 12" Mix) / Rep U Dub 1 / Rep U Dub 2 (Parlophone 12R 6253. May 1990)

Reputation (the Alternative Mix) / Reputation (Lots of Fun Single Mix) / Getting It Right (Parlophone 12RX 6253. May 1990)

Arrested by You (Extended version) / Born This Way (12" Remix) / Arrested by You (Instrumental) (Parlophone 12R 6266. November 1990)

EPs

I Only Want to Be with You: I Only Want to Be with You / He's Got Something / Twenty-four Hours from Tulsa / Every Day I Have to Cry (Philips BE 12560. March 1964)

Dusty: Can I Get a Witness / All Cried Out / Wishin' and Hopin' / I Wish I'd Never Loved You (Philips BE 12564. September 1964)

Dusty in New York: Live It Up / I Want Your Love Tonight / I Wanna Make You Happy / Now That You're My Baby (Philips BE 12572. April 1965)

Mademoiselle Dusty: Demain Tu Peux Changer / L'Été Est Fini / Je Ne Peux Pas T'En Vouloir / Reste Encore Un Instant (Philips BE 12579. July 1965)

If You Go Away: If You Go Away / Magic Garden / Sunny / Where Am I Going (Philips BE 12605. August 1968)

Star Dusty: In the Middle of Nowhere / Twenty-four Hours from Tulsa / I Only Want to Be with You / I Just Don't Know What to Do with Myself (Philips 6850 751. 1972)

Dusty Springfield: I Only Want to Be with You / You Don't Have to Say You Love Me / Little by Little / In the Middle of Nowhere (Philips CUT 111. 1980)

CD singles

What Have I Done to Deserve This (Extended Mix) / A New Life (Pet Shop Boys) / What Have I Done to Deserve This (Disco Mix) (Parlophone CDR6163. August 1987)

Nothing Has Been Proved (Dance Mix) / Nothing Has Been Proved / Nothing Has Been Proved (Instrumental) (Parlophone CDR 6207. February 1989)

In Private (12" version) / In Private (7" version) / In Private (Instrumental version) (Parlophone CDR 6234. November 1989)

Reputation / Reputation (Lots of Fun 12" Mix) / Rep U Dub 2 (Parlophone CDR 6253. May 1990)

Arrested by You (7" version) / Arrested by You (Extended version) / Born This Way (12" version) / Getting It Right (Parlophone CDR 6266. November 1990)

Heart and Soul (duet with Cilla Black) / Heart and Soul (A Cappella Remix) / Heart and Soul (Instrumental) / A Dream Come True (Cilla Black) (Columbia 659856 2. October 1993)

Goin' Back / Son of a Preacher Man / Let Me Love You Once Before You Go / What Are You Doing the Rest of Your Life (Philips SPRCD 1. April 1994)

Wherever Would I Be (duet with Daryl Hall) / All I Have to Offer You Is Love / Reputation / Wherever Would I Be (Dusty solo) (Columbia 662059 2. May 1995)

Wherever Would I Be (duet with Daryl Hall) / Daydreaming (edited 12" master) / Arrested by You / Wherever Would I Be (Walter A Mix) (Columbia 662059 5. June 1995)

Roll Away / Old Habits Die Hard / Your Love Still Brings Me to My Knees / Born This Way (Columbia 662368 2. October 1995)

Roll Away / Old Habits Die Hard / Baby Blue / What's It Gonna Be (Columbia 662368 5. October 1995)

I Only Want to Be with You / You Don't Have to Say You Love Me / I Close My Eyes and Count to Ten / Roll Away (Night & Day) (Philips PSPCD46. July 1997) (Special Edition)

Vinyl albums

A Girl Called Dusty (April 1964)

Mama Said / You Don't Own Me / Do Re Mi / When the Lovelight Starts Shining Thru His Eyes / My Colouring Book / Mockingbird / Twenty-four Hours from Tulsa / Nothing / Anyone Who Had a Heart / Will You Love Me Tomorrow / Wishin' and Hopin' / Don't You Know (Philips BL7594 and stereo SBL 7594, rerelease 1990 on CD 842 699–2, MC 842 699–4)

Everything's Coming Up Dusty (September 1965, gatefold sleeve with booklet)

Won't Be Long / Oh No! Not My Baby / Long After Tonight Is All Over / La Bamba / Who Can I Turn To (When Nobody Needs Me) / Doodlin' / If It Don't Work Out / That's How Heartaches Are Made / It Was Easier to Hurt Him / I've Been Wrong Before / I Can't Hear You / I Had a Talk with My Man / Packin' Up (Philips RBL 1002 and stereo SRBL 1002, rerelease 1990 on CD BGO Records BGOCD 74, MC BGOMC 74 and on LP BGOLP 74)

Golden Hits (October 1966)

I Only Want to Be with You / I Just Don't Know What to Do with Myself / In the Middle of Nowhere / Losin' You / All Cried Out / Some of Your Lovin' / Wishin' and Hopin' / My Colouring Book / Little by Little / You Don't Have to Say You Love Me / Goin' Back / All I See Is You (Philips BL 7737 and stereo SBL 7737)

Where Am I Going (November 1967)

Bring Him Back / Don't Let Me Lose This Dream / I Can't Wait Until I See My Baby's Face / Take Me for a Little While / Chained to a Memory / Sunny / They Long to Be Close to You / Welcome Home / Come Back to Me / If You Go Away / Broken Blossoms / Where Am I Going (Philips BL 7820 and stereo SBL 7820, rerelease 1990 on CD 846 050–2, MC 846 050)

Dusty Springfield (1968)

Twenty-four Hours from Tulsa / Anyone Who Had a Heart / Go Ahead On / Every Day I Have to Cry / Now that You're My Baby / The Corrupt Ones / The Look of Love / Live It Up / I Wish I'd Never Loved You / Reste Encore Un Instant / Who Can I Turn To / I Want Your Love Tonight (World Record Club T 848 and stereo ST 848)

Dusty ... Definitely (November 1968)

Ain't No Sun Since You've Been Gone / Take Another Little Piece of My Heart / Another Night / Mr Dream Merchant / I Can't Give Back the Love I Feel for You / Love Power / This Girl's in Love with You / I Only Wanna Laugh / Who (Will Take My Place) / I Think It's

Gonna Rain Today / Morning / Second Time Around (Philips SBL 7864, rerelease 1990 on CD 846049–2, MC 846 049–4)

Stay Awhile (December 1968)

I Only Want to Be with You / Stay Awhile / Mama Said / Anyone Who Had a Heart / When the Lovelight Starts Shining Thru His Eyes / Wishin' and Hopin' / Mockingbird / You Don't Own Me / Something Special / Every Day I Have to Cry (Wing WL 1211)

Dusty in Memphis (April 1969)

Just a Little Lovin' / So Much Love / Son of a Preacher Man / I Don't Want to Hear It Any More / Don't Forget About Me / Breakfast in Bed / Just One Smile / The Windmills of Your Mind / In the Land of Make Believe / No Easy Way Down / I Can't Make It Alone (Philips SBL 7889, rerelease 1990 on CD 846252–2)

Stay Awhile (February 1970)

Rerelease of 1968 compilation (Fontana SFL 13189)

From Dusty ... With Love (February 1970)

Lost / Bad Case of the Blues / Never Love Again / Let Me Get in Your Way / Let's Get Together Soon / Brand New Me / Joe / Silly, Silly Fool / The Star of My Show / Let's Talk It Over (Philips SBL7927 and 6308 004, rerelease 1990 on CD 846 251–2)

A Girl Called Dusty (September 1970)

Rerelease of 1964 original minus Mama Said and Nothing (Fontana 6438 024)

This Is Dusty Springfield (October 1971)

Twenty-four Hours from Tulsa / Son of a Preacher Man / Every Day I Have to Cry / If You Go Away / Anyone Who Had a Heart / Mockingbird / Do Re Mi / When the Lovelight Starts Shining Thru His Eyes / Don't You Know / Nothing / You Don't Own Me (Philips 6382 016)

A Girl Called Dusty (1972)

Rerelease of 1970 issue (Contour 6870 555)

Star Dusty (1972)

In the Middle of Nowhere / Twenty-four Hours from Tulsa / I Only Want to Be with You / Little by Little / Mama Said / Do Re Mi / I Just Don't Know What to Do with Myself / You Don't Have to Say You Love Me / All I See Is You / Anyone Who Had a Heart / My Colouring Book / Wishin' and Hopin' (Philips Audio Club 6850 002)

Sheer Magic (1972)

Rerelease of *Ev'rything's Coming Up Dusty* (Philips Audio Club 6856 020)

See All Her Faces (November 1972)

Mixed Up Girl / Crumbs off the Table / Let Me Down Easy / Come for a Dream / Girls Can't Do What the Guys Do / I Start Counting / Yesterday When I Was Young / Girls It Ain't Easy / What Good Is I Love You / Willie & Laura Mae Jones / Someone Who Cares / Nothing Is Forever / See All Her Faces / That Old Sweet Roll (Hi-De-Ho) (Philips 6308 117)

Cameo (April 1973)

Who Gets Your Love / Breakin' Up a Happy Home / Easy Evil / Mama's Little Girl / The Other Side of Life / Comin' and Goin' / I Just Wanna Be There / Who Could Be Loving You Other Than Me / Tupelo Honey / Of All the Things / Learn to Say Goodbye (Philips 6308 152)

This Is Dusty Springfield Vol 2: The Magic Garden (April 1973)

Magic Garden / In the Land of Make Believe / They Long to Be Close to You / This Girl's in Love with You / The Look of Love / I Think It's Going to Rain Today / Where Am I Going / How Can I Be Sure / The Windmills of Your Mind / Broken Blossoms / I Can't Wait Until I See My Baby's Face / Who (Will Take My Place) (Philips 6382 063)

Dusty Springfield Sings Burt Bacharach and Carole King (January 1975)

Compilation of songs by these songwriters (Philips 6382 105)

You Don't Have to Say You Love Me (June 1976)

You Don't Have to Say You Love Me / You Don't Own Me / Do Re Mi / When the Lovelight Starts Shining Thru His Eyes / My Colouring Book / Mockingbird / Twenty-four Hours from Tulsa / Anyone Who Had a Heart / Will You Love Me Tomorrow / Wishin' and Hopin' / Don't You Know / Son of a Preacher Man (Contour CN2016)

It Begins Again (February 1978)

Turn Me Around / Checkmate / I'd Rather Leave While I'm in Love / A Love Like Yours / Love Me by Name / Sandra / I Found Love with You / Hollywood Movie Girls / That's the Kind of Love I've Got for You (Mercury 9109 607)

Living Without Your Love (May 1979)

You've Really Got a Hold on Me / You Can Do It / Be Somebody / Closet Man / Living Without Your Love / Save Me, Save Me / Get Yourself to Love / I Just Fall in Love Again / Dream On / I'm Coming Home Again (Mercury 9109 617)

Greatest Hits (October 1979)

Hits compilation (Philips 9109 629)

Memphis Plus (September 1980)

Rerelease of *Dusty in Memphis*, plus four extra tracks: I Want to Be a Free Girl / I Believe in You / What Do You Do When Love Dies / Haunted (Mercury 6381 023)

The Very Best of Dusty Springfield (October 1981)

Hits compilation (K-Tel NE 1139)

Greatest Hits (October 1983)

Reissue of October 1979 album (Philips PRICE 45)

Son of a Preacher Man (February 1984)

Hits compilation (Spot SPR 8539)

Memphis Plus (September 1985)

Reissue of 1980 version (Philips PRICE 83)

The Silver Collection (January 1988)

Hits compilation (Philips DUSTY 1, also on CD 834 128-2 with two extra tracks: Anyone Who Had a Heart and Am I the Same Girl)

Reputation (June 1990)

Reputation / Send It to Me / Arrested by You / Time Waits for No One / Born This Way / In Private / Daydreaming / Nothing Has Been Proved / I Want to Stay Here / Occupy Your Mind (Parlophone PCSD 111, CD on CDPCSD 111, TCPCSD 111)

Songbook (1990)

Hits compilation (Pickwick CN 2107, CD on PWKS 580, MC CN4 2107)

A Girl Called Dusty

BGO reissue of original 1964 album (BGO Records BGO LP46)

Ev'rything's Coming Up Dusty

BGO reissue of original 1965 album (BGO Records BGO LP74)

Songbook (May 1990)

Compilation of single and album tracks (Pickwick CN 2107)

Reputation (June 1990)

Reputation / Send It To Me / Arrested By You / Time Waits For No One / Born This Way / In Private / Daydreaming / Nothing Has Been Proved / I Want To Stay Here / Occupy Your Mind (Parlophone PCSD 111)

A Very Fine Love (June 1995)

Roll Away / Very Fine Love / Wherever Would I Be (duet with Daryl Hall) / Go Easy on Me / You Are the Storm / I Can't Help the Way I Don't Feel / All I Have to Offer You Is Love / Lovin' Proof / Old Habits Die Hard / Where Is a Woman to Go (Columbia 478508 1)

CD albums

Love Songs

Compilation of single and album tracks (Philips 814 990–2)

The Silver Collection (January 1988)

Hits compilation (Philips 834 128–2)

Dusty's Sounds of the Sixties

Compilation of single and album tracks (Pickwick PWK 104)

Love Songs

Compilation of single and album tracks (different track listing from Philips CD of the same title; Pickwick PWK 120)

Songbook (May 1990)

Compilation of single and album tracks (Pickwick PWKS 580)

Reputation (June 1990)

Reputation / Send It to Me / Arrested by You / Time Waits for No One / Born This Way / In Private / Daydreaming / Nothing Has Been Proved / I Want to Stay Here / Occupy Your Mind (Parlophone CDPCSD 111; mid-price release, Parlophone CDFA 3320)

A Girl Called Dusty

Identical track listing to original 1964 album (Philips 842 699–2)

Ev'rything's Coming Up Dusty

Identical track listing to original 1965 album (BGO Records BGOCD74)

Where Am I Going
Identical track listing to original 1967 album (Philips 846 050–2)

Dusty ... Definitely
Identical track listing to original 1968 album (Philips 846 049–2)

Dusty in Memphis
Identical track listing to original 1969 album (Philips 846 252–2)

From Dusty ... with Love
Identical track listing to original 1970 album (Philips 846 251–2)

Blue for You
Compilation of single and album tracks (Spectrum 5500052)

Goin' Back: The Very Best of Dusty Springfield (May 1994)
Hits compilation (Philips 848 789–2)

Dusty: The Legend of Dusty Springfield (June 1994)
93-track compilation (4-CD box set; Philips 522–254–2)

A Very Fine Love (June 1995)
Roll Away / Very Fine Love / Wherever Would I Be (duet with Daryl Hall) / Go Easy On Me / You Are the Storm / I Can't Help the Way I Don't Feel / All I Have to Offer You Is Love / Lovin' Proof / Old Habits Die Hard / Where Is a Woman to Go (Columbia 478508 2)

Dusty in Memphis (1995)
Identical track listing to original 1969 album with bonus tracks: Willie and Laura Mae Jones / That Old Sweet Roll (Hi-De-Ho) / What Do You Do When Love Dies? (Mercury 528 687–2)

Am I the Same Girl (March 1996)
Compilation of single and album tracks (Spectrum 552 093–2)

Something Special (April 1996)
48-track compilation (Mercury 528 818–2) (2-CD set)

We Wish You a Merry Christmas (December 1996)

O Holy Child* / Jingle Bells** / Bambino** / Star of Hope** / The Twelve Days of Christmas** / Mary's Boy Child** / Away in a Manger** / We Wish You a Merry Christmas** (Zone X001) (*Dusty Springfield Bulletin* charity CD) (*Dusty Springfield; **the Springfields)

A Girl Called Dusty (February 1997)

Identical track listing to original 1964 album with bonus tracks: I Only Want to Be with You / He's Got Something / Every Day I Have to Cry / Can I Get a Witness / All Cried Out / I Wish I'd Never Loved You / Once Upon a Time / Summer Is Over (Mercury 534 520–2)

Hits Collection (May/June 1997)

Compilation of single and album tracks (Spectrum 537 549–2)

Reputation and Rarities (September 1997)

Identical track listing to *Reputation* album with bonus tracks: Any Other Fool / When Love Turns to Blue / Getting It Right / In Private (12" version) (EMI GOLD 1077 (7243 8 59882 2 6))

Songbooks (February 1998)

Compilation of Bacharach/David and Goffin/King tracks (Philips 552 863–2)

Ev'rything's Coming Up Dusty (March 1998)

Identical track listing to original 1965 album with bonus tracks: Live It Up / I Wanna Make You Happy / I Want Your Love Tonight / Now That You're My Baby / Guess Who? / If Wishes Could Be Kisses / Don't Say It Baby / Here She Comes (Philips 536 852–2)

Where Am I Going (March 1998)

Identical track listing to original 1967 album with bonus tracks: I've Got a Good Thing / Don't Forget About Me / Time After Time (Philips 536 962–2)

Dusty: The Very Best of Dusty Springfield (October 1998)

24-track compilation (Mercury 07314 5383452 1/cassette also – 07314 5383454 5)

The BBC Sessions (March 1999)

I Can't Hear You / Wishin' and Hopin' / Losing You / In the Middle of Nowhere / Mockingbird / Little by Little / Up Tight (Everything's Alright) / Chained to a Memory / We're Doing Fine / Every Ounce of Strength / You Don't Have to Say You Love Me / Good Loving / To Love Somebody / Son of a Preacher Man / Higher and Higher (Your Love Keeps Lifting Me) (Zone X002) (*Dusty Springfield Bulletin* charity CD)

Cassette-only releases

Dusty (double cassette) (Philips 7564 001)

Stay Awhile (Philips 7176 004)

Hits of Dusty Springfield (Philips MCP 1004.EP)

Hits of the Walker Brothers and Dusty Springfield (Philips MCP 1004.EP)

I Close My Eyes and Count to Ten (Philips MCP 1016.EP)

Songs released in the US but not in the UK

Sweet Ride / No Stranger Am I (Philips 40547. A side not released in UK; different recording from that issued in UK on soundtrack album *Sweet Ride*)

It Goes Like It Goes / I Wish That Love Would Last (20th Century Fox TC-2457. B side not released in UK)

Bits and Pieces (included on soundtrack to film *The Stunt Man*. 20th Century Fox T-626)

As Long as We Got Each Other (credited as Steve Dorff and Friends, featuring B. J. Thomas and Dusty Springfield) / As Long as We Got Each Other (Instrumental) (Reprise 7-27878)

White Heat (1982)

Donnez Moi (Give It to Me) / I Don't Think We Could Ever Be Friends* / Blind Sheep / Don't Call It Love* / Time and Time Again / I Am Curious* / Sooner or Later* / Losing You / *Gotta Get Used to You* / Soft Core (*recordings not released in UK) (Casablanca Album: NBLP 7271)

A Brand New Me (1992)

Identical track listing to album *From Dusty ... with Love* with bonus tracks: I Wanna Be a Free Girl / What Good Is I Love You / What Do You Do When Love Dies / Haunted / Nothing Is Forever / Someone Who Cares / I Believe in You / I'll Be Faithful* / I Can't Give Back the Love (Rhino CD: R2 71036) (*recording not released in UK)

The Burt Bacharach Songbook (1998)

17-track various artists compilation including alternate version of I Just Don't Know What to Do with Myself (Varese Vintage VSD-5873)

Dusty in Memphis (Deluxe edition) (1999)

Identical track listing to album *Dusty in Memphis* with bonus tracks: What Do You Do When Love Dies / Willie and Laura Mae Jones / That Old Sweet Roll (Hi-De-Ho) / Cherished* / Goodbye* / Make It with You* / Love Shine Down* / Live Here with You* / Natchez Trace* / All the King's Horses* / I'll Be Faithful* / Have a Good Life Baby* / You've Got a Friend* / I Found My Way* (Rhino R2 75580) (*recordings not released in the UK)

Dusty in London (Deluxe edition) (1999)

24-track compilation including Sweet Inspiration (recording not released in the UK) (Rhino R2 75581)

Stay Awhile – I Only Want to Be with You (1999)

Original US album with 3 bonus tracks including Standing in the Need of Love (recording not released in the UK) (Mercury 314 538 902–2)

Dusty (1999)

Original US album with 3 bonus tracks including unedited version of Heartbeat (this version of recording not released in the UK) (Mercury 314 538 909–2)

The Look of Love (1999)

Original US album with 4 bonus tracks including I've Got a Good Thing (alternate version) and It's Over (recordings not released in the UK) (Mercury 314 538 912–2)

Selected compilation releases 2000-2024

The BBC Sessions (Zone X002) (1999)

Good Times (The Best of Dusty Springfield's BBC TV Performances 1966–1979) (Zone X003) (2001)

Live at the Royal Albert Hall (Eagle EAGCD310) (2005)

The Dusty Springfield Story (Mercury 9833223) (2006)

Goin' Back: The Definitive Dusty Springfield (Mercury boxed set 0600753304990) (2011)

Featuring The Lana Sisters and The Springfields – The Early Years (Jasmine Records JASCD 759) (2014)

The Complete Atlantic Singles 1968-1971 (Real Gone Music/ Atlantic RGM 1166) (2021)

Dusty Sings Soul (Ace CDCHD 1612) (2022)

The Springfields

Little by Little / Waf-Woof (Springfields, A-side released in UK) (Philips 40092)

Italian songs

Tanto So Che Poi Mi Passa (Every Day I Have to Cry) / Stupido Stupido (Wishin' and Hopin') (Philips BF 326 679)

Tu Che Ne Sai / Di Fronte All'Amore (original songs) (Philips 363 699PF)

German songs

Warten Und Hoffen (Wishin' and Hopin') / I Only Want to Be with You

Songs from films

The Corrupt Ones (from *The Corrupt Ones* (US title) / *The Peking Medallion* (UK title))

The Look of Love (from *Casino Royale*)

I Don't Want to Hear It Anymore (from *Love or Money*, recording not released)

Sea and Sky (from *Time for Loving* (UK title) / *Paris Was Made for Lovers* (US title))

Give Me the Night (from *Corvette Summer* (US title) / *The Hot One* (UK title))

Bits and Pieces (from *The Stunt Man*)

But It's a Nice Dream (from *Kiss Me Goodbye*, not released)

Nothing Has Been Proved (from *Scandal*)

Getting It Right (from *Getting It Right*, not released)

Songs from TV series

Learn to Say Goodbye (from *Say Goodbye, Maggie Cole*, ABC Movie of the Week)

As Long as We Got Each Other (from *Growing Pains*)

Six Million Dollar Man (from *The Six Million Dollar Man*) (not released)

Miscellaneous releases

Son of a Preacher Man (live recording; CD TVT 9429–2) (from *The Sullivan Years: The Mod Squad* 1990 TVT Records) (US release)

Baby It's Cold Outside (duet with Rod McKuen, live recording from the Rod McKuen special *Christmas in New England*; CD 12 778) (from *Christmas in London* 1996 Laserlight) (US release)

Quiet Please There's a Lady on Stage (live recording from *The Tom Jones Show*; CD 9016) (from *Great Solo Performances Volume II* 1997 Classic World) (US release)

Upside Down (duet with Tom Jones; 2-CD set; live recording from *The Tom Jones Show*) (from *Tom Jones: Greatest Performances* 1998 32 Pop) (US release)

Picture Credits

Page one: top: Pictorial Press Ltd/Alamy Stock Photo; middle and bottom: David Hartley/REX/Shutterstock.

Page two: Pictorial Press Ltd/Alamy Stock Photo (both).

Page three: top left: Pictorial Press Ltd/Alamy Stock Photo; top right: GAB Archive/Redferns/Getty Images; bottom left: M. McKeown/Express/Getty Images; bottom right: Personal collection of Pat Rhodes.

Page four: top: Mirrorpix; middle: CA/Staff/Redferns/Getty Images; bottom: Trinity Mirror/Mirrorpix/Alamy Stock Photo.

Page five: top: Fiona Adams/Redferns/Getty Images; middle: Photograph by Terry Manning, © 2019, All Rights Reserved. Used by permission; bottom: Everett Collection Inc./Alamy Stock Photo.

Page six: top: Michael Putland/Hulton Archive/Getty Images; middle: Everett Collection Inc./Alamy Stock Photo, bottom: ANL/REX/Shutterstock.

Page seven: top: All Action/EMPICS /PA Images; bottom: Andrew Csillag/REX/Shutterstock.

Page eight: top left: Gerry Penny/REX/Shutterstock; top right: Fiona Hanson/PA Archive/PA Images; bottom left: Toby Hancock/REX/Shutterstock; bottom right: Tony Kyriacou/REX/Shutterstock.

Index